Sport, Culture aɪ Modern State

Edited by
Hart Cantelon
Richard Gruneau

UNIVERSITY OF TORONTO PRESS
Toronto Buffalo London

© University of Toronto Press 1982
Toronto Buffalo London
Printed in Canada

ISBN 0-8020-6493-0 (paper)
ISBN 0-8020-2494-7 (cloth)

Canadian Cataloguing in Publication Data

Main entry under title:
Sport, culture and the modern state

Papers presented at a conference held at
Queen's University, Kingston, Ont., Oct. 1979.
ISBN 0-8020-6493-0 (pbk.)
ISBN 0-8020-2494-7 (bound)

I. Sports and state – Congresses. I. Cantelon, Hart,
1944– II. Gruneau, Richard S., 1948–

GV706.5.S66   796'.01   C82-094747-4

Sport, Culture and the Modern State

HART CANTELON is assistant professor in the School of Physical and Health Education at Queen's University.
RICHARD GRUNEAU is associate professor in the Department of Sociology at Queen's University.

Although there has been considerable attention paid to the study of sport and politics, the complex nature of sport's relationships to the state remains largely unexplored.

This book presents a unique collection of essays by an international group of political theorists, sociologists, and physical educators on the nature of sport and its relationships to power and cultural production in capitalist and socialist state systems. The opening papers focus on sport, and the violence often associated with certain sports, in the context of broader debates over the nature and role of the state and over theories of violence and social control. Subsequent essays examine sport as a feature of ideological hegemony, the labour process, and dependency. Three are devoted specifically to sport and the state in the Soviet Union.

CONTENTS

PREFACE

Over the past decade there has been a notable growth of interest in the study of sport and politics. Numerous developments have undoubtedly contributed to stimulate this interest but three sets of considerations appear to have been of decisive importance. First, socialist countries with fully state-supported sports programs have experienced remarkable "successes" in international sport from the 1950's to the present. Second, and partially in response to the programs in socialist countries, sports activities have become increasingly incorporated into the welfare-state domestic policies of most of the capitalist liberal democracies. Finally, the growing use of sport as an element of foreign policy by certain countries has frequently disrupted the so-called "normal" exercise of international sporting contests as witnessed in the recent controversies over anti-apartheid campaigns directed at South Africa and over the boycott of the 1980 Moscow Olympic Games.

What is common to all of these considerations is that they dramatize in the area of sport the increasingly large and visible role the state has come to play in post-war industrial societies. Yet, ironically, it is not the state itself, or the question of the state's role as a constitutive feature of culture and society, that has commanded the attention of most

people who have been moved to write about sport and politics.
Indeed, with few exceptions, one is hard pressed to find in
this literature much concern about what the state actually
is (although hidden assumptions abound), whose interests it
serves, and how it articulates with people's cultural prod-
uctions. Rather, the apparent "statization" of modern sport
tends to be evaluated, condemned, or applauded only from the
standpoint of the vested interests of varying groups in the
sporting community. As a result, the consequences of sport's
changing association with the state are rarely discussed in
terms of their links to the production and reproduction of
social and cultural relations as a whole.

Consider, in this regard, three major research emphases
that have characterized the bulk of the literature on sport
and politics. Most common among these emphases is the long-
standing debate over the inherently apolitical nature of sport
-- a debate that is rooted in romanticized conceptions of sport
and idealized visions of cultural forms. Sport ought to be
"above" politics, we are often told, and its inherent essence
is corrupted and debased by state "interference". Other writers,
less inclined to use the idealized language of essences, have
claimed to ask more "pragmatic" questions about how particular Sports policies have emerged and how state policies in
sport might democratize opportunities for participation, offer

centralized and more effective planning and create better conditions for maximizing athletic performances. Still other writers have sought to examine the nature of state-supported sport policies with respect to their implications for reinforcing patterns of bureaucratization and system rationalization which coerce and overly constrain sports participants, especially at the highest levels of athletic competition.

The problem in all of these cases, however, is that they are most often limited to a focus on sport as an independent object of study rather than as a mediated cultural form located in an ensemble of social relations. This focus has generally led people interested in sport and politics to overlook the much broader politics of sport. That is, in the quest to understand the effects of certain political transformations on sport people have tended to gloss over any political role that different sporting practices themselves play in social and cultural life. Thus, paradoxically, what is usually left out of the account in discussions of sport and politics are precisely those issues which have always defined the core of political theory: the issues of power and domination.

This latter statement can be clarified by returning to the three examples discussed above. Idealist polemics against the "corruption" of sport by the state, or the "politicization" of sport that ostensibly derives from state "intervention", simply ignore all other forms of social determination in sport and their political implications. Proponents of the idealist view seek restoration of a separation of sport from political practice that has never existed. Problems of how sport might figure politically in class, racial, ethnic or colonial struggles, for example, are simply wished away in the nostalgic pursuit of a transcendent world of pure form. In the second case, studies of the history of government sport policies or on government decision-making in sport have often been conducted in a fashion that virtually takes for granted the nature of the social, economic, and cultural structures within which decisions are framed. Accordingly, this research lends itself to trivialization in a way that never contends with the hidden face of state power. Finally, the focus on the personal troubles of milieu experienced by athletes as a result of the demands of state-sport are all too rarely studied in the context of public issues of social structure; that is, the implications of athletes' personal troubles are not located in broader analyses of the nature of human possibilities and their denial in different socio-political contexts.

The few significant attempts to think more broadly about the politics of sport have tended to focus primarily on the question of sport's contribution to ideology and have been developed by a handful of iconoclastic Marxist writers and left-wing cultural critics. In these analyses the politics of sport are tied to questions of power and domination ex-, pressed as a feature of the struggle for consciousness between social classes. Sport, the argument usually runs, is an important feature of a dominant ideological system that has legitimated advanced capitalism and has acted as a mechanism of incorporation with respect to the working class. But this simple equation of sports with bourgeois ideology seems far too easy and is greatly limited by its reductionist conception of cultural forms and its overemphasis on the incorporative power of ideology itself. Moreover, the emphasis on sport's articulation as ideology has actually tended to direct attention away from the state as a mediating feature in the cultural expression of sport and the struggle for class consciousness.

One might hope such deficiencies could be easily overcome given the great increase in recent years of Marxist writing on the state and its role in ideology and cultural production. The long-standing Marxist tendency to view the state in reductionist terms as a simple manifestation of dominant class interests has been much debated in a

theoretical movement which has sought to demonstrate the
"specificity of the political" and the importance of state
power as something distinct from class power. An important
part of this movement has been an examination of the complex
relationships between class and state influences on ideology
and cultural production as a whole. Yet, remarkably, there
is a very real silence in this literature on the role of sport
in cultural production and its relationships to class and
state power. Given the great visibility of sport in modern
life, its increasing association with the state, and its centrality in working class culture in the majority of capitalist societies, this silence is absolutely mystifying. That
such a silence exists may indicate something about the effectiveness of sport's ideological character in general and about
the extent to which Marxist writing has chronically devalued
questions about the centrality of play, the body, and the drama
of the contest in human cultural production.

The essays which make up the volume at hand have been
written, for the most part, with a view to redressing the
theoretical imbalances described above while simultaneously
expanding our understanding of the world wide politics of
sports. The first three essays by Rick Gruneau, Ian Taylor
and Wally Clement outline some background issues on state
and class relationships and their ties to sport and the

violence often associated with certain sporting contests.
The following papers by John Hargreaves, Rob Beamish and
Alan Ingham offer more detailed (and somewhat conflicting)
examinations of the nature of sport's insertion as a cultural
form into processes of social reproduction and transformation
in advanced capitalism. In the next three essays by Henry
Morton, Hart Cantelon and Jim Riordan the focus shifts to a
debate over the implications of sport's association with the
state in the Soviet Union. Finally, the book concludes with
essays by Bruce Kidd and Colin Leys which examine sport in the
context of cultural imperialism, nationalism and dependency.

Any critic will readily discern that the contributions
which appear in this volume do not add up to anything like a
comprehensive theory of sport, culture and the modern state.
But they do, we believe, contain important guidelines for future research and open up important areas of discussion and
debate. Empirical research, as a number of the contributors
to the present volume indicate, is obviously a necessity here,
but before effective research of this type can be done we need
to do the equally necessary task of theoretical ground-
clearing. In any case, our belief is that future research
on the relationships between sport and politics must always
be interpreted against the backdrop of general problems of

classes, cultural production and the state. In this way it can help to further our understanding not only of the specific dilemmas that face athletes and sports enthusiasts themselves, but will in addition serve to contribute to the ongoing debate over the direction and development of contemporary industrial societies as a whole.

Rick Gruneau
Hart Cantelon

Kingston, May, 1982.

ACKNOWLEDGEMENTS

All of the papers and discussions of papers which appear in this book were presented at a conference held at Queen's University, Kingston, Ontario in October of 1979 and sponsored by the Queen's Sport and Leisure Studies Research Group, the School of Physical and Health Education and the Department of Sociology. The purpose of the conference was to bring together sociologists, sport scientists and political theorists in an attempt to stimulate debate and develop some working models on the topic of the relationships between sport as an element of cultural production and the modern state. On their own behalf, and on behalf of the authors represented in the book, the editors wish to thank the Social Sciences and Humanities Research Council and the National Administrative Centre for Sport and Recreation for grants which allowed the conference to be held and which helped in preparing the papers for inclusion in this volume. Thanks are also due to the staff of the Donald Gordon Centre, Queen's University and to Cathy Bray, Bob Hollands, Janine May and Kevin Whitaker for their help in staging the conference. Special thanks are also due to John Albinson, Don Macintosh and John Meisel who chaired various conference sessions and to Dorothy Daley for typing the final manuscript. Finally, we want to thank R.I.K. Davidson at University of Toronto Press for his interest and support of this project. Royalties from the book will go to the Queen's Sport and Leisure Studies Research Group to promote further critical work on the nature and role of sport in capitalist and state socialist societies.

1
Sport and the Debate on the State

Richard Gruneau

Introduction [1]

State involvement of some type has long been an
important feature of the development of sport and popular
recreation in the western industrial societies. As examples,
one need only think of the numerous municipal ordinances
that have been created in order to specify where and when
people might play, of the conscious and persistent use of
sport in military training, and of the creation of licensing
and other regulatory commissions designed to control
"gaming" of different types. Over the last two decades,
however, the scope of state involvement in sport appears to
have become even broader. The early municipal, judicial and
military aspects of state-involvement have been increasingly
supplemented by more formalized national and sub-national
programs in recreation, community sports and, more notably,
international athletic competition.

In recent years, this increasingly complex and visible
association between sport and the state has come to be the
subject of a great deal of scholarly attention. Studies of
sport and domestic government policies, sport and international relations, or sport and political ideologies are
now quite common and have contributed greatly to our
understanding of the close relationship between sport and
politics.[2] Yet, there is an important sense in which the
majority of these studies have been seriously deficient.
Very little of the recent work on sport and politics has
attempted to situate sport in the context of any coherent
theory of the state and there has been virtually no
sensitivity among students of sport to the significant
debates in social and political theory about the nature
of the state and its role in social and cultural life. I

2

should add, however, that most social and political theorists have tended to be equally insensitive to the importance of sport as an aspect of the state's involvement in cultural production and social reproduction.

My purpose in this paper is to outline a set of considerations that will provide both a groundwork for future research on sport and the state and a general introduction to some of the key theoretical problems that are discussed by the contributors to this volume. In order to accomplish this objective my discussion will be divided into two parts. In the first part of the paper I shall review some of the debates that have arisen in social and political theory about the nature of the state and its relationships to civil society. In the second part of the paper I shall try to show how some of these debates provide important points of departure for understanding the politics of sport in contemporary cultural life. Most of my discussion in the second section of the paper will focus on an examination of sport in the capitalist state, however, I do plan on introducing one key theme in conclusion that will also be relevant for assessing sport's relationship to the state in socialist societies.

The Debate on the State

Let us begin with two general questions. What is the state and what is its role in society and culture? Perhaps the most popular response to these questions is to define the state as that complex of instititions which politically embodies the values and interests of the people of any given society.[3] It is along these lines that people generally refer to the Canadian state, the British state, the American state and so forth. Yet, this definition is not really very satisfactory. For one thing, it fails to specify the exact ways in which the state embodies the values and interests of people in society and it fails to delineate the various institutions that would be the backbone of any state structure or system. At the same time, the definition in no way differentiates between the various types and strengths of values and interests that exist in social life. In other words, it does not allow us to see the state as an embodiment of only some values and interests rather than all values and interest.

This latter failing is especially important, I believe, because it hints at the degree to which a view of the state as the political embodiment of people's values and interests contains a number of implicit assumptions both about the nature of power and its distribution in societies, and about the nature of the limitations that political and social structures place on human agency. These assumptions, as Ralph Miliband has noted,[4] have often served to deflect analysis away from the state as a factor in social and political theory and they have largely obscured an understanding of its basic features.

For the most part, there are two ways in which this deflection of interest away from the state can occur. First, by assuming that the state is nothing more than the political embodiment of collective interests and values one faces the risk of blurring any conceptual distinction that might be maintained between state and civil society. Where such blurring has occurred in social and political theory the state has often been elevated to some vaguely organic form of collective political expression whose goals are ostensibly co-extensive with and indistinguishable from those of society itself.[5] A second way in which interest can be deflected away

from the state is to argue that the state's role in society
is simply one of neutral co-ordination. The state remains
the political embodiment of values and interests, not because
it is indistinguishable from society, but rather because it
stands outside of and "above" society. Given the existence
of a multitude of conflicting interests and values in human
existence, the state's role is to reconcile and accommodate
them all and thereby preserve the collective good. Under
such circumstances what is politically relevant for social
scientists is not the state itself so much as its internal
workings and organizations, the tensions that occur within
it, the political cultures that characterize it and the ebb
and flow of political preferences within it.[6]

One obvious feature of much of the writing on modern
politics is the extent to which variations on each of these
particular views have been widely accepted by partisan
political theorists in capitalist liberal democracies. For
apologists of the capitalist state it makes good ideological
sense to view the state as some kind of "positive" or
"neutral" embodiment of collective values and interests.
But, supporters of existing socialist states have also
adopted their own version of this thesis. This socialist
version is classically laid out by Engels in Anti-Durhring
and reaffirmed forcefully in Lenin's The State and Revolution.
The argument simply is that after the socialist revolution
the state, in Engels' words, simply becomes the "real
representative of the whole of society" and therefore renders
itself unnecessary. The "government of people" supposedly
becomes surpassed by the "administration of things, and by
the conduct of processes of production."[7] Thus, the
repressive bourgeois state "withers away" and is replaced by
an effectively neutral co-ordinating mechanism. The view

5

that the state has taken on, or is about to take on, this form in society is a key feature of "official" policy in most of the "state-socialist" societies.

Now in each of the two cases that I have described, the state can be understood, in some way, as the embodiment of collective values and interests and in each case the analytic importance of the state is down-played. But, at the same time, there is one sense in which the significance of the state is not completely overlooked, for it is often suggested by partisan political theorists in both state systems that their political enemy's state system "deviates" in some way from the role of co-ordinator or custodian of the collective good. From the perspective of writers in east European socialist states, and many western Marxists as well, capitalist liberal democracy simply embodies the values and interests of a ruling class more than any sort of generalized interest. On the other hand, from the perspective of the committed liberal democrat, socialist states (and, by implication, any future socialist projects) are seen simply to embody the interests of a bureaucratic elite. The ultimate projection of these views is the argument that in capitalism the state is nothing more than an instrument of class rule and that in socialism the state-structure simply replaces class as the force of domination in human existence.

Regardless of the truthfulness of either of these projections the question which presents itself immediately is that we now have two definitions of the state--one where the state is defined as a complex of institutions which are the political embodiment of the general interests and values of the people in any given society and the other where, under certain circumstances, the state is defined to be the embodiment of only some interests and values. How we decide

between the two contrasting views is a deeply serious concern.
It is scarcely adequate, for example, merely to accept the
idea that one's definition of the state's nature and role
depends upon an acceptance of some ideological stance. What
we need, it seems, are some set of "objective" empirical
procedures upon which we might "ground" our theoretical
speculation.

Admittedly, empirical evidence can help us here. For
instance, it might be possible to establish empirically that
no one group of people in a society is in a position to
effectively control the state. On the other hand, it might
be possible to establish empirically that some group of people
in a society have appropriated the state system and are using
it as an "instrument" to advance their own interests. Yet, too
much faith should not be placed on the ability of such
procedures to resolve our dilemmas over choosing an adequate
definition of the state. The argument that such an issue can
be resolved purely on the basis of empirical findings tends to
overlook both the degree to which empirical findings must be
"interpreted" and the degree to which many of the assumptions
which underlie the definitions in question are hotly contested
issues at the levels of philosophy and epistemology. To cite
just one example, the marshalling of empirical support for
views of the capitalist state as the political embodiment of
people's values and interests has often been built on
philosophical assumptions about power and structure that
virtually guarantee conclusions that are ideologically safe.

The point requires some clarification. Most views of
the capitalist state as the political embodiment of generalized
values and interests are built on a number of "essentially
contestable" assumptions about voluntarism and the inevitability
and effectiveness of "counter-vailing" power in liberal
democracy.[8] In capitalist liberal democracies, the argument

runs, power is generally attributable to human agents who characteristically perform voluntary acts in the presence of open alternatives.[9] Such limits as there are on human agency develop as a result of the social necessity of insuring that no one agent, or collection of agents under some self-chosen leader, finds themselves in a position to monopolize power and impose their interests upon others. Power then, is like a resource, a commodity in the system, and the state is the mediating central bank within which the circulation and exchange of power proceeds.[10]

This view of power, coupled with its "entrepreneurial" view of political decision-making, has recently been referred to by C.B. Macpherson as the "equilibrium" model of democratic politics.[11] It has also been referred to variously as the "pluralist" or "elite pluralist" view of political organization. In Macpherson's words:

> It is pluralist in that it starts from the assumption that the society which a modern democratic political system must fit is a Plural society, that is, a society consisting of individuals each of whom is pulled in many directions by his many interests, now in company with one group of his fellows, now with another. It is elitist in that it assigns the main role in the political process to self-chosen groups of leaders. It is an equilibrium model in that it presents the democratic process as a system which maintains an equilibrium between the demand and supply of political goods.[12]

Macpherson goes on to show how, at the descriptive level, much of this model rings true, but at the explanatory level, the model is less defensible and less readily supported in empirical terms. The power that is assumed to be the capacity of agents, the assumption that agents are utility maximizers, and that the limitations on human choices which exist in the system are in people's best interests,

are as much epistemological and philosophical problems as
they are empirical ones. Certainly, there are other views of
power and structure that are no less credible as assumptions
upon which to build an understanding of politics and a
definition of the state.

The most notable source of these "other" views is
Marxism, for Marx always emphasized the degree to which the
actions of human agents are severely limited by the structures
they create as they produce and reproduce the conditions of
their existence. In the case of the development of an
adequate definition of the modern state the decisive Marxist
intervention was to show how the bourgeois state had emerged
historically in a fashion that offered considerable personal
freedom but only on the basis of "rights" that were intimately
connected to an asymmetrical system of class relationships.
This system of class relationships was "objectively"
determined by the structure and logic of wage labour and its
accompanying capitalist form of value. As Anthony Giddens
notes:

> In capitalism authority relationship in . . .
> (industry and the state) . . . ultimately rest
> upon the rights inherent in the possession and
> deployment of capital. In neither case are these
> rights legitimized, as in feudal society as the
> natural rights of a specific minority; their
> legitimacy derives from newly recognized concepts
> of freedom and equality. In the sphere of the
> economy itself, freedom of contracts effectively
> sanctions the dominance of the owner of capital,
> since the wage-labourer is forced to deliver
> himself into the hands of the capitalist by dint
> of economic necessity. This position of nominal
> freedom and actual bondage is reinforced and
> stabilized by the modern state, which recognizes
> 'political' rights of citizenship, but separates
> these from industry. Thus, in Marx's analysis,
> the authority structure of capitalist industry
> is treated as flowing from the rights, and there-
> fore the powers, of capital as bolstered or

sanctioned by the bourgeois state.[13]

In other words, Marxist theory views the state as an important part of the means of class domination. The bourgeois state is not some neutral "thing" that is above struggle, it is part of class relations and, as Miliband suggests, its involvement in everyday social and cultural practices is "crucial, constant and pervasive."[14] Indeed, the classic Marxist definition of the bourgeois state dramatically captures its supposedly partisan nature: The state, Marx and Engels argued in The Communist Manifesto, is "a committee for managing the common affairs of the whole bourgeoisie."[15]

Now in recent years Marxists have debated this latter formulation with some intensity. What is fundamentally at issue in these debates is the degree to which the ruling class, designated by virtue of the fact that it owns and controls a predominant part of the means of material and mental production in society, can be seen to control the state as well. In other words, can class power be translated automatically into state power? As a response to this question I want to outline three broad positions taken by Marxist writers, each of which takes a somewhat different view of the class/state relation.[16]

The first of these positions focusses on the issues of shared personnel and the social origins of well-placed individuals in the state system. Taking the case of the capitalist state, if it could be shown that members of a "state elite" were recruited from the ruling class or that the members of any "state elite" were also members of a "corporate" elite drawn from the ruling class, then one would appear to have an empirical basis for the claim that the state is subordinate to class interests.

As Ralph Miliband has noted,[17] there is certainly a good deal of persuasive evidence that has been collected in different capitalist states which shows that: (a) key personnel in the elites of the major economic, political and cultural institutions in capitalist societies tend to have been recruited primarily from the bourgeoisie and its allies; and (b) that patterns of recruitment to positions within the state system follow similar tendencies (although different fractions of the bourgeoisie may be drawn upon depending upon the institutional "elite" in question). On this basis it has been argued that state power is instrumentally connected to class interests because of common social backgrounds and shared experiences among elite members, actual social contacts and networks of friendships between elite members, and a generalized sharing of broad perspectives and world views. This is not to say that members of the corporate elite, state elite and other elites in society are necessarily seen to be conspirators or that there are not important and persisting conflicts and differences between elite members individually and collectively, the argument simply is that these are differences in degree rather than kind. A common class interest is shared and, related to this, are approximately similar ideas about the nature of freedom and justice, about what is in people's best interests, and about what is best in the "national" interest.

There are many objections that can be made to such views but for present purposes I only want to touch on a few of the problems that are raised by this type of thinking. One problem stems from the great amount of competing empirical work in different societies that points a lack of co-ordination between elites and the fact that positions in the state system are rarely held by capitalists. Another problem arises when

11

one focusses upon the impact of supposedly "neutral"
managerial personnel on decision-making in the corporate and
state systems--managers who are not considered as part of the
elites in question. In the view of most "pluralist" writers
the fundamental lack of elite co-ordination and the power of
technocrats and managerial personnel is sufficient to cast
doubts on the importance of finding links between a ruling
class (and its corporate elite) and the holders of key
positions in the state system.

I do not want to spend a great deal of time examining
these problems except to say that pluralists have usually
underestimated the degree of overlap between institutional
elites in capitalist societies. Moreover, as both Wallace
Clement and Ralph Miliband have shown,[18] the argument that
managerial personnel have more power over state policies than
capitalists, or that managers and technocrats are completely
neutral in these matters, is belied by considerable evidence
to the contrary. Yet, at the same time, it is true that key
personnel in the state systems of capitalist societies are
not always recruited from the capitalist class. In Canada,
for example, Dennis Olsen has noted that even though "the
upper class has an advantaged position in the (state) elite,
the elite as a whole is largely drawn from the 'middle class'
in Canadian society."[19] Moreover, as Miliband notes, there
can be no denying that when the question of personnel and
class bias is viewed historically there are many instances
when the policies of a given state have seemed to be incompatible with the class interests of power holders in the
state system. For example, there are many cases where
aristocrats and the petit bourgeoisie have supported
capitalism and this suggests the fallacy of arguing that the
class bias of any (state) is conclusively determined by the

12

social origins of its leading personnel.[20]

What one can add to strengthen arguments about the class bias of the capitalist state, however, is the great amount of evidence that reveals the strengths of large business interests in influencing state policies. This evidence in no way suggests that the capitalist state is at the beck and call of powerful business interests, but it does seem to show fairly convincingly that in areas ranging from government social programs to environmental policies, capitalist enterprise is the most powerful "pressure group" in society. Nonetheless, it must be made clear that to argue that capitalist industry is the strongest "presence" in capitalist society is not tantamount to saying that the state is simply the instrument of the dominant class. Again, to quote Ralph Miliband:

> . . . the pressure which business is able to apply to the state is not in itself sufficient to explain the latter's actions and policies. There are complexities in the decision-making process which the notion of business as a pressure group is too rough and unwieldy to explain. There may well be cases where that pressure is decisive. But there are others where it is not. Too great an emphasis upon this aspect of the matter leaves too much out of account.[21]

Each of the two arguments that I have just provided seeks to establish empirically that the state is a direct instrument of class rule. The arguments focus on human agents, either individually or collectively and they empower some agents with the capacities to exercise collective pressures on the basis of class privilege. Yet, it has been suggested by Nicos Poulantzas that such arguments run the risk of attacking bourgeois conceptions of the capitalist state "on their own epistemological terrain."[22] This tendency, Poulantzas argues, "imports" an acceptance of the capacities of human agents that is supposedly not compatible with Marxism. The state is not reducible to individuals, to a "problematic" of the subject where individuals are the initiators of social action; rather in Poulantzas' view, the state is defined by ". . . objective structures, and their relations as an objective system of regular connections, a structure and a system whose agents . . . are in the words of Marx, 'bearers' of it."[23] In other words, Poulantzas is arguing that the state cannot be understood in the context of a view of class based on "inter-personal relations"; rather class should be defined on the basis of "objective determinations." The state must ultimately be the purveyor of class power in this formulation because it cannot be anything else given the "requirements" of the capitalist mode of production.

Now I would argue that this view is certainly debatable as are the assumptions that are contained within it both about Marx's understanding of human agency and about the possibility of totally rejecting empirical procedures as offering an avenue for us to develop an adequate definition of the state. Marxism, as Raymond Williams argues so clearly, is based on some sense of "determination" but it does not fit well with a view that human agents are simply the "bearers" of objective forces.[24] Moreover, while empirical procedures may not be able to guarantee the development of an adequate analysis of the extent to which class power can be transferred into state power, they certainly cannot be dispensed with altogether.

Yet, however one may feel about the epistemological and theoretical limitations of his work, what Poulantzas has done is to point out rather dramatically the necessity of understanding those moments in the analysis of the state that must

14

be seen as decisively "objective" because of their relationships to the mode of production. The virtue of this, to
paraphrase Ralph Miliband, has been to show how reform-
minded governments in capitalism, pledged to wide-reaching
changes, often carry out only a small part of their promised
political program.[25] In other words, this view suggests the
degree to which the institutions which comprise the state go
well beyond governments. A social democratic government,
even a Marxist government, may not completely hold state power.
As Leo Panitch notes in the case of Chile, Salvador Allende
led a Marxist government in Chile but despite this Chile
remained a capitalist state.[26] The extent to which a
government effectively controls the power of the state, or the
extent to which it can speak on behalf of the state, will
depend upon broader class forces and the balance of power
that exists between the various institutions in the state
system such as the bureaucracy, the judiciary and the military.
The classes that each of these institutions represent and the
values that members of these institutions hold will generally
define in which measure governmental power is circumscribed
by state power.

Another feature of Poulantzas' discussion is the extent
to which it has stimulated an awakened interest among western
Marxists about the capacity for the capitalist state to
distance itself from direct ties to the capitalist class.
Building on the work of Louis Althusser,[27] Poulantzas has been
greatly responsible for calling attention to the extremely
provocative (and much debated) concept of the "relative
autonomy" of the state.

Marx's own writings on the nature of the state definitely
contain both an emphasis on the state as a direct instrument
of class domination and an awareness of the administrative

significance of the state as a supervisor of the operations of capitalist production.[28] These two aspects of the state were not in any way incompatible since in order to ensure and regulate the contractual obligations upon which the free market in labour depends, the state obviously had to remain at least partially free from direct class bias. In the case of modern capitalist liberal-democratic states, the effectiveness of state functioning is very much contingent upon widespread acceptance of the "neutrality" of the state and this apparent neutrality cannot be manufactured if the state is too closely identified with the ruling class. Thus, as the very popular Marxist dictum goes, while the modern capitalist state can be seen to act on behalf of the ruling class, it does not act at its behest.[29] Poulantzas has even gone as far as to argue that the most "effective" capitalist state will be one where the members of the ruling class "do not participate directly in the State apparatus, that is to say when the ruling class is not the politically governing class."[30] None of this suggests, of course, that the so-called "relative autonomy" of the state is a quality that is only specific to capitalism. Different state systems have varying degrees of direct and indirect attachment to the interests of dominant classes and status groups. The strength of these attachments and the ways in which they are expressed in social and cultural production and reproduction cannot be established adequately by abstract theoretical formulae; rather they are matters for historical investigation.

I will return to a more detailed critical examination of the concept of "relative autonomy" in the discussion of sport that follows in the next section of this presentation. However, at this point I want to return to the two questions that I raised at the outset of this brief discussion of basic

16

theoretical debates on the nature and role of the state. What is the state and what is its role in social and cultural life? Recognizing the limitations of abstract definitions, I shall summarize by noting that the one thing which all Marxists do agree on is a definition where the state is best thought of as a complex of institutions that is the political embodiment of ruling or dominant interests in societies. Included in this definition is the view that the state's main historical role has been to give institutional, legal and coercive support to the rules and procedures which define the distribution of human choices and material advantages in societies. Another facet of this role has been to give cultural and ideological support to these rules and procedures and to provide opportunities for periodic reforms in their interpretation and implementation. In liberal democratic states the various institutions within the state system which perform these roles are the central government, the "public" administration and bureaucracy, the military, the police, the judiciary and various forms of sub-central (e.g., provincial, municipal) government and administrative assembly.[31] In fascist and socialist states the range of formally incorporated state institutions has often broadened to include the various networks of voluntary organizations that remain comparatively "autonomous" in liberal-democratic states.

Sport, Culture and the State

Where does sport fit into all of this? I would suggest that there are actually two related sides to this question. One side of the question focusses upon the degree to which sport's formal and informal incorporation into the institutional apparatus of the state influences the nature and meaning of sport in social and cultural life. The other side of the

17

question focusses upon the extent to which the nature and meaning of sport in different state systems aid in the reproduction of the rules and procedures which define class power and the overall distribution of privileges in society. The theoretical perspectives on the state and civil society that I have just outlined all offer different answers to these questions and it is to a consideration of some of these answers that I now want to turn.

Let us examine first the case of sport viewed from the perspective of liberal pluralist theories about culture, the state and civil society. In such theories sport would generally be seen as a voluntary set of social and cultural practices that allow for periodic releases from the tensions of everyday existence (e.g., play and recreation) and which provide for collective representations of diverse community interests (e.g., neighbourhood or ethnic teams). The potential multiplicity of collective representations that may occur, however, is mediated by the fact that sport is seen to be institutionalized in a consensual way. That is, it is assumed that sport's main organizational structures, systems of rules and collective meanings are shared by the majority of the members of society. The basic institutional framework here is defined by a long history of sporting practices whose regulation and legitimation is tied to a network of voluntary associations which act to co-ordinate the goals and interests of participants and fans. State involvement in sport is generally assumed to be limited to specifying the manner in which sporting activities can be accommodated to existing laws which pertain to public order and morality, the use of public space, and the production of taxable revenues. A more "indirect" feature of state involvement might include the "use" of sport in the training of social control agents (e.g., the police or

the military) who act in those areas where the state has
sovereignty.

For purposes of the discussion at hand there are two
aspects of this view of sport, culture and the state that are
analytically significant. First, institutionalized sport is
seen to be an expression of a consensus that has been
developed, and is currently shared, by voluntary actors.
Secondly, sport is not seen to be a formal part of the state
system. The state may have occasion to "regulate" some aspects
of sporting practice but sport is not generally recognized to
be part of the state apparatus. Indeed, this version of the
pluralist view of sport, culture and the state is often
accompanied by a moral corollary which suggests, not only that
sport is separate from the state system, but that it ought to
be separate from the state system. Sport is, in short, assumed
to belong to an ideal realm of unrestrained voluntary action,
expressive meaning and cultural creation, and state "intervention" is seen to be an unjustified intrusion into this
realm. According to this view, sport should be an area of
life that is somehow set-off from the "realities" of politics
and government.

Of course, such views about the metaphysical separation
between sport, civil society and politics are not only limited
to liberal pluralism, but they are especially compatible with
the view of human agency that defines the liberal pluralist
frame of reference. Operating from this frame of reference,
people in so-called "voluntary" sporting associations have
often felt compelled to decry the expansion of state-involvement in sport and the "politicization" of sport that has
ostensibly accompanied this expansion. In Canada, for example,
members of Canada's national (voluntary) sports associations
encouraged the expansion of the state's role in sport during

the 1960's and 70's as long as this role was seen to be
limited to "lending a hand" or to "neutral" co-ordination.
However, when state agencies have attempted to insert their
own aims and objectives in place of the traditional and
emergent goals of the national associations there has been a
great deal of tension.[32] Partisan members of national sports
associations have argued that, by limiting the scope of actions
open to the associations, the state has not only "politicized"
sport but has also gone beyond its mandate to act as the
"neutral" embodiment of the interests of its citizens.

Yet, if certain partisans in the sports associations in
Canada and other western societies have utilized one interpretation of liberal pluralist assumptions in order to criticize
state involvement, other people have used different interpretations of these assumptions in order to explain and
legitimate this involvement. In certain areas of public
welfare, the argument runs, voluntary associations cannot be
relied upon to represent the interests of all citizens, and
the state, as the so-called real representative of generalized
interests, must play a role. Along these lines, it is argued
that state involvement in sport can be seen historically as
part and parcel of the general movement in society toward more
equitable opportunities in a welfare-oriented world order.
The move, in T.H. Marshall's words, from an emphasis on civil
and political rights to increasing social rights of citizenship
in western democracies has necessitated a certain expansion of
the responsibilities traditionally managed by the state.[33]
Thus increased state involvement in sport is seen simply as an
expansion of the state's mandate to act on "behalf" of its
citizens in the areas of health, welfare and cultural life
and has even been seen by some people as an indicator of the
"progress" made in the growth of citizenship rights. From

this perspective, the state is seen to act in concert with the plurality of interest groups in society and in sport, balancing their various needs in a way that is universally beneficial.

Now I would argue that most of the literature about politics and the state in sport tends to adopt (either tacitly or directly) one or another of these variants of liberal-pluralism. The fact that the supporters of these perspectives often appear to be in such fundamental disagreement with one another tends to disguise the common assumptions that unite them. That is, we are led to overlook the degree to which proponents of each view tacitly assume that society is composed of voluntary actors who interact freely within a framework of a broad institutional consensus and where the state is seen largely as the embodiment of generalized interest. What is at issue between the various proponents of these views is the ways in which the state can best achieve its mandate to represent its citizens without putting limits upon their capacities to act in the various voluntary associations that are central to a pluralist society.

Earlier in this paper I attempted to suggest some of the limitations of the pluralist view of civil society, politics and the state and I do not see any real need to rehash this critique again. Similarly, since I have so often attacked the sport literature's many ideological corollaries to liberal pluralism in other papers (most notably, the ideas of unre-strained voluntarism in sports and of classlessness in sports), I do not think it necessary to point out once again the ways in which liberal pluralist assumptions about sport in society are simply not consonant with our historical experience.[34] I shall only say here that liberal pluralist discussions of politics and sports do not really engage the problems that are raised when one sees the state not as the embodiment of general interests, but rather as the embodiment of only some interests--especially those interests that can be identified as a result of social class relations in liberal-democratic societies.

Marxist studies of politics and sports have been far better in engaging these problems even though they have not always done so in a completely satisfying way. As indicated earlier, there is a great range in Marxist perspectives on the nature of the state and this range extends to discussions of the state's relationships to civil society and culture. I want to turn now to a consideration of some of the Marxist perspectives that were discussed in the previous section of this paper and show how aspects of the Marxist "debate on the state" influence an understanding of sports and politics in capitalist societies.

The most common approach to sport taken by Marxists is based on the view that all forms of culture and political expression are "superstructural" elements of existence. In this view, the state, as a political formation, and sport, as a type of cultural practice, are both seen to be direct reflections of class interests and the material forces and relations that define capitalism as a mode of production. Furthermore, work in this mainstream Marxist tradition tends to assume that all superstructural phenomena are, in some way, instrumentally connected to class interest. In the case of sports, it is argued that sports are largely controlled by members of the dominant class and that their institutional and ideological features have developed in a way that corresponds with, and helps to reproduce, the conditions upon which class power is based.[35]

Sport's role in reproducing the class structure can be understood from this perspective largely on the basis of its

22

capacity to act as an area of social contact for the ruling
class and as an area of political socialization which
legitimates the capitalist system of allocating rewards. This
has the dual effect of teaching "appropriate" values to
prospective capitalists and of legitimating the existing
system of allocating rewards and privileges for other groups,
thereby minimizing the necessity of the implementation of
coercive measures by the state. Along these lines it is
argued that sport reflects all phases of bourgeois ideology.
Most notably, sport ostensibly glorifies meritocratic standards
of hierarchy and success based on skill, celebrates commercialism, and presents a false view of social progress through the
continued assault on the record books. At the same time, the
argument runs, the popularity of sport among the under-classes
is simply a manifestation of their incorporation into the ideological system which binds them. Sport supposedly provides a
false sense of escape and functions as a compensatory mechanism
to an alienated existence. In this way sport supposedly retards
the development of working class consciousness and undermines
the socialist project. The state's role in all of this is
simply to help in coordinating and popularizing sport while
surrounding its involvement in mystifying notions of the
collective good that mask its class bias.

Now there can be no denying, I believe, that this type of
analysis has a great deal of explanatory power. One of its main
strengths is to emphasize the class character of sport in
capitalist societies and make this a central feature in assessing sport's relationships to politics and the state. There is
certainly little doubt, for example, that where researchers
have examined patterns of ownership and control in commercial
sport or patterns of recruitment to voluntary associations in
sport, working class individuals have been notably under-
represented.[36] Similarly, the central role of sports in the

23

life-styles and childhood socialization of the capitalist class
has been amply documented, and there have been several studies
which have shown that sport has on occasion been used as an
ideological weapon in class conflict.[37] Moreover, there also
seems to be at least some merit in the argument that sports and
other forms of popular entertainment often do substitute in
working class life at the expense of an intense involvement in
politics and related forms of social participation. Added to
this, and on a somewhat different level, one cannot help but
be struck by the degree to which so much of the organization
and culture of modern sport seems to have been influenced by
capitalist productive forces and relations. For example,
"amateur" sports at their highest levels have almost become
monuments to such new sciences as biomechanics, exercise
physiology, and sport psychology where a market rationality
is expressed in a mechanical quest for efficiency in human
performance that is indentured to state and commercial sponsorship. Professional sports, meanwhile, have gone a great distance
toward reducing the meaning of athletic contests to a simple
dramatization of commodity relations.

Yet, it is important, I believe, not to push this line of
reasoning too far. The argument advanced by Paul Hoch and
others that sports effectively socialize their participants
with reactionary elitist, sexist, racist, and consumatory views,
or else simply act as large scale opiates which induce apathy
among the underclasses, are far from reasonable and appear to
be belied by considerable evidence to the contrary. An equally
problematic formulation that is often common to the Marxist
views that I have described is the argument that the state
merely acts as a handmaiden to capital in its use of sport as
an instrument of big business, and capitalist interests.

We need to be cautious about all of these arguments for

they seem to be based on highly questionable assumptions. In the first case, most of the mainstream Marxist views that I have described are overly reductive and non-dialectical. They fall prey to a mechanistic view which reduces cultural formations to passive "reflections" of reality rather than meaningful dramatizations of it.[38] Moreover, these arguments also assume incorrectly that members of the dominant class actually do exercise complete control over sport and that they are able to use it (especially through state programs) in an instrumental way as a defense of class interest.[39] There may be a widespread under-representation of the working class in key corporate and state positions in sport, but there is also a good deal of evidence to suggest that a good number of these positions have historically been held by petit bourgeois individuals, skilled labourers and professionals (e.g., shop-keepers, clerks, artisans, teachers) whose interests have not always been identical to those of the capitalist class.[40] Furthermore, it seems particularly unreasonable to assume, as many Marxist arguments seem to do, that participants in working class culture who consume sport are somehow unreflective dupes or that a deep interest in sports is incompatible with either militant trade unionism and the pursuit of the class struggle.[41]

What can be added to remedy these theoretical deficiencies? Let us consider the "structuralist" position that I described earlier. From this perspective it is irrelevant to even debate about such questions as who owns or who controls sports, or about the degree to which state sport programs can be seen to be expressions of class interests. It is argued, from this perspective, that individuals ("subjects") are not important. The state and sport both have a degree of "relative autonomy" from the class structure. Structuralists would concede, for example, that sports have their own ideological traditions,

meanings and styles and that these features cannot be understood as a simple reflection of class interests and the infrastructural categories of capitalism. Nonetheless, in the
"last instance" as Althusser might say, these autonomous
traditions, meanings, and styles are ultimately tied in
"structuralist Marxism" to the reproduction of forces that are
generated abstractly in the mode of production. This
reproduction is sport's main ideological function in capitalism
and the state is the medium through which this reproduction
occurs. For instance, both Louis Althusser and Nicos
Poulantzas have argued that sport is not a part of the ideological system or cultural apparatus of civil society, it is,
rather, part of the cultural "Ideological State Apparatus."[42]

Let us consider some of the general strengths and
weaknesses of this view. On the positive side, it has the
virtue of nominally maintaining some sense of separation
between membership in the dominant class and participation in
organization or institutional elites in sport, and it recognizes
that state-supported sport programs need not operate at the
behest of capitalists in order to function on their behalf.
Yet, while this view nominally grants cultural and political
formations a degree of "autonomy" and while it recognizes the
indirect way in which the state acts to support capitalism, it
confuses class power and state power in a way that simply
transforms the idea of relative autonomy into a set of
assertions about functional interdependence. The state (and
sport as a "relatively autonomous field" within it) is
relatively autonomous because it needs to be in order to
function properly as an area of social reproduction and meet
the"requirements" of the capitalist mode of production.

Now as John Rex has recently argued,[43] this kind of
abstract teleological thinking has been criticized for some

time in sociology in the long-standing debate over the status
of functional analysis in sociological theory. And, Rex
continues, functionalism is not any more palatable when it comes
from the left than when it comes from the political right. In
its left-wing versions a functionalist perspective commits us to
an abstract emphasis on the reproductive functions of sport
almost completely to the exclusion of the range of often
oppositional meanings that sport has for members of different
classes.

In contradistinction to structural determinism and the
functionalist premises which surround it, I would endorse
Raymond Williams" argument that the reduction of meaningful
cultural creations to a purely reproductive status is not at
all adequate for analytic purposes.[44] Whether we are talking
about the state itself, or of the place of sport in relation
to the state, we are dealing with contested and conflict-
filled areas of human experience. Sport in particular has
occasionally, let us say often, been instrumentally connected
with the expression of dominant class interests in the
development of capitalism and there is a strong sense in which
its traditions, styles and major practices, its meanings and
metaphoric qualities can be logically, abstractly, connected
to the constitutive logic of the capitalist mode of production.
But have these connections always been present and clearly
defined in the institutional development of sport in capitalist
societies? Are these connections necessarily inevitable and
can we say that all state programs in sport have simply tended
to support such connections?

I think if we pose these questions in historical terms
that the answers to them are far from clear. For my part I
would be inclined to answer them with a qualified no. Sports
are historically constituted and contested features of human

27

experience and their meanings, institutional shape, relations
to class and the state are literally defined by the struggles
that have characterized lived social experience at different
historical moments. In this way it can be argued that the
changing definition and organization of sport in the development of the capitalist societies is indissolubly connected to
class conflicts and the conflicting cultural creations of
different classes. It is clear, for example, in Bryan Palmer's
discussion of baseball in the culture of the working class in
Hamilton, Ontario in the late nineteenth century,[45] that baseball had the potential to take on a set of oppositional meanings
within the developing bourgeois hegemony. Similarly, this is
seen in my own work on the social development of Canadian
sport.[46] There is no doubt that the struggle between class
fractions within the bourgeoisie over the social definition
and control of sport in the nineteenth century was an active
process of contesting instrumentalities rather than a simple
unified expression of bourgeois dominance. What I take to be
significant about such examples is the degree to which they
illustrate the oppositional features of the cultural expressions
of subordinate classes and class fractions--features that are
part and parcel of the relationships that the subordinate
classes and class fractions have to the dominant hegemony.
The reduction of sport to the instrumental control of a ruling
class or state elite, or to an abstract feature of some vague
ideological state apparatus, loses the dynamic elements of the
constitutive role that sport has played in history.

Some Concluding Remarks

     I want to conclude this presentation by emphasizing once
again that the kind of understandings of sport and politics that
I am calling for are historically-based types of analyses that
are sensitive to the active role that sport has played (and

continues to play) in social reproduction and transformation in capitalist societies. As I have already noted, if we focus on the place of sport in the state's role in the struggle over the reproduction and transformation of capitalism it seems true to say that most often direct and indirect state involvement in sport or in related forms of popular recreation has been associated in some way with class interests in capitalist societies (e.g., rules over where and when to play, over the "conduct" of popular recreations, or rules which have protected the monopoly position of professional team sports). There is also evidence to suggest, however, that in most capitalist societies class struggles and the expression of class interests in sport (e.g., the struggle over the definition of amateurism) have been carried on outside of the sphere of widespread state involvement. Even now the nature of state involvement is often limited and focussed on the development of some kind of liaison with traditionally established and restrictive voluntary associations.[47] In this regard, modern state policies often have an important reformist character to them in their capacity to influence and broaden the goals of these associations. On the other hand, state interests expressed in the creation of "national" goals and the production of high level athletic performances which have ideological payoffs in the international athletic marketplace hardly work towards the long-range transcendence of capitalism.

All of this suggests, I believe, that it is much too much to say that the ruling class, or the state, has always used (or is now using) sport directly and instrumentally toward its own ends or that sport in modern society can only "function" in some sort of reproductive way. In addition to their broader theoretical shortcomings each of these views on sport, culture and the capitalist state over-emphasizes sport's role in

regulation and repression and underplays its role in indirect
rule and reform (e.g., state funded recreation opportunities,
movements for the democratization of sport, etc.). People are
not falsely conscious dupes and sports under the best
circumstances can combine the exercise of creative physical
mastery with self-development and enjoyment in a way that is
matched by few activities in contemporary life. What is at
issue, however, is the degree to which the pursuit of sports
organized in specific ways and possessing certain "dominant"
or "oppositional" meanings aid in social reproduction. Of
particular relevance is the relationship of state action to
these dominant or oppositional meanings and organizational
modes. In what way, it might be asked, have the dramatizations
of class conflicts, expressed in and through the development
of sport, been mediated and influenced by the changing nature
of state programs? In what direction have most state programs
in sport been geared (e.g., the intended or unintended use of
sport for legitimation or capital accumulation)?[48]

Answers to these and other questions that I have raised
throughout this paper are complex and difficult. The responses
that we give to them will depend upon the particular definition
of the state that we use, on our assumptions about the relationships that exist between class interests and state interests,
and on the methodological strategies that we use in our research
My position would be to adapt and apply Miliband's views and
argue than any balanced analysis of sport's relationship to the
state would combine some of the considerations that derive
from each of the various sides in the Marxist debate on the
state. For example, I would suggest that any adequate analysis
of sport and the state would have to give some recognition to
the social class backgrounds of individuals in the state "elite"
and of those who have influenced and contributed to state

30

programs in sport. Also relevant would be some analysis of the ideological content of the specific practices (e.g., rules, moral codes, technical features) being advocated in these programs at different historical moments, that is, the "culture" that these practices seem to represent, and it would be necessary to assess how this culture compares to other definitions and meanings attributed to sport by various con-flicting groups in the society. Added to this must be some considerations of the more "objective" questions of the chang-ing limits and pressures on state agencies that stem from changes in the mode of production itself. All of these considerations will help us to understand the politics of sport in a changing state system that has variously consolidated and mediated the forces of class domination in capitalism through complex and changing strategies of regulation, repression and reform.

Now there is one last thing that I want to comment upon in closing. I mentioned that I was not going to deal only with the capitalist state in this paper and thus far I have concentrated exclusively on it. What about sports in modern socialist states? Well, there are three papers later in this volume that are exclusively devoted to this topic so I do not intend to do anything more than raise one issue that I see to be at the core of analyses of the politics of sports in state socialist societies.

I mentioned earlier how Marx talked about the state both as a direct instrument of class domination and as a more detached "supervisor" of the administration and regulation of capitalism. Now related to this latter notion is an issue that Marxists have not been very good at responding to or confronting. I am talking here of the question that was constantly raised by Bakunin in his many debates with Marx and was later put forward (in a much different way) by Max Weber. That is, to what

extent are the demands of production in highly-rationalized
industrial societies such that they inevitably require degrees
of co-ordination and control which virtually guarantees domination by some kind of administrative, political or bureaucratic
elite?[49] At the theoretical level this question demands that
Marxists struggle with the prospect that the state may indeed
be incapable of "withering away" under current or even future
conditions. At the practical historical level the question
demands an examination of the degree to which the state systems
of modern socialist societies embody the practical political
interests of the communist party more than the interests of
the citizens who comprise these societies.

The implications of these concerns for the study of
sport in state socialist societies seem clear and prompt
several questions. What is the role of sport in the state
system of socialist societies? What are the political
implications of the highly-rationalized systems of athletic
production that have characterized the sport programs of
state-socialist societies? Can it be argued that sport in
these societies is organized in a way that serves the general
interest or only some interests and how does this compare to
the sport/state relation in capitalist societies?

That there are both similarities and major differences
between sport in capitalist and state-socialist societies is
certain. Moreover, the questions that I have raised should
not be confused with those tired liberal pluralist defenses
of capitalist sport which point an accusing finger in the
direction of socialist states and cry out that "things are
no better over there!" Rather, such questions seem inevitable
if one is to seek out and develop an adequate understanding
of the world-wide politics of modern sports. If Marxist
analyses of such politics are to have any credibility whatsoever, Marxists can no longer afford to leave the critical

32

analysis of sport in socialist states uncontested to the vast numbers of apologists for bourgeois sport.

NOTES AND REFERENCES

1. I got the idea for this paper while listening to Ralph
    Miliband speak at Queen's University in the spring of
    1979. Miliband's talk was directed at a non-specialist
    audience and he sought to draw out in very basic terms
    some of the implications of various Marxist "debates"
    on the state. This talk made a great impression on me
    and I thought that I might try to write a similar
    "introduction" for people in the sociology of sport who
    only had a passing familiarity with the broader critical
    literature on politics and the state. Moreover, I
    thought that such an introduction might be the best way
    to introduce the other topics and papers included in the
    program of this symposium. It will be apparent to anyone
    with any familiarity with the various "debates on the
    state" that the position put forward in this paper leans
    very much on Miliband's work. However I have "mediated"
    my use of Miliband with concepts drawn from Raymond
    Williams, Marxism and Literature (London: Oxford Press,
    1977) and my own historical research on sports and the
    Canadian class structure (see my "Power and Play in
    Canadian Social Development," Working Papers in the
    Sociological Study of Sports and Leisure, Kingston:
    Queen's University, Volume 2, No. I, 1979.

2. See, for example, Brian Petrie, "Sport and Politics," in
    D. Ball and J. Loy (eds.), Sport and Social Order
    (Reading: Addison-Wesley, 1975) and B. Lowe, et al.,
    Sport and International Relations (Champagne, Illinois:
    Stipes Publishing, 1978) and Paul Hoch, Rip Off the Big
    Game (New York: Doubleday, 1972). In addition to these
    studies are numerous articles and chapters on sports and
    politics in scholarly journals (including such "specialist"
    journals as the Arena Review and the Journal of Sport and
    Social Issues) and in the popular "anthologies" and texts
    in the sociology of sport such as J. Coakley, Sport in
    Society: Issues and Controversies (St. Louis: C.V.
    Mosby, 1978), J. Loy and G. Kenyon, Sport, Culture and
    Society (New York: Macmillan, 1969), and M. Hart, Sport
    in the Sociocultural Process (Dubuque: Wm. C. Brown,
    1976).

3. There are countless variations of this view in writings on
    politics and society. One of the most influential sources
    of "scientific" justification for the few was developed
    by liberal functionalist theorists in the 1950's and 60's.
    See, in particular, Talcott Parsons' "The Distribution of
    Power in American Society," in Structure and Process in
    Modern Societies (New York: The Free Press, 1960).
    Parsons defines the state as the social institution that

specializes in a society's "collective goal attainment." That is, it is an "institutionalized power system" within which certain categories of commitments and obligations are treated as binding. Thus, the state helps to achieve functionally important ends and goals defined in terms of ideas, values and conscious goals. See also _The Social System_ (New York: The Free Press of Glencoe).

4. See Ralph Miliband, _Marxism and Politics_ (Oxford: Oxford University Press, 1977) p. 66, and _The State in Capitalist Society_ (London: Quartet Books, 1973), p. 4.

5. The classic example of this, of course, occurs in Hegel's philosophy of the state. See Anthony Giddens discussion of this and Marx's famous critique of Hegel in _Capitalism and Modern Social Theory_ (Cambridge: Cambridge Press, 1971). Somewhat different variations of this view were also part of functionalist analyses of the state as an "institution" in social life (see note 3 above).

6. See Miliband's discussion and critique of this view in _The State and Capitalist Society_.

7. Cited in V.I. Lenin, _State and Revolution_ (New York: International Publishers, 1932) p. 16.

8. The concept of "essentially contestable" assumptions is discussed with specific reference to the concept of power in Steven Lukes, _Power: A Radical View_ (London: Macmillan, 1974).

9. See Steven Lukes' discussion of "voluntarism" in "Power and Structure," _Essays in Social Theory_ (New York: Columbia University Press, 1977).

10. For an excellent criticism of the view of power as a "circulating resource" see Anthony Giddens, "Power in the Writings of Talcott Parsons," in _Studies in Social and Political Theory_ (New York: Basic Books, 1977).

11. C.B. Macpherson, _The Life and Times of Liberal Democracy_, (Oxford University Press) p. 77.

12. C.B. Macpherson, _The Life and Times of Liberal Democracy_, p. 77.

13. Anthony Giddens, _Class Structure of the Advanced Societies_ (London: Hutchinson, 1973) p. 90.

14. Ralph Miliband, _Marxism and Politics_, p. 67.

15. See Miliband's in-depth discussions of this view in "Marx and the State," _The Socialist Register_ (1965) and in _Marxism and Politics_.

16. My position on these perspectives has been taken almost directly from Miliband, _Marxism and Politics_, pp. 68-74. There are, of course, a number of different interpretations that fall outside the limits that I have set myself for this discussion. In particular see the articles on the recent "state derivation debate" in John Holloway and Sol Picciotto, _State and Capital: A Marxist Debate_ (London: Edward Arnold, 1978).

17. Ralph Miliband, _Marxism and Politics_, pp. 69-70.

18. Wallace Clement, _The Canadian Corporate Elite: An Analysis of Economic Power_ (Toronto: McClelland & Stewart, 1975), and Ralph Miliband, _The State in Capitalist Society_, op. cit.

19. Dennis Olsen, "The State Elites," in Leo Panitch, _The Canadian State: Political Economy and Political Power_ (Toronto: University Press, 1977).

20. See Miliband, _Marxism and Politics_, p. 70.

21. Miliband, _Marxism and Politics_, p. 72.

22. Nicos Poulantzas, "The Problem of the Capitalist State," in R. Blackburn, _Ideology in Social Science_ (New York: Vintage Books, 1973).

23. Poulantzas, "The Problem of the Capitalist State," p.242.

24. Raymond Williams, _Marxism and Literature_ (see part II).

25. Miliband, _Marxism and Politics_, p. 73.

26. Leo Panitch, "The Role and Nature of the Canadian State," in Leo Panitch, _The Canadian State: Political Economy and Political Power_,

27. See Louis Althusser, _For Marx_ (Middlesex: Penguin Books, 1969), and _Lenin and Philosophy and Other Essays_ (London: New Left Books, 1971).

28. See Miliband, _Marxism and Politics_, pp. 75-90.

29. The popularity of this dictum is easily documented. For instance, it is cited in Miliband's _Marxism and Politics_, in Panitch's "The Role and Nature of the Canadian State," and in Wallace Clement "The Corporate Elite, the Capitalist Class, and the Canadian State," in Panitch, _The Canadian State: Political Economy and Political Power_.

30. Nicos Poulantzas, "The Problem of the Capitalist State," p. 246.

31. This definition is taken from Miliband, _The State in Capitalist Society_, pp. 49-55.

32. See, for example, Nora McCabe, "Volunteers being pushed from amateur sport," Toronto Globe and Mail (Saturday, January 7, 1978), p. 45.

33. T.H. Marshall, Citizenship and Social Class (London: Cambridge Press, 1950).

34. See my discussion in "Power and Play in Canadian Social Development," Working Papers in the Sociological Study of Sports and Leisure (Vol. 2, No. 1, 1979).

35. Examples of this approach (with slightly different emphases) can be found in Paul Hoch, Rip Off the Big Game (New York: Doubleday, 1972), Jean-Marie Brohm, Sport: A Prison of Measured Time (London: Ink Links, 1978), and Gerhard Vinnai, Football Mania (London: Ocean Books, 1973).

36. See R. Gruneau, "Elites, Class and Corporate Power in Canadian Sport," in F. Landry and W. Orban, Sociology of Sport (Miami: Symposia Specialists, 1978), Paul Hoch, Rip Off the Big Game, and R. Hollands and R. Gruneau, "Social Class and Voluntary Action in the Administration of Canadian Amateur Sport," Working Papers in the Sociological Study of Sports and Leisure (Volume 2, No. 3, 1979).

37. On the role of private clubs and their related sports activities in "elite" socialization, see W. Clement, The Canadian Corporate Elite: An Analysis of Economic Power. On sports as ideological weapons see my "Power and Play in Canadian Social Development," and also Francis Hearn, "Toward a Critical Theory of Play," Telos (Winter 1976).

38. This point is also made in Christopher Lasch, "The Corruption of Sports," The New York Review of Books (April 28, 1977).

39. Consider, on the other hand, Orlando Patterson's discussion of "The Cricket Ritual in the West Indies," New Society (June 26, 1969) as a demonstration of the oppositional qualities of the dramatizations presented in sport. Citing Patterson's analysis of the riots that are provoked when the West Indian team loses to a visiting English team, Steven Lukes makes the following observations:

> In the West Indies, a test match is not so much
> a game as a collective ritual--a social drama in
> which almost all of the basic conflicts within
> the society are played out symbolically. At
> certain moments this ritual acquires a special
> quality which reinforces its potency and creates

a situation that can only be resolved in violence. Cricket is the Englishman's game, and yet it also gives the West Indian masses 'a weapon against their current aggressors, the carriers of the dominant English culture in local society.'

40. See Alan Metcalfe, "Organized Sport and Social Stratification in Montreal, 1860-1895," in R. Gruneau and J. Albinson, Canadian Sport: Sociological Perspectives (Toronto: Addison-Wesley, 1976).

41. This point is made in Miliband, Marxism and Politics, p. 52.

42. See Louis Althusser, Lenin and Philosophy and Other Essays.

43. John Rex, "Threatening Theories," Society (Volume 15, No. 3, March/April, 1978).

44. This position is developed further in Williams, Marxism and Literature.

45. See Bryan Palmer, A Culture in Conflict: Skilled Workers and Industrial Capitalism in Hamilton, Ontario, 1860-1914 (Montreal: McGill-Queen's University Press, 1979).

46. This tension is discussed in "Power and Play in Canadian Social Development," Working Papers in the Sociological Study of Sports and Leisure (Volume 2, No. 1, 1979).

47. For a discussion of the class-restrictive nature of the control of national "volunteer" sports governing bodies see Robert Hollands and Richard Gruneau, "Social Class and Voluntary Action in the Administration of Canadian Amateur Sport," Working Papers in the Sociological Study of Sports and Leisure (Volume 2, No. 3, 1979).

48. It is possible that the apparent "statization" of sport in some of the capitalist societies is simply part and parcel of a general movement on the part of state agencies away from the simple "supervision" of capital accumulation to a somewhat different concern over welfare-statism and legitimation. An interesting (although limited by its functionalist assumptions) framework for such an analysis is provided in James O'Conner's The Fiscal Crisis of the State (New York, 1973).

49. Anthony Giddens makes this problem a central focus in the latter sections of The Class Structure of the Advanced Societies.

2
Class, Violence and Sport

The Case of Soccer Hooliganism in Britain

Ian Taylor

In this paper I wish to provide some kind of overview of the existing sociological literature on the notorious question of violence and sport, and then to show the relevance of recent developments in so-called "theories of the State" and in "class-theory"[1] to the more useful explanation of the sport-violence nexus. Clearly, however, as the manager of any British soccer club might say, we shall have to find some short cuts to that goal.

I shan't be examining here the question of violent tactics and behaviour amongst professional sportspeople, although this has been a matter of widespread concern, I know, in popular discussions of North American ice hockey (for example) in recent years,[2] and also in the official delibera- tions of the bodies that control European soccer.[3] I shan't attempt to range too broadly even over "spectator" or "fan" violence in all the societies where it has been reported, since to do so would take us into discussions of phenomena as far removed as the "football war" of 1970 between the poor third-world nation states of Honduras and El Salvador, on the one hand,[4] and the growth of violent interventions by fans in baseball games in urban North America, on the other.[5] Spectator violence is fairly widespread through many advanced and third-world societies,[6] and has indeed been reported in the Soviet Union,[7] but it is not universal, and its form is to some extent specific to the context in which it occurs.

We shall be concerned here to deal primarily with the question of violence amongst supporters of soccer clubs in Britain, and the attempts made to control and to account for that violence. Some sideways reference will be made to the North American situation, but no real claim is being made as to the generalisability of the remarks made about Britain, and specifically about soccer. Our concentration on British

40

soccer can be justified pragmatically in terms of my earlier
work on soccer hooliganism in that country (1971a, 1971b and
1976), and the need for that work to be revised and updated.
But I think it can also be justified in terms of the advanced
degree of degeneration in the class relations in Britain, and
the rapid emergence of a strong State, at all levels of the
British social formation, as a means of policing the crisis
in civil society. In that country, the social contradictions
which we shall want to identify later have perhaps "matured"
to a rather more urgent extent than they have, as yet, in
North America. I shall return to this use of language and
perspective later in the paper.

I want first to narrate a simple history of the recent
history of soccer violence in Britain, and then to examine the
accounts advanced for these developments by both 'accredited'
and lay social scientists. In other words, I shall want to use
the question of soccer violence in its relatively specific,
and British, form as an occasion for a more broadly based set
of theoretical reflexions..

The Development of Soccer Violence in Britain 1961-1979

"Violence" amongst soccer supporters in Britain has been
publically identified as a serious social problem in the mass
media and amongst social control agencies generally, since
1961, subsequent to a series of invasions of the playing pitch
by spectators. Prior to that year, and, specifically, the
invasion of the pitch at Sunderland after the home team had
equalized in a "quarter-final" of the F.A. Cup against the
leading club of the First Division, Tottenham Hotspur (the
first televised pitch invasion), there are very few recorded
instances of spectators "trespassing" on to the playing arena.[8]
Popular folklore, indeed, insists that the pitch was always

41

understood, in the period from the first world war through to
the late 1950's, as sacred, an area reserved for the club's
players only: in effect, the stage on which the people's
game was to be regularly played. In the early to middle
1960's, the pitch invasions escalated, on occasion, into
attempts to occupy the pitch in order to force postponement of
games, when the supporters' team were threatened with defeat.[9]
There were also new attempts by the crowd to distract the
attention of goal-keepers whilst they took goal-kicks, as well
as of players taking penalties (interventions which would also
have not been thought of by spectators prior to the 1960's).
The more aggressive forms of crowd response to the game, and
also the increasing evidence of property vandalism prior to
and after the game, resulted in some anxious press reportage,
although it was not until 1969 that any official enquiry was
carried out into "crowd behaviour at football matches" (The
Lang Report).[10]

The Lang Report is a treasury of commonsense accounting
of the 1960's middle-range "sociology", in particular the
sociology of the crowd. It runs through a wide variety of
factors which had been thought of as responsible for the growth
of incidents of 'hooliganism' at soccer grounds during the
1960's (from the bad example provided by players who challenge
referees' decisions to the influence of "alcohol consumption"
in the grounds) and concludes that:

> No single simple solution (can be found) for
> a problem which is often due to a combination
> of factors, which is liable to arise on any
> occasion when large crowds assemble, especially
> if the circumstances are exciting, and which is
> a form of social malaise not at all unusual in
> the state of relaxed discipline which is a
> feature of modern society. (Lang (1969)
> Introduction)

The Report's proposals centred around the need for expansion of the amount of seated accomodation available, especially in the old, and frequently decrepit, football stadia that are characteristic of working class British towns, especially in the North of England and in Scotland; on the need for 'maximum cooperation between a football club and the police' (specifically, in introducing official detention rooms and central police control points at all grounds, but also in the stationing of police on the terraces as well as round the playing pitch). It also, symbolically, re-emphasized the need for players and spectators to accept the authority of the referee.

The Lang Report was published in an atmosphere of re-newed and amplified concern around violence at soccer, occasioned by the appearance of the Skinhead. Emerging out of the East End of London at the start of the 1968-9 soccer season, the Skinhead was an object initially of a bemused form of press reportage[11] and indeed contradictory analysis, even, in the lively radical press of the period.[12] There was general agreement, however, that the emergence of the Skinhead signalled a new phase in the development of forms of crowd behaviour of soccer games (Clarke, 1973). In particular, the Skinhead was accused of being at the centre of 'fighting gangs' of young football supporters whose first purpose on entering a football stadium was to attempt to "take the ends". (Cohen, 1976). The ends were the areas of the terrace behind each goal, which had traditionally been a favourite standing place for spectators who wanted to be close to the "goal-mouth action": they were now transformed into "territories" over the occupation of which rival supporters would do physical battle prior to, and during, the game itself.

With the emergence of the Skinhead, too, the repertoire

of the football hooligan was allegedly expanded. To the acts
of vandalism against rival stadia (ranging from the writing of
graffiti to actual physical destruction of seats, terrace
barriers, and other items of property) were added major
incidents of vandalism to shops and other buildings in city
centres en route to and from the game, and also buses and
trains transporting supporters to away games.[13] And the
Skinhead's racist-populist politics spilled over into campaigns
of physical violence against the migrant Asian population in
Britain (the so-called "Paki-bashing" phenomenon) (cf. Pearson,
1976).

On 2 January 1971, in the meantime, 66 people died at
the Ibrox Stadium, Glasgow (the home ground of Glasgow Rangers
F.C.) whilst leaving the ground at the end of the game, and
being crushed to death on a narrow stairway. Public attention
was drawn to the question of the safety of the grounds on
which more than two million people watched soccer every week;
and the ensuing official Report, the <u>Report of the Inquiry
into Crowd Safety at Sports Grounds by Lord Wheatley</u>, published
in May 1972, recommended <u>inter alia</u> that local city authorities
should be given the power to licence soccer grounds in the way
that they were able to licence night clubs, public houses, and
other places of local entertainment. Failure of the football
clubs to bring their grounds up to specified levels of safety
should result in refusal of licence, and temporary closure of
the club.[14] The other proposals of the Wheatley Inquiry concerned the provision of new crush barriers on soccer terraces,
and at exits, with a generalized emphasis in the report being
on the need to further 'contain' and control the crowd on the
terracing.

The early 1970's witnessed a series of "initiatives"
and "new measures" against soccer hooliganism, ranging from

the introduction of specially-trained snatch squads of police
to make arrests in football crowds on the terrace, to
programmes undertaken to "involve" young supporters more
intimately with the affairs of the local club.[15] There were
also several major policy conferences at regional and national
level[16] and also a further official report on Crowd Behaviour,
specifically in Scotland (The McElhone Report, 1977). (cf.
discussion by Ingham, 1978). And, a major paradox, a
continuing theme in the discussions and reports was that
hooliganism was "about to be beaten". In November 1972, Mr.
Walter Winterbottom, Director of the Sports Council, told the
national conference on soccer hooliganism held in Glasgow
that:

> There are isolated incidents which have been
> very, very severe, but the wave that we are
> supposed to be seeing, the wave that reached
> its crisis about two and a half years ago,
> according to information and figures is not
> coming up again. (Evening Citizen, Glasgow,
> 29 November 1972)

As Home Secretary, and later as Prime Minister, Mr James
Callaghan, announced the impending defeat of soccer violence,
in 1969 and later again in 1974. The 1974-9 Labour Government's
Minister for Sport, Mr Denis Howell, observed, on 8 May 1977,
that the numbers of people being arrested at soccer matches
was an indication of "a success for the police":

> The object of the exercise was to reduce
> the size of the problem to one the police
> could manage. This clearly happened.
> (Morning Telegraph, 9 May 1977)

The optimism of these assessments was often justified in
terms of the great benefits to be gained from each new
initiative by the Government or by other responsible (i.e.
State) authorities. In 1973, these initiatives took the form
of encouraging magistrates to impose the maximum level of fine

on soccer hooligans (of £100) under existing criminal legislation; and the use of mobile cameras by police (at Coventry, Derby and elsewhere) in order to identify trouble-makers in the crowd. (Guardian 14 August 1973). In 1974, attention turned to the erection of fencing around the perimeters of the playing area, (beginning at Manchester United in June) and to the introduction of identity cards for "under-17s" (which would have to be produced to gain entry at grounds, but which could be confiscated by police subsequent to arrest). This was initiated, with a great deal of newspaper coverage, at Cardiff in September. (Daily Express, 7 September 1974). In 1975, a Labour MP, Walter Johnson, called for young people arrested at soccer games to be automatically detained overnight in police-cells (Guardian 21 April), and in July, the Minister for Sport called for "bars on drink" on coaches and trains taking supporters to games. (30 July). In September, British Railways suspended their practice of offering cheap fares on special trains to football matches; and, in November, the Labour Government's new Criminal Law (Conspiracy Bill) included provisions for fines for "threaten-ing behaviour" (the offence with which most young soccer supporters are charged) to be increased to £1,000 (for over 18's) and £200 for 'juveniles'. (Guardian, 25 November 1976). In 1977, the major initiative, promised by Merlyn Rees, the new Home Secretary, was for an expansion in the provision and use of Attendance Centres (which are centres run for young offenders by the police themselves on weekends, at the same time as the Saturday afternoon game). In addition, in 1977 and 1978, serious action began to be taken against particular clubs, in attempting to prevent people who were identifiable supporters from entering opponents' stadia (Manchester United and Chelsea supporters respectively were banned in these years),

46

and in forcing clubs to play their "home" fixtures on their opponents' grounds or on neutral grounds. In 1979, the responsibility for new initiatives fell to the new Conservative Government, with its general commitment to increases in police power and support for the magistracy and judiciary, as well as its specific commitment to the use of 'short, sharp shock' punishments for young offenders. (see footnote 19).

Each of these initiatives was taken as grounds for optimism about the possibility of winning "the war against soccer hooligans"; and, equally importantly, each of them was presented as a planned and coherent response to individually serious incidents. These precipitating incidents included for 1974 (in April) the invasion of the Manchester United ground just prior to the end of their final game of the season against Manchester City (subsequent to a goal which ensured United's relegation; the first death in the history of soccer hooliganism (of 17 year old Kevin Olson, at a Second Division game in Blackpool, in August, from a stabbing); and the riot of Tottenham Hotspur fams in Rotterdam after "the Spurs" had been beaten in the UEFA Cup Final in May. In 1975, a similar "riot" amongst British fans occurred on the continent of Europe when Leeds United were beaten in the Final of the European Cup, the major European tournament at club level. In 1976, further deaths occurred of young fans (in August, of a Glasgow Celtic supporter, subsequent to a game in Arbroath; and in September, a young Millwall supporter, found dead on a London railway track after a fight with a supporter of a rival London team, West Ham United). In 1976 and 1977, a series of massively violent incidents occurred at games involving Manchester United; and in 1977, the achievement of this violent reputation by the fans of 'the Reds' was challenged. in particular in similar incidents involving fans

47

of Chelsea, Millwall and other teams in the English and
Scottish League.

By 1978 and 1979, indeed, several more English and
Scottish League clubs had developed violent reputations, which
their "fighting gangs" were no doubt concerned to maintain.
The repertoire of some of these gangs now extended far beyond
the "taking of the ends" and the property vandalism of the
1960's to involvement in National Front-inspired attacks on
blacks (especially in South and East London), to terrorising
bus-crews and the staff of the London Underground (both of
which public service occupations are very heavily black), to
destroying the interiors of public houses and shops in the
vicinity of soccer grounds, in city centres and near railway
stations. By the end of the 1970's, a midweek evening or
Saturday afternoon soccer match was an event which occasioned
fear and anxiety <u>in significant sections of local working
class communities themselves</u> (and not just amongst the shop-
keeper population and the agencies of social control). This
new reality of life for working class populations was
recognised in 1979 <u>not</u> by liberals and social democrats (who
tended, with the implicit or explicit support of sociologists
of the centre and the left, to argue that the picture of
soccer violence in the press was a product of "amplification"
through labelling) but by the New Right leadership of the
British Conservative Party in its successful use of a (complex)
"law and order ticket" from 1977 onwards, but especially in
its successful campaign during the General Election of May
1979 (Taylor, 1980a).

We shall return to the question of the New Right and the
form of the State (and State discipline) a little later. Some
comments are necessary, however, on the character of the press
reportage of soccer hooliganism since 1961, since, as nearly

all sociologists now correctly insist, social problems like soccer violence are known to many people only through the treatment they receive in the media.[17]

The Mass Media's Treatment of Soccer Violence

A cycle of stimulus and response is observable in both Governmental and mass media reactions to the development of soccer violence in Britain. Each new incident is taken by the media in general (from the popular newspaper to the highbrow weekly magazines) as evidence of the need for a new initiative which is almost invariably described as a "clamp-down"; and each new initiative is a panacea which obviates the need for more "extreme measures". Calls for the use of the stocks (made by Lady Emmet of Amberly in the House of Lords on 7 October 1976) or for football hooligans to be sprayed with indelible dye (a suggestion put by a Labour M.P., Mr. Arthur Lewis, in 1977), can in this way be described as "batty" (the adjective used about Mr. Lewis, in quotation obtained from another ageing Labour MP, Mr. Marcus Lipton, by the Liberal Guardian newspaper). (Guardian, 13 April 1977).

The cycle of stimulus and response within which official responses to football violence have been formulated also serve to focus attention on the areas in which action can (immediately be taken.[18] Actions which might be useful, from the point of view of social democrats, in tackling the deepening nexus of deprivation in the inner cities and in the ghetto areas from which rank-and-file supporters may come, or in reversing the upward spiral of youthful unemployment, are, in this respect, not strictly or immediately relevant.

Far Right conservative measures, like the re-introduction of the stocks, whilst acceptable in the sense of being 'practicable' without involving fundamental economic or social change, tend to be given prominence in the committedly right-wing newspapers (The Daily Telegraph, and the Daily Mail), but to be ultimately eschewed on condition that the existing apparatus of penal discipline is used with an appropriate severity.[19] Thus, whilst the level of policing and the severe sentencing of soccer fans has increased, and therefore the intensification of penal discipline as a political solution to soccer violence, the process has necessarily been accomplished with a due regard to the necessity for some social concensus. The pressure exerted by press treatment of incidents of soccer violence is exerted primarily on liberals and social democrats, in the form of a demand that they recognise youth violence as evidence of a need for the penal discipline of individuals, and that they suspend or bracket their other "humanitarian" or (long-term) reformist concerns. The concensus around the need for a penal response to soccer violence is in part a product of the demand for immediate and practical action, with the practicability and immediate availability of other measures (to combat unemployment, or to bring about fundamental changes in the life chances of rough working class youth, etc., etc.) closed off in advance. In this way, both the liberal and conservative press in Britain wrench soccer violence out of the social relations in which it has been generated, and without being avowedly 'political', make penal discipline the obvious and necessary measure. They leave untouched the question of when it will be appropriate to address the humanitarianism and reformist concerns of liberals and social democrats.

Press reportage of the struggle against soccer hooligans successfully undertakes some other major ideological projects. In particular, it has to react to the claims of

State authorities that they can deal with the problem of soccer violence (and violent youth generally) whilst also acceding to the commonsensical view that "the youth are getting more troublesome, violent, difficult, etc....". The liberal media seem to achieve this task by taking on the role of a neutral arbiter between the State control agencies, and 'the people', who claim that things are getting worse. This is most notable in the many television documentaries which have been produced, throughout the 1960's and 1970's, on soccer violence;[20] as well as in the "in-depth analyses" of the quality liberal daily and weekly press. It is indeed precisely in this use of "expert" evaluation, and distancing from a particular viewpoint, that the _liberal_ media make their claim to "balance" and neutrality. The answer in each individual article or television programme is to some extent produced in advance by the choice of experts, but it is also "genuinely" dependent on the ability of the expert to persuade his audience and/or his questioner.[21]

The Conservative media are not so sanguine. For them, the answer to the ideological conundrum is that youth _are_ getting worse (because "authority" continues to be soft etc., etc.) but that youth can nonetheless be _controlled_ by the proper use of coercion. The problem is that there are liberal and social democratic agencies who continue to be committed either to the treatment of recalcitrant individuals or to improving their life chances. The pursuit of these other goals has weakened the effective pursuit of social control over troublesome and un-socialized youth. The key to the deteriorating situation is therefore to shift the responsibility for the exercise of social control for the forces of law and order (police, prison, probation service), and to cease conflating social control with the project of social reform.

51

As the soccer violence of the 1970's has continued and developed, the Conservative press in Britain has increasingly effectively argued this case as the case of the people, directed against the 'experts' in the quality press and, especially, the reformers associated with the State social welfare institutions. So that, in general terms, the real anxieties of working class populations at the decline in their standards of commumity are taken up and levelled as indictments of postwar social democratic pretensions of a reconstructed social order; and the specific instance of violent attacks by soccer hooligans on the working class' own community on a regular weekly basis are taken, repeatedly, as confirmation of the people's own need and demand for a return to law and order. (The most predictable of headlines in the popular press on days following major soccer games are of demands for State action to "smash these thugs", "stamp out violence", "Thump and be Thumped" or even "cage the animals". (Sun 4 October 1976, Sheffield Star, 1 December, 1972, Daily Express, 25 November, 1976 and Daily Mirror, 21 April 1976). And the reality of popular experience of soccer violence in 1979 ensures that this particular penal connection, for all that it is connected into an attack on the existing form of the State from the Right, is much more resonant in working class community than the responses we have outlined from the liberal press and "concensual" television documentaries.

We need to emphasise that both the Conservative and Liberal press have developed their ideological paradigms on soccer violence (a) without reference to the massive material changes that have been occurring in the economic and social experience in the situation of working class youth in Britain in the last thirty years, and (b) within the context of a

52

journalistic language that almost guarantees the playing out of violent responses to the (unspoken, unproblematicized) experience of a readership that includes the working class youth themselves.

Mass media accounts of soccer violence are silent, for example, in the virtual collapse that began in the juvenile labour market in Britain in the late 1960's and early 1970's.[22] They are also silent on the absence of any future improvement in the employment possibilities for the "reserve army" of youth, and indeed on the clear recognition of a future of "worklessness" and hopelessness signalled in the culture of Punk, for white youth in particular, and in street crime, on the part of young West Indians.[23]

As liberal sociologists have frequently observed, in this connection and generally, the mass media are guilty of a fixation with "violence", with "incidents" and with "personality", and are also guilty of reporting the events they do select as newsworthy as if they have no history and no complex contradictory context. So the 'thugs' in the reports of soccer violence are stereotypical figures, presented without a history in school, in the declining housing market, in the labour market or in a class society. The closest they get to humanity is when their ages and occupations (which are so frequently non-existent - simply "unemployed") appear in subsequent reports of courtroom appearances, in the week following arrest. The media's account of soccer violence, although it emphasises that "things are getting worse" has actually been curiously static throughout the 1960's and 1970's, and, in the popular press in particular, has been primarily articulated around a stereotypical picture of the growth of "thuggery" and "violence" in society (connected, implicitly, to the growth of permissiveness within "authority").

The use of stereotypes as an explanation of the
activities of hooligans is perfectly mirrored by the popular
press' use of what Stuart Hall calls "a language of violence".
The treatment of soccer violence in the British press has been
characterized by an "editing for impact", characterized by:

> graphic headlines, bold type-faces, warlike
> imagery and epithets, vivid photographs
> cropped to the edges to create a strong
> impression of physical menace, and the
> stories have been decorated with black
> lines and exclamation marks.
> (Hall, 1978, p.26)

The embrace of this form of language by the press is,
however, general to its reportage of sport: it is the
general form of discourse in the back pages of the popular
newspaper. The game itself is increasingly reported in
such terms. Hall notes the continuity between a story
headed - 'FANS GO MAD' in the Sunday People, on 3 March 1977,
and a story, on the following page about a tackle on a
Birmingham City half back, Howard Kendall, by Jeff Nulty of
Newcastle, under the lead headline 'C-R-U-N-C-H'. The
language of violence extends in the same edition even to
discussions of league tables ("THE OTHER BIG FIGHT")and
elsewhere even to "struggles" between clubs over transfers of
players, or between managers and coaches. And since the back
page in the popular press is an "alternative front page",
which is for many readers the starting point of the paper
(and, for many, the only "worthwhile" part), it is not
difficult to see the importance of this editing for impact.
What is for male working class youth its own, relatively
autonomous "life world", soccer, the people's game, is
increasingly depicted as being a world in which "violence"
is a means both literally and metaphorically to goal. As
Hall observes:

> If the language of football reporting
> is increasingly the language of thrills
> and spills, hard tackles and tough games,
> of struggle, victory and defeat, studded
> with images drawn from the blitzkrieg
> and the military showdown, it is not so
> difficult to understand why some of what
> is going on on the pitch, and recorded
> with such vivacity in the newspapers,
> spills over onto the terraces. Here the
> line between the sports reporter glorying
> in the battle on the pitch, and expressing
> his righteous moral indignation at the
> battle on the terraces, or between the
> managers who drill and rehearse their lads
> in tough and abrasive styles of play, but
> who think their faithful and involved fans
> should be birched or caged in or hosed
> down ("DRENCH THE THUGS" - Mirror 4.4.77) -
> is a very fine and wavery one indeed.
> (Hall, 1978, p.27).

We shall address the significance of these features of
the press reportage of soccer hooliganism - of what is
present in the reportage, and what is not - in the final
section of this paper. But we need first to look at the
moral and analytical position of sociology itself, for, fond
though sociologists have recently been of indicting a liberal
press for its failings, 'sociology' has a case of its own to
answer.

Sociology and Soccer Violence

Professional (and amateur)[24] sociology in Britain have
been progressive in their accounting of soccer violence and
associated youthful delinquency insofar as they have provided
critiques of outlandish psychological and even physical
explanations of social violence in general,[25] of some of the
more simpleminded attempts to account for juvenile delinquency
in general as "an effect" of exposure to television,[26] and,
finally of "explanations" of youthful dissidence by the Right

55

as a result of a decline in social discipline.[27] It is not
clear however that the various sociologies can really claim
to have provided an alternative explanation of their own of
all that requires to be explained in this field.

Specifically sociological accounts of soccer violence in
Britain may be said to fall, basically, into five categories:
(1) subcultural theories of youthful fashion or style, (2)
theories of changes in the structure of the game, (3) social
anthropological theories of ritual violence, (4) labelling
theories and (5) more or less empiricist amalgams of the
above. Each of these theories is capable of providing a
powerful critique of the limitations in theories of violence
as being the results of the physical or psychological
possession of individuals, the spread of some contagion in a
crowd, or the effects of watching certain kinds of television.
But they are lacking in other crucial respects.

1.   Theories of Subcultural Style

For John Clarke (1978), football hooliganism (and other
forms of working class youthful deviance) must be understood
as a symbolic social intervention by an age cohort of youth,
caught in a subordinate position vis-a-vis "adult society" in
general and vis-a-vis the parental cohort, also, of its own
class, in an attempt to develop a sense of its distinctive
identity. These interventions involve the development and
diffusion of a style of each working class youth subculture.
In post-war Britain, these styles have comprised, respectively,
the Teddy Boys (1953-1957), the Mods and Rockers (1964-6), the
Skinheads (1967 to 1970), and, latterly, in rapid sequence,
Glamrock, Punk Rock and New Wave.

The style is evolved as a means of signifying subcultural
membership, and as a means of signifying the difference of

the subculture from its perceived oppressors (in the age and
class structure) and from its competitors in the age cohort.
It is a symbol of an identity, certainly, but also, according
to Clarke et al, the highly ritualized and stylized
identifications of each of the post-war youth subcultures in
Britain suggest that

> they were attempts at a solution to....
> problematic experience: a resolution
> which, because pitched largely at the
> symbolic level, was fated to fail. The
> problematic of a subordinate class
> experience can be 'lived through',
> negotiated or resisted; but it cannot
> be resolved at that level or by those
> means .... (Clarke et al, 1975, p.47)

The symbolic adaptations of the post-war youth subcultures,
in style, are in this sense attempts to solve the concrete
problems experienced by each generation of lumpen working
class youth in a declining class society. They are attempts
at "imaginary" or, indeed, "magical" solutions to material
problems. So the Skinheads, for example, developed a style
which, in its use of clothing style (boots, workmen's jeans,
and rolled up sleeves etc.) and its core values (sexism,
racism, toughness, self-reliance within a group), was a
caricature of the working class community, increasingly
destroyed by the post-war housing redevelopment and by
massive changes in the internal structure of the industrial
workforce. It was an attempt at the "magical recovery of
community". (Clarke, 1975). Each of the post-war youth
subcultures may be analysed, it is argued, more or less in
such terms.

There is no doubt that the "reading" of subcultural
style, advanced by Clarke and the Subcultures Group at the
Centre for Contemporary Cultural Studies at the University

of Birmingham is an important advance on earlier, more
formal observational accounts of youth subcultural formations
in Britain. But it is a reading of the more visible,
'violent' and therefore spectacular subcultural adaptations
of youth: and it has been criticised, rightly, for its
silence on the situation of the mass of working class youth,
only a minority of whom make firm subcultural adaptations,
but many of whom do get involved, periodically, in soccer
violence, and in the "clampdowns" that follow on from moral
panics in the media. There is also an associated tendency
to posit what Simon Frith has called "a false freezing of
the youthful world into deviants and the rest". (Frith,
1978, p.53). Evidence suggests that the vast bulk of British
youth "pass through groups, change identities and play their
leisure roles for fun." (Ibid).

It is also a form of analysis that is relatively silent
on the source of the stylistic adaptations. The Teddy Boys'
styles were clearly derived from a very different source to
those of the bike-riding Rocker ten years later, though
many would argue that the social composition of the group was
similar. So that the reading of style tends, occasionally,
to be descriptive and celebratory, almost, across the board:
an important failing at a moment of increasing congruence
between some youth subcultures in the rough working class
and the youth groups of the National Front and the British
Movement.

But, thirdly, as Simon Frith has observed, there is a
tendency for subcultural analysts (of this character and of
others) to articulate their account of youth around the
symbol, or around the subculture itself, rather than to see
the youth question as a displacement of a broader dynamic of
the relation of the classes (a displacement at both the

behavioural and ideological level). The behavioural point
may be more clear in North America where the reproduction of
class relations, and the need for the policing of class
relations by the State, is routinely accomplished, as it
were, "on the street corner", in the public, political
concerns over the delinquencies of the "corner boy"; black
or white, unemployed or under-employed, but always troublesome. North American class relations have reproduced, with
some regularity, a large reserve army of youthful labour, an
increasing proportion of which was until recently excluded
from production in college, but a significant proportion of
which was "left behind" at the street corner, as a potential
source of trouble in local civil society. The Schwendingers
have shown the centrality of this continual reproduction of
the youthful reserve army to the high rates of delinquency in
North America, whether of what early subcultural theorists
called an 'expressive' or an 'instrumental' variety.
(Schwendinger and Schwendinger, 1976). The ideological
displacement which is accomplished in both North American
and British society is to make the youth question the central
conceptual problematic (as a problem of socialization,
discussed de-contextually; or as a constant, naturally
occurring class of the generations): class is displaced
into generation.

In Britain, which was until the late 1960's an economy
with low unemployment, compared with North America, the
subcultural solutions of each working class youth cohort were
therefore solutions for 'fractions' of the class, with the
"mass of the class" existing in a situation of some incorporation, by virtue of employment. It is in the 1970's, indeed,
with the beginnings of rates of unemployment of a North
American level that violent adaptations on the part of

larger numbers of youth, without a clearly identifiable
subcultural style, have spread beyond the marginal fractions
of the class; and it is precisely this dynamic (of political
economy) and this context (of class relations) which is
absent in many subcultural accounts of soccer violence.
Crudely speaking, with their conceptual emphasis on culture
and style, these accounts cannot indeed explain why "things
are getting worse".

2.   Theories of the Game

Broadly speaking, attempts to explain soccer violence as
a function of features of the game itself fall into two
categories. In my own early writing, for example, I placed
considerable emphasis on changes in the social organization
of professional football (and in particular, the decomposition
of the football club as a neighbourhood institution of the
class, with football being increasingly reorganized, after
the second World War, as a locally based national entertainment sport aimed at "paying spectators"). (Taylor, 1971a,
1971b). This thesis has been extended by Clarke, 1978.

In both these versions, and also in the work of
journalistic commentators on soccer violence like Hunter
Davies (1972), the examination of the relations of clubs
and supporters, in historical time and in the recent period,
tends to deteriorate into specious and anecdotal debates
("were the clubs in the 1930's really experienced as
democratic organizations to which all supporters belonged?"
etc. etc.), in which the club is abstracted artifically
from its surrounding social relations. It was no part of
my original intention in the 1971 papers to argue that
membership of the football club in the interwar period was
any more or any less "ideological" than membership of any

other institution that occupied a significant position in class experience in that period (whether that institution was a sporting institution for spectators (like the greyhound stadium) or for players (the billiard hall), or whether it was a leisure institution of the neighbourhood (like the pub). All these institutions were physical territories of the class, and a part of the social relations of the class. They were a part of the ensemble of class relations. Similarly, the "alienation" of the football supporter from his local club, in the 1960's and 1970's, is not unrelated generically to the overall alienation of fractions of the working class that has resulted from changes in the structure of the labour market and the 'class map' generally, and, specifically, from the decomposition of working class community.

Calls for the "democratization" of football clubs of the kind made by myself, and later by Hunter Davies, albeit made for a polemical purpose, have not met with an active response from professional football as a whole, despite token schemes for participation of youngsters in club training and related activities. Professional football is a part of local political economy, and, perhaps more importantly, local civic power: and is no more available for real democratization than the political economy and structure of power at the level of the State itself. Analyses of the violence amongst football spectators and diagnoses of a solution which have been focussed on the club in isolation from the ensemble of class relations in which they are located in practice have fallen, in other words, into a form of idealist politics of the left, or even of the liberal centre. They have also been analytically guilty, as it were, of 'reifying' football's social significance in the relation, simply, in the relation of the club to the spectator.

A second category of work on soccer violence as a
function of the game itself is that which concentrates on
some physical features of the game; and, in particular, the
fact that the game is played in front of large crowds,
caught up in the excitement of the competition, and, as we
indicated earlier, increasingly exhorted to think of the
game in physically violent terms. This perspective has
been advanced, inter alia, by researchers working for the
police (Jones, 1969, 1970), by the Harrington Enquiry of
1968, and, to some extent, in the eclectic Report of the
Social Science Research Council, "Public Disorder and
Sporting Events" which we will discuss later. (SSRC, 1978).
Each of these reports places considerable emphasis on the
irrationality of human beings in crowd situations (the
collective behaviour thesis, which is also discussed for
sport in general, ultimately rather ambiguously, by Smith,
1975). In the case of British soccer, the crowd's essential
irrationality has been exacerbated by the same social factors
spoken of in sociological accounts of changes in the game
(the decline in attendance at football since the 1940's has
left the remaining supporters more committed; the massive
number of domestic European and international games has
introduced further prizes and successes to be prized and
given 'symbolic significance'; and television and press
coverage has given the crowd a sense of being 'on camera' or
'in the news'). The abolition of the maximum wage (1961)
and the introduction of new forms of wage bargaining are
said to have made players more cynical in their quest for
success, and their use of violent tactics have been
relatively badly controlled by referees, who have not been
given the power and authority to control the increasingly
instrumental athletes in their charge. All of these changes

in the sociology of the game have acted as 'bad examples'
to the individuals who make up the crowd, and thus there
are few controls in the form of customary bonds tying
spectators to the club (its tradition, values etc.) when a
crowd begins to get out of hand.

All of these social "facilitators" may be aided,
however, by the presence of psychologically-disturbed
individuals in the crowd, who, for reasons which are not
explained, may act as leaders of groups in the crowd; by
the need of particular groups of supporters to uphold a
fighting reputation; by the results of games themselves
(in the context of long rivalries between clubs, especially
within localities) or by particular incidents within the
games themselves.

Whatever the balance of precipitating factors, it is at
this point that the "contagion" which is a quality of
collective behaviour incidents starts to operate, and, so
the argument proceeds, the conditions become present for
violence in the crowd. Fights and pitch invasions are
likely developments: and a sequence is fulfilled, in rather
the fashion described in the various collective behaviour
theorists (from le Bon to Ralph Turner and beyond).

The originating source of these violent developments
is, however, ultimately the irrational, primitive and more
or less pathological crowd. What is never stated, but always
implicit, is that the crowd is very largely composed of
lower and working class youth - "the dangerous classes" -
who have not been immune from the general "climate of
permissiveness" in civil society, on the mass media etc.

The problematic in accounts focussing on changes in the
game itself is ultimately located, and localized, in particular

collective behaviour situations or, in other terms, in
particular, problematic contexts of social control. It
should immediately be clear that this localization serves
certain important functions. Whilst certainly allowing the
professionalization and commercialization of spectator sport
to become problematic, in the sense of directing attention
to the breakdown in the nexus of neighbourhood fan, club
ownership and management, and player, the thesis tends to
translate the problem of the relation of the class to its
sporting institution into a problem of social control. So
those who speak of changes in the relation of the crowd to
the game tend also to have argued, along with architects
and others, for the introduction of seating right throughout
the football stadium, for the introduction of purpose-built
entries from the pitch to enable the police to make arrests,
and for entries and exits into the stadium which enhance the
safety of the crowd and also its availability for control.[28]
So where my own earlier work on the football as a social
relation tended to "problematicize" the club, and to bring
forward an entirely idealist plea for democratizing reforms,
the work on football as a set of social relations in
physical space "problematicizes" the crowd, and tends tó
bring forward a set of proposals, simply, for the coercive
control of the working-class crowd. Any more ambitiously
societal and political, or indeed analytical concern is
eschewed.

3. Social Anthropology and Ritual Violence

Closely connected with sociological and psychological
work on collective behaviour and on the crowd are the social
anthropological traditions of investigation into the nature
of animal and human violence and aggression and also into
group formation. Some of this work is usefully summarized,

64

for sports of all kinds, in Smith (1975) and also in SSRC (1978) section 7.2.

There has recently been a rash of work into British soccer violence, and into other forms of youthful disorder, from writers using a particular mix of animal ethology, social anthropology and sociological empiricism (Marsh, Rosser and Harre, 1978; Marsh 1978a). Our concern here will be with the application of "the theory" to soccer violence.[29]

The argument advanced by Marsh is the product of a close observation of actually occurring behaviour at soccer grounds; and his claim to knowledge is indeed in part based on the deductions drawn from these observations. Football violence is said, at close range, properly observed, to be ritual violence (a slowing-down of films of fights at football matches will show that the fist, or the boot, rarely hits home). This has always been the case with both early (folk) and modern (professional, spectator) forms of football, according to Marsh; and indeed he provides some interesting detail on the gestures, songs, and crowd rituals of earlier forms of the game. The essential function, therefore, of what is now called 'aggro' is, and, importantly, always has been (in its earlier forms), a means of signifying member- ship of what Marsh calls "micro-cultures", and thus a way of affirming identity of otherwise amorphous "cultural unities". This observational lesson is then illustrated in historical time ("aggro in history") with particular attention being given to the symbolic struggles of the Blue and Green charioteers in the Roman and Byzantine circus (recently reported on by Alan Cameron in Circus Factions); to duelling in seventeenth-century France and to the symbolic and instrumental violence of American culture in general (Marsh seems to be convinced of the inherent violence of the

United States, which in its early settlement "lacked a culture on which to fall back", Marsh 1978, p.82). Aggro in some form, however, is universal in all societies, in being a symbolic and ritual form in which real conflicts can be sublimated, or "re-represented". Aggro is useful in maintaining a requisite level of dynamism in a culture, and thereby renovating the basis of cultural cohesion during periods of social change.

The Durkheimian cast of Marsh's explanation of "aggro" is arrived at, in part, as a result of his attempt to construct a "sociological" critique of the socio-biologists and cultural anthropologists for whom territorial struggles, and other instances of human aggression, are determined, specifically, by the fact of differential genetic endowments amongst the species. For Marsh, explanations of this order could only be true at the level of struggles over the most basic features of human existence. "Once culture has taken over the role of transmitting life-styles and social values there is no reason to suppose that the genetic imprint will remain" (Marsh 1978, p.34). By the same token, animal studies are unhelpful in explaining what Marsh calls the "secondary level of aggression management" - the ritual violence which exists in all cultural totalities (or societies).

The point about Marsh's excursion into cultural anthropology is that it constitutes an attempt to con-textualize the "moral panics" of the last 15 years over soccer hooliganism and associated instances of violence and vandalism in a theory of the fundamental character of the human species. Aggro is a product of human beings' struggle to express identity, in forms of interpersonal ritual, the rules governing which are well understood at a micro-cultural level. Thus, there are good anthropological reasons to justify the adoption of a policy of non-intervention (or at least liberal treatment rather than punitiveness) vis-a-vis troublesome youth. Labelling theory's benign conslusions are given an anthropological justification. Attempts by "society" to repress aggression ("to the extent that (the) useful function of aggression is negated") - of the kind that have been proposed by the magistracy, by the police and by the media in recent months, and years, as a way of "dealing with the problem of soccer hooliganism" are unhelpful, for if aggression is repressed rather than "socialized", it will merely be transferred onto other targets, and also there will be an accompanying destruction of "the groups and micro-societies in which ritualized aggression is acted out". The point here is that these "groups and micro-societies" are man's own natural solutions (in symbolic form) to conflicts over material interest and human identity; they alone have the capacity to socialize and thus to contain the real potential for violence in the species which led Desmond Morris, in The Naked Ape, to speak of the inevitability of Armageddon.

We can usefully relate this exposition, and our criticism of this, to the accounts of soccer violence offered out by labelling theorists and by interactionists.

4.   Labelling Theory and Soccer Violence

A significant number of the accounts of soccer violence written by both professional and amateur sociologists have utilized a more or less straightforward version of the notion of deviancy amplification derived from North American labelling theory of the early 1960's; or, alternatively, a slightly more 'theorized' framework derived from Stan Cohen's reformulation of this theory in his classic study of the Mods and Rockers (Cohen, 1972).

In the deviancy amplification version, the concentration
is on the sequences of rule breaking, social reaction,
labelling and ostracism that occurred vis-a-vis youthful
disturbances of all kinds in the 1960's, and the particular
impact of this process of 'sensitization' on the football
terraces. The sequence is seen to have been speeded up by
the emergence of the Skinhead, whose behaviour and presentation
of self resulted in powerful reactions from a broadly based
"social audience" of teachers, social workers, police and
magistrates, aided by the media. A spurious dramatization
is thought to have occurred, whereby the wearing of the
Skinhead garb was sufficient to excite the attention of
"agencies of social control", and probable arrest. A
classic cycle of stimulus and response was initiated,
resulting in the signalling of the original Skinhead style
(whose adherents were by now firmly 'cast' as social outcasts)
as the uniform of committed deviants. Ultimately, the
"societal reaction to Skinheads" was so all-pervasive as to
produce, on the one hand, an alientated but increasingly
committed group of outcasts (who had now no other option),
and, on the other, the deterrence of the mass of youth. The
result, artificially, was to define violence at soccer games
as an activity of a "hard core" of commitedly anti-social,
untypical, and dangerous youth (which, in turn, gave soccer
violence a spurious attractiveness to working-class adolescents
seeking adventure and diversion).

The slightly different account advanced by Stan Cohen
involved what might be called the "recasting theory" of
youth culture. Here, the argument is that "society"
continually creates new "folk devils" over time, relegating
earlier devils to "relatively benign roles in the gallery of

social types" (Cohen, 1972, p.200). For Cohen, the production of youth as folk devils is in large part explicable by the facts of the generational conflict (that youth are relatively powerless, that they must always attempt to establish identity, that their attempts to break free of adult authority will result in responses of moral indignation etc.) as well as by resentments provoked, in the 1950's especially, by the partial emergence of possibilities of relative "affluence" for sections of working-class youth.

Both versions of labelling theory are in themselves silent, however, on the questions addressed by our earlier theories: the source and contexts of the initial youthful adaptations. They tend, indeed, to imply (like all labelling theory) that the initial behaviour is irrelevant, arbitrary or, in Becker"s term, 'random'; or, even worse, a 'fad', fashion, or indeed imitation (in the manner of other species). This would be a severe omission in any period, but has become all the more severe with the recent increases in recruitment into fighting gangs, and in the blurring of some New Wave music and fashion into the thematics of fascist political groups. In so doing, labelling theory ignores the extent to which the initial behaviour is in some sense an attempt on the part of working-class youth "magically" to recover and to symbolize "community" against outsiders, and ignores the way in which this problem is available for a racist and populist translation into the problem of defending and celebrating the community of white working-class youth, against an alien horde of black immigrants.

Labelling theory also argues that the continuation of soccer violence results from the continuingly over-sensitive intervention of agencies of social control in youth activity, and argues a policy of non-intervention. This is true, also,

of Peter Marsh's social anthropological contextualization
of labelling theory, where the insistence is on the ritual,
unreal, and functional character of the "aggro" on the
terraces. In so doing, the labelling theorists and the
anthropologists desert the ground of social control altogether.
They argue, still, for "radical non-intervention". This is
a crippling error, especially in the current moment, with
vast numbers of working class people being won, via populist
political appeals, to parties of the Right in a desperate
attempt to find a means for guaranteeing 'order' and
security in their personal lives and living environments.
It is also a major departure from the classical concerns
of liberals with the protection of the lives and liberties
of all sections of the broader community, since many of the
worst incidents around soccer games, and in the weeks between
soccer games, have involved attacks on immigrants, women
and the elderly, other enemies of the "fighting gangs",
mostly within the fighting gang's own class.

Many of these attacks, perpetrated by youths who are
affiliated with football's fighting gangs, go unreported in
the national press and misleadingly, or incompletely,
reported in the local press.[30] And this alerts us to
labelling theory's other failure here. Almost as a catechism,
labelling theorists have written of the role of the mass
media in terms of the theory of "deviancy amplification".
The press and television are thought of as being over-
sensitive to even the most minute of incidents, and as
tending to amplify it and accord it a spurious significance.
Individual crowd happenings are written up as though they
were general to the crowd, or the terrace, and as if they
were occurring throughout the game.

Labelling theorists in Britain have however remained

silent in the face of recent accusations made by the Right
vis-a-vis the role of the media in the reporting of youthful
delinquency generally, and soccer violence in particular.
According to Patricia Morgan (1978), Mary Whitehouse and the
National Union of Licensed Victuallers, amongst others, the
mass media have under-estimated the extent and the character
of youthful violence in Britain in the late 1970's. In
particular, the media have mainly tended to report incidents
inside the football grounds (occurring in the presence of
their sports reporters) and they have largely ignored
incidents of interpersonal or property violence occurring
before and after the game, because they have not witnessed
them. Thus, there have been few reports in the national
press in the 1960's and 1970's of incidents between supporters
on the route to and from football grounds, in public houses,
or on public transport.

The New Right are correct here, in more ways than they
realize. It is common knowledge amongst football supporters
that the fighting gangs at many games engage in a series of
confrontations on the streets prior to most weekend games;
as well as in ritual confrontations surrounding the "taking
of the ends". There are also frequent confrontations at
railway stations throughout Britain en route to and from
games, as groups of supporters encounter other supporters
travelling to support their own team. And a key element in
the behaviour of the fighting gangs on arrival at the city or
town of their opponents is to terrorize members of various
target groups (ticket-collectors at stations, public transport
personnel, local women and blacks, local publicans, and
turnstile operators at the stadium). It is not for nothing
that bus crews in the traditionally tough city of Glasgow
have recently refused to run their buses on days of the
Celtic versus Rangers confrontation, or that Underground

staff have refused to man trains to and from certain football stadia in London.

Some of these incidents do get reported in the local press in Britain, and there has been a great deal of ideological work (of a generally right-wing variety) taking place in the press on the question of juvenile behaviour and violence. But there is a real sense in which the sporting journalist in recent years has under-reported the broad context of breakdown in the traditional relations between youthful spectators, and the development of a culture of violence amongst an increasing number of young football supporters. Labelling theory, in the meantime, insists as an act of faith that a constant process of exaggeration has occurred, and by implication that the structure of working-class community is troubled primarily by inaccurate reportage of its activities, rather than any real or essential decomposition.

The blindness in both labelling theory and social anthropology appears to arise out of their respective failure to deal in any specific way with the historical moment of soccer hooliganism. This may seem to be a paradoxical accusation to make of Marsh's work, in particular, which is in fact based in part on an examination of long "sweeps" of existing historical evidence. But the point is indeed that the historical perspective advanced by Marsh is so general (almost, unsurprisingly, the history of "the species") as to be unable to identify the social and political character of particular moments of "history". This epochal conception of history, coupled with a concentration on the nexus of Man and Culture as the essential character of "the social", avoids or at least does not address the material basis of historical development (Man's struggle to produce)

72

and the material character of the social relations that result (the relations of classes). It fails to recognize the relation of Capital and Labour in general, or the playing out of this relation in particular moments of time, like the present. In labelling theory itself, in the meantime as we have indicated, a constant process of production and reproduction of "folk devils" occurs, irrespective almost of cycles of economic boom and slump, the development of a crisis of profitability, the shift from one basic mode of production to another. Labelling is presented as a cultural inevitability, though undesirable nonetheless.

5. Eclecticism

The concerns of subcultural theorists and theorists of the game with the origins of the behaviour are linked to the concerns of the labelling theorist and the social anthropologist in a recent revival of a 1950's form of empiricist sociology, published by the Social Science Research Council in conjunction with the Sports Council (SSRC, 1978).

This Report was written by a committee, subsequent to consultations with many social scientists, and, partly as a result of this, but also out of an evident a priori belief in the inevitable interplay of many 'factors' in the constitution of any social phenomenon, the Report takes the form, more familiar now to North American social science than to British, of a multifactorial account, in which the different and often contradictory accounts offered by others are placed together in a (sociologically false) integration. The literature on theories of aggression, on crowd behaviour, on "culture" and on sport and society lead into a "possible synthesis" in which the particular features of football as "natural arena" for the exercise of masculine qualities, for the creation of group bonds and the development of localized forms of social organization are posited as the key to its contemporary importance. The Report then proceeds to call for a more cautious form of press reportage, "a major new programme" for the provision of facilities of leisure and recreation, and research into the relation between football hooliganism and the decline in attendance at football matches, as well as into the provision of better information for police purposes on the relation between the types of matches and the degrees of violent incident to be expected.

One of the most obvious features of this "synthesis" is that it appropriates almost all of the descriptive elements in the other theories; but removes them from the theoretical perspective in which they were originally given meaning. Peter Marsh has indeed already complained of the way in which his work on group formation and ritual in "the ends" was misappropriated without accurate recognition of the liberal non-interventionism which he derives from this work. (Marsh, 1978b). The point is, of course, that the SSRC Report's eclecticism is profoundly theoretical. It is a liberal social scientific version of the popular demand for practicable action for the control of youthful dissidence, through the informed actions of the State, including, as it does, in the end, a discussion of the existing state of the relevant criminal law. The "discussion" of existing literature in the SSRC report is the moment where the Committee de-constructs and then reconstructs the "knowledge" that has been produced by researchers working in the area of soccer violence, in order to make them available (a) to commonsense, in all its conservative and stereotypical forms, and then (b) by dint of persuasion, to the State, in the hope of encouraging the acceptance of liberal recommendations for improvements in the leisure, work and other provisions of disadvantaged youth.

Soccer Violence, Class and the State

Existing sociological accounts of soccer violence -
like the journalistic reports they deplore - can all be
indicted for their tendency to extrapolate a single feature
of the phenomenon (its style, its ritual character, its
essential violence, its existence as a feature of 'the crown',
its connectedness with the violent language of the media,
and/or its "existential dependency" on the fact of social
reaction) and to treat this feature in isolation from the
"ensemble" of social reactions in which they occur. Equally
seriously, they can be indicted for the assumption they
nearly all share, namely that the object of analysis is
properly to be found in the "soccer-violence" couplet: that
this is what is to be explained, via a "theory of soccer"
(the history and sociology of the game etc.), via a "theory
of violence", or via a sociology that "integrates" the two.

Even radical sociologies are guilty here of dealing
analytically primarily with soccer violence, even though
they may reference the violence as a symptom of the larger
ensemble, when the problem must be to theorize the
significance of soccer violence in Britain (and sports
violence in general) within the primary relations of the
class and the State. This is necessitated not merely by the
fact that limits have been encountered within the sociological
accounts themselves, but also by the demand we must
increasingly answer during the crisis of western society to
make our theoretical work responsible. This responsibility
(and the crisis in social and economic relations in the
West) increases forced recognition of the fundamental
inequalities and significance of class relations in Western
society. We have to develop analysis that begins and ends

75

with the fundamentals of class in its simple and complex divisiveness, and which is competent to recognize in events like the soccer violence panic a particular kind of decomposition within a class at a particular moment in the history of that class within one nation state. It is a task which has been initiated in a recent text by Dave Robins and Phil Cohen, who address a wide variety of features of decomposition in the British working-class, from the physical character of its neighbourhoods to the dislocations in its long-standing sporting traditions of boxing and street-fighting; and who begin the task of explaining the growth of nihilism and racism in the white youth of that class. (Robins and Cohen, 1978). It is a task which must be under-taken, however, across the broad terrain of the existence of that, or any other, working class' experience.

Moreover, to speak of the need for class analysis is not to argue for a return to what C. Wright Mills called the 'labour metaphysic', or what others have called ouvrierism; the romanticization of "the working class" as the prime agent in history. It is to the credit of structuralist writers like Althusser and Poulantzas that they have alerted us to the need for a close analysis of the developing contradictions within the class, as well as across the "class map" as a whole. The account we offered of the social composition of the football gangs should remind us of the role of sexual and racial divisions within the class, and also alert us to the problematic question for Capital of the reserve army of labour in moments of economic recession and decline. The diffuseness of class formations, especially in ideology, and the conflation of class into race and gender, should need no more emphasis in front of a North American audience.

We do insist, however, that the key to explaining the decomposition in the social order of this working-class sport, and other popular sports also, must lie in the attempt to follow through the class relation in which the sport has developed and continues to be embedded. Any such analysis will depend, initially, on the correct identification of the "origins" of the class' involvement with the sport and the later transformations in that relation (work that has been suggested, also, by John Alt in speaking of forms of industrial leisure, organized for workers' consumption outside the hours of production, (Alt, 1976) and which I attempted to encompass in speaking of the historical creation, development, and decline of the "working-class weekend" (Taylor, 1976). It is work which will become more complex in moments of decomposition of the class, or which depends, in North America, on the continuing elaboration of what it means to speak analytically of "class" at all. And it is work which will have to take account also, as we suggested earlier, on the use of sports like football in newspapers, in television and in popular discourse as a neutral, non-political terrain, an arena in which the contradictoriness of class experience is repressed and simultaneously displaced (into other loyalties).

The importance of this kind of class analysis, however, is that it suggests a way out of the agnostic and un-historical responses of labelling theory and other schools of sociology to "the crisis", and here, specifically, the crisis in the lived experience of the reserve army. Specifically, there are grounds for believing that the lived experience of this "under-class" in Europe and North America is one of material and psychic frustration also resentment at the continued reproduction of inequality of material and existential possibility. There are also grounds for believing that the logic of capitalism's recent development throughout the West is one which must place an increasing proportion of "the class" in such a marginal situation; and that the "revolution of rising expectations" cultivated, in popular ideology, in the period of the long boom, has now, decidedly, to be reversed. Something more than the routine reproduction of sociological anomie is involved in moments of this kind: a fundamental decomposition of the expectations of life-style and possibility that have been continually encouraged over the thirty years of the Keynesian boom is occurring, alongside of a decomposition of the institutions and communities of that class. Comtemporary sociology, still undertaken in an analytical form set apart from political economy, and caught in an empiricism which mistakes the <u>appearance</u> of things (or their symbolic representation) for their <u>essence</u>, is an inappropriate base for such a project.

Most of the sociological accounts (and especially labelling theory) can also be faulted for their continuing reproduction of the language of pluralist political science as a means of conceptualizing the way in which soccer crowds are 'policed', and the agency through which societal reaction against soccer violence articulated. The general reliance is on something like Edwin Lemert's notion of the "societal control culture" as a means of identifying the bodies with the responsibility for defining, labelling and controlling soccer hooligans. For Lemert, the societal control culture comprises

> the laws, procedures, programs, and
> organizations which, in the name of
> a collectivity, help, rehabilitate,
> punish or otherwise manipulate deviants.
> (Lemert, 1950)

But, as Hall et al observe in an already classic passage in their recent important collective work on "mugging and law

78

and order" in Britain in the 1970's:

> The 'control'culture' approach ... appears
> too imprecise for our purposes. It identifies
> centres of power and their importance for the
> social-control process; but it does not locate
> them historically, and thus it cannot designate
> the significant moments of shift and change.
> It does not differentiate adequately between
> different types of state or political regime.
> It does not specify the kind of social formation
> which requires and establishes a particular kind
> of legal order. It does not examine the
> repressive functions of the state apparatuses
> in relation to their consensual functions. Thus
> many different types of society-'plural' societies,
> where some are more plural than others, or 'mass
> societies', where power is alleged to be
> distributed between the elites, or a 'democratic
> society' with countervailing powers - all are
> made compatible with the concept of a 'social
> control culture'. It is not a historically
> specific concept. In short, it is not premised
> on a theory of the state: even less on a
> theory of the state in a particular phase of
> capitalist development - e.g. class democracies
> in the era of 'late capitalism'.
> (Hall et al, 1978, p.195)

The agenda for analytical work presented here is
formidable enough. But Policing the Crisis goes beyond this,
and argues for the recognition that the institutional
apparatus of the State is the basis of an ideological
structure. The argument is initially put in an abstract
form:

> ....the conditions for (capitalist) production
> or what has come to be called social
> reproduction - are often sustained in the
> apparently 'unproductive' spheres of civil
> society and the state; and in so far as the
> classes, fundamentally constituted in the
> productive relation, also contend over this
> process of 'social reproduction', the class
> struggle is present in all the domains of
> civil society and the State. It is in this

> sense that Marx called the state 'the
> official resume of society', the 'table'
> of contents of man's practical conflicts'
> .... (Hall et al, 1978, p.202)

and then, more directly,

> .... the state (has) another and crucial
> aspect or role beside the legal and coercive
> one: the role of leadership, of direction,
> of education and tutelage - the sphere, not
> of 'domination by force', but of the
> 'production of consent!. (Ibid.)

The State is seen, following Gramsci, as an apparatus within
which the exercise of both coercive and consensual forms of
power is articulated: both types of domination being present
in all social formations. But the production of hegemony,
which for Gramsci was the form of class power that was
legitimated primarily in popular consent, was best achieved
in the liberal-democratic state with its elaborate apparatus
of 'representation' and the organization of social interests
via parliamentary parties, pressure groups, "independent"
mass media, etc. etc. The achievement of hegemony (or the
universalization of the particular interests of a class)
depends on what Gramsci calls "the decisive passage from the
structure to the sphere of the complex superstructures", or,
in other words, the achievement of authority over civil
society as well as over production. In this perspective,
analytical work on the mass media or on the organization of
State welfare or, indeed, sport is important in uncovering
the ideological connections upon which such hegemonic
domination depends. In particular, it is through our
examination of the activities of State authorities and the
organizations (like the free enterprise media, or privately
owned sports club) which are allowed existence within the
formal, public arena of the State that we can begin to

understand how a dominant class attempts, through the State, to take the side of the people, and, thus, to produce popular consent to its rule.

This version of State theory is not without its critics: it has indeed been accused of a variety of analytical sins (from functionalism to idealist revisionism) and empirical mistakes (over periodiciaation).[31] But it is a theory of State which makes sense of the extent to which the British State, in particular, increasingly attempted until 1979 to move into the direct position of control over the economic problems being experienced by British capital and into the direct control over social policy at large. For the particular "conjunctural" situation of British capital is one in which hegemony has become more and more precarious, at the level both of the economy and of civil society. The progressive liberalization that has occurred in Britain (as well as in other societies) has unpacked and dislocated the traditional and substantially unreformed relations of the classes, but this reform of civil society has not been accompanied by a successful reform of the traditional economic base. The post-war period of social reconstruction and its promise of a new age of affluence has been followed by a succession of currency crises, by regular and deepening cycles of boom and slump within the national economy and by the entrenchment of capital and labour in regular struggles over their share of profits in a context of continuing low wages and low industrial productivity.

Gramsci identified a situation of this kind as a "crisis of hegemony", occurring

> ....because the ruling class has failed in some major political undertaking for which it has requested, or forcibly extracted, the consent of the masses .... A 'crisis of

> authority' is spoken of: this is precisely
> the crisis of hegemony, or general crisis of
> the State. (Prison Notebooks, quoted in
> Hall et al, 1978, p.216)

For Hall et al, the British State has been in the throes
of such a crisis since the end of the 1960's, and in
particular since 1968, the year "of the parting of the waters".
(Ibid, p.240). The crisis in civil society is thought, also,
to have had reached high tide in 1972, a year in which a
Conservative Government's Industrial Relations Act was
introduced and immediately and violently resisted by the
organized trade union movement, and a year of general panic
in the media, amongst Headteachers, Psychiatrists, Police
and other guardians of the social order, over "pupil
violence" in schools, "violence" among adolescent girls and
mugging in the streets. (Taylor, 1980b, c.3).

The point about such moments of moral panic, for Hall
et al, is that they are instances of the activities of the
State itself (and not merely the over-anxious interventions
of social control agencies, spurred on by moral entrepreneurs).
They are part of the transformation of the State as an
ideological structure (resulting from an internal recomposition
of the social forces) in the direction of the coercive pole:
towards the attempt to construct a consensus around the need
for an authoritarian form of State. The "law and order
campaigns" of the 1970's are no simple repeat of the
instances of right-wing moral enterprise or morally indignant
societal reaction of the form familiar in the 1960's. They
are a constituent element of the work that is required to
reconstitute the relation of the State to civil society.

The emergence of this strong, authoritarian state, in
Britain precisely parallels the panics over soccer
hooliganism and over youthful behaviour in general. The

parallels are indeed so close as to invite further
speculation, for it was in the year of political "cataclysm",
(1968), that the Skinhead first emerged within the youthful
cohorts of the class: and it was quite definitely in 1972,
the year of entry into world recession and also of the Heath
Government's confrontations with the unions that the
"threshold of violence" amongst working class youth was
encountered in the mass media. Once again, Hall puts the
overall argument astutely:

> .... the sharp reaction against football
> hooliganism has been paralleled by a
> striking toughening in popular social
> attitudes - marked by a return to traditional
> standards and practices in education, a call
> for stricter social discipline, a stern
> defence of the family and traditional ethical
> and sexual codes, an abrasive stance towards
> anyone who is "scrounging" on the welfare
> state ... support for tougher sentencing
> and policing policies and harsher prison
> regimes and so on. This general background
> against all forms of social permissiveness
> has already produced active grass-roots
> campaigns of vigilance and discipline,
> attributing our economic plight to the
> weakening of our moral fibre as a nation - a
> theme which has become an active element in
> the mainstream of political life, as well as
> being taken up and exploited on the extremist
> fringes of the far-Right. Though football
> hooliganism was certainly not dreamed up by a
> conspiracy of strict disciplinarians, the
> excuse it has offered for the airing of
> traditionalist remedies has played a significant
> part in the construction of a popular social
> consensus which .... can only be called
> authoritarian. (Hall, 1978, p.35)

We could not improve on this formulation, but we have
chosen in this paper to leave the revisions made to labelling
theory formulations of the moral panic by theorists of the
State and of ideology (like Hall) until this point in our

argument, giving earlier prominence and emphasis to the real "decline" in the behaviours of working-class youth. In speaking of hooliganism (rather than mugging) we want to insist that the responses of the media and the State are not merely metaphorical, and that they are not based, in the 1970's, on a resentment of the affluence and freedoms of youth. The responses of the State are necessitated by the weakness of "traditional" controls of the working-class family and community, which are both undermined by the restructuring of post-war urban space and by the destruction of "traditional" labour markets, and by the requirement that the State act effectively as policemen defending the precarious and valued property and insecure persons of the working class itself.

With the exception of the period between 1970 and 1974, the authoritarianism of the British State, in the last 15 years, has however been justified, in terms of the "general interest" as defined by the ruling social-democratic Labour Party (in terms of the interests of "both sides of industry" and, therefore the "national interest"). Social democracy's ability to talk of class was lost at some point in the late 1940's, on the assumption of the first Labour Government of the post-war period to State power on a massive majority, of the mass of all the British people. The increasingly desperate Keynesianism of the nation's political governors has been matched throughout the 1960's and 1970's by an authoritarian response (on behalf of the people and the State (the nation)) towards unruly youth, and in particular towards unruly working class youth, whose activities fundamentally threaten the social democratic vision of the Utopian consequences to be expected from the gentle reform of a class society.

But in Britain and in other European societies like Italy and, increasingly, Germany, such a form of authoritarian statism meets the limits of its appeal. Failing to guarantee order and security (and material benefits) even for the class on which its electoral base is founded, the social-democratic State is open to massive attack from the Right, and especially by any Right which can speak for the people _against_ the existing structures of State. It is precisely this appropriation of the authoritarian theme which has been accomplished by the British Conservative Party in Britain. State power is achieved by a party now fundamentally wedded to a desperate form of ruling class economic policy, on the bases of its use of a form of _authoritarian populism_ directed against the extravagance and the demoralizing influences of the social democratic welfare state, and the inability of such a state to protect the citizenry from street crime (in particular) and from "violence" and lawlessness (amongst youth, and, as if as an afterthought, amongst trade unionists).[32] The ideological work is undertaken whereby a new ruling fraction of British capital begins to make "the decisive passage from the structure to the sphere of the complex superstructure".

In an era of an alliance between authoritarian populism and the State, the coercion that underpins the relation of the ruling class to the rest of civil society will be all the more apparent, and yet also more difficult to challenge, for it _is_ a State form that rests however conditionally on popular consent. But it is likely to mean in terms of our purposes here that the policing of the sporting activities of the class will continue to require the use of Special Patrol Groups, special fencing, detention rooms and moral panics in the national press with demands for further 'clampdowns': all of which will be justified by implicit reference to some future social situation in which "order"

will be restored and guaranteed. It has been the concern of
this paper to show that such a possibility of order depends
on the solution to a more fundamental question: the
construction of a society that is not based on the divisions
of Man from Man on the basis of the needs of economic
production. It may also entail a rupture in the involvement
of the class with passive, spectator sport dominated by
capital, and with the routine reproduction of "sport news"
in the mass media of capitalist societies. The "Utopianism"
of such a vision may be fairly compared in the Britain of
1979, with the consequences of the "realism" of liberalism,
social democracy and, indeed, of empiricist sociologies
which make recommendations to and for "the State".

NOTES

1. We are thinking of the distinction advanced by Altvater between "class-theoretical" and "capital logic" approaches to the analysis of capitalist societies.

2. Ice hockey may be the "joker in the pack" in discussions of violence around sport, since there is a long history of violent incidents amongst both players and spectators, pre-dating the covering of the sport on the mass medium of television. Michael Smith, and others, have discussed the instance of the Montreal hockey riot in March 1955 (Smith, 1975; Lang and Lang 1961). Some indication of the severity of the situation in professional ice hockey may be gained from the fact that the sport's troubles are now receiving coverage in the British press. A good example is the piece by David Lacey on the New York Rangers - St. Louis Blues fixture of March 1979 ("Slap Shot League" Guardian 20 March 1979).

3. Major discussions took place, for example, into "indiscipline among players and spectators" at the congress of the European Union of Football Association (UEFA) held in Edinburgh in May 1974 (consequent on a fall in attendances at European tournament soccer games during 1972 and 1973). (Guardian, 23 May 1974).

4. The 'soccer war' between El Salvador and Honduras was precipitated by spectator riots during the three match regional finals of the World Soccer Cup in those countries in June 1970. For discussions of the role of soccer in the maintenance of soccer relations in two Latin American societies, see Lever (1969) and Taylor (1970).

5. Violence amongst baseball spectators has been the subject of an increasing number of journalistic reports and assessments. cf. "The Ugly Sports Fan" Newsweek 17 June 1974, pp.93-5, and P.S. Greenberg and Clark Whelton "Wild in the Stands" New Times 9(10) 11 November 1977.

6. Spectator violence has even been reported in the relatively sedate instance of a cricket "Test" match between India and West India in 1967 (cf. Smith, 1975, footnote 19).

7. A syndicated report in British newspapers in 1975 indicated that riots had recently occurred in games in Nalchick (in the North Caucasus), in Dushanbe (capital of Tadzhikistan) (when the home side, Pamir, were losing to the Red Army club of Rostov) and at the Radzan stadium in the Armenian capital of Yerevan, whose home side Ararat

had just won the Soviet Cup. Even in "more well-behaved" Moscow, the authorities use uniformed troops to keep order during games (and even in the 100,000 seat Lenin stadium). ("Hooliganism hits soccer in Russia" The Star, Sheffield, 26 September 1975).

8. In particular, there is evidence of pitch invasions by fans in both Scotland and England in the years immediately after the First World War. In Scotland, many of the soccer fans were members of "brake clubs", whose commitment to violent support of their teams was at least as great as the fighting gangs of the 1970's. Members of the "brake clubs" were known for their wearing of steel helmets painted in club colours and for their use of weapons retrieved from the Great War. cf. correspondence from T. Paris et al, Sunday Times 6 April 1969.

9. One high point of this crowd 'tactic' was the invasion of the Newcastle United playing pitch by supporters of Glasgow Rangers, on 21 May 1969. This 'occupation' of the pitch occurred as a result when 1,000 Rangers' fans realized that their team was likely to be eliminated from the Inter-Cities Fairs Cup competition (Newcastle had just scored their second goal, with ten minutes left of normal time). Newcastle was again the scene of a pitch invasion in March 1974, when home supporters moved on to the playing area after Nottingham Forest went into a 3-1 lead in an F.A. Cup-tie. After resumption of play, Newcastle scored three goals to 'win' the game 4-3; but the game was later declared void and replayed.

10. The Lang Report was preceded by an unofficial enquiry by a team of psychiatrists from Birmingham, published in 1968. The Harrington Report, presented to the Minister of Sport in that year, was a characteristic example of psychiatric positivism, with its primary concern being to differentiate the (arrested) hooligan from the non-hooligan in terms of the possession of certain individual psycho-pathological characteristics. (cf. discussion in Taylor 1971a, Taylor 1971b and Ingham 1978). The Report seems to have been a largely individual initiative, and to have had no major significance for State policy at the time.

11. The ad hoc accounts in the press of the origins of the Skinhead ranged from the assertion that the Skinhead 'uniform' was a development of naval uniforms (and thus a phenomenon of the South Coast of England) to the view that the Skinhead style was an imitation of contemporary American teenage styles. The considered view - that the style was a complex caricature and celebration of the

blue collar worker - was only to emerge a little later. For a fuller discussion, see Taylor and Wall 1976.

12. This major difference in the analysis of the Skinhead is caught in the contrast between what can now be seen as a premature but far-sighted analysis of the potentialities of rough working class youth's narrowing range of options by John Hoyland (1969), and the attempt of Project Free London (a middle class anarchist group) to link into Skinhead culture, in the free leaflet "Up Theirs" (Agro Pilot Issue, December 1969).

13. On September 20, 1969, a trainload of Tottenham Hotspur supporters who "had become destructive" were turned off a train at Flitwick and left to walk the remaining fifty miles to London. As a consequence of this incident, the Home Office announced that there would henceforth be "stewards" on all trains carrying fans to football games, and the circulation of a code of good practice for supervising supporters on trains. (Home Office Press Notice, 20 November 1969).

14. On 19 September 1973, the Minister for Sport under the then Conservative Government, Mr. Eldon Griffiths, announced that the recommendation of the Wheatley Enquiry would only be enforced in the case of grounds capable of holding 10,000 or more spectators; and that the first grounds to be modified for safety purposes would be those used for internation, English First and Second Division and Scottish First Division Matches, (68 in total). Even they "would be put to no unnecessary expense". (The Star, 19 September 1973).

15. Notable for a time amongst the clubs who tried to "involve" their young supporters were Coventry City (with their Sky Blues Club), Sheffield United, and Notts County. Many of these youth organizations are now defunct; and the short history of these initiatives requires research and analysis. The democratizing gestures of the club managements were in many cases compromised by the attempts of the club to involve local police in 'making contact' with local working class youth.

16. These conferences included the national conference organized by Glasgow Corporation in November 1972 and a series of conferences organized by other local authorities and by police organizations throughout the 1970's. Once again, these initiatives seem to have encountered a series of contradictions, not least of which was the primary role of the police, with their paramount concern for 'crowd control', public order and arrests. By the late

1970's, many police forces were using their mobile
snatch squads, the Special Patrol Groups, for the control
of football games: a development that would suggest a
departure by the police from collaboration with other
agencies in the field.

17. We argue later, however, that it is incorrect to think
of all popular experience of soccer violence as deriving
from the mass media. The very common sociological
treatments of delinquency and the mass media which are
couched in these terms underestimate the extent to which
the professional journalist's implicit knowledge of what
is newsworthy depends on his or her knowledge of the
sources of popular anxiety in any particular historical
moment. This is true, in particular, of the popular,
tabloid press with its professional commitment to
entertain its readership primarily by reference to its
direct (and contradictory) experience of life. (This is
also true of popular television, a point that is
brilliantly brought out by Gittlin (1979).

18. The demand for immediate, practical action in combating
social problems is central to the western professional
journalist's preference for commonsense solutions to
problems and also to the social policy programmes of
the New Right. The avowed a-theoreticism of both these
constituencies is underpinned by a profound, and unstated,
belief in the tenets of nineteenth-century liberalism
updated and revamped in recent years in order to enable
attacks on social-democratic state interventionism. In
criminology, the clearest exponent of New Right
'commonsense' as a means of attacking social democracy
is J.Q. Wilson (1975).

19. In practice, State responses to soccer violence in Britain
for the 1970's have not simply involved the use of
"existing penal disciplines". They have contributed to
the continuing use (and revival) of institutional measures,
like the Attendance Centre, the Remand Centre, and the
Detention Centre, which were scheduled for attrition or
abolition (in the Children and Young Persons Act of 1969);
and they are also in part responsible for the re-introduction (experimentally) on two sites of a military
glasshouse version of the Detention Centre by the
Conservative Government, announced at the Party Conference
in October 1979. Arrested soccer hooligans may also be
a significant proportion of the youthful populations of
the "secure' units' (lock ups) in the Community Home
System, where places increased from 60 (in 1969) to 600

in 1977, and are likely to escalate further.
(cf. Taylor, 1980a, c.5).

20. There have been innumerable documentaries of this sort
    on soccer violence, on British television, in the last
    ten years. I have personally participated in half a
    dozen, including a Man Alive special on BBC-2 in
    November 1974, a Scottish Television special in
    November 1976. On each of these occasions, the agenda
    of the programme has been set in terms of an initial
    evaluation of the "seriousness" of the issue, with an
    implicit bias against any participant who wanted either
    to deny its seriousness or to place its seriousness in
    an explicit context (for example, the contemporary
    situation of working class youth). The third stage of
    each programme (guaranteed in advance by the inclusion
    of police officers, representatives of football clubs
    etc.) was an evaluation of existing practical policy
    alternatives.

21. The existence of this area of "freedom", within which all
    is dependent on the experience or agility of the expert
    gives individuals who are experienced in the implicit
    rules of television debate (like professional politicians
    of high-standing) very considerable advantage. Cf. the
    examination of the rules underlying party-political
    exchanges in current affairs television by Hall, Connell
    and Curti (1976).

22. Between 1969 and 1973, the percentage of the total
    numbers of unemployed in Britain aged 19 or under increased
    from 10.4 per cent to 14.3 per cent, and a Department of
    Employment Study in 1974 projected that the percentage
    of under 20's in the labour force would decline from 8.6
    per cent in 1971 to 4.6 per cent in 1991. (The 1921
    figure had been 18.7 per cent). Most of these pessimistic
    estimates are currently being revised, downwards, in the
    context of the 1979 recession, and recognition of the
    likely impact of the new micro-technology.

23. Although "worklessness" is the key to the current crisis
    of working-class youth in Britain, it is clear that there
    is a broader withdrawal of legitimacy for 'liberal-
    democratic' politics taking place (resulting from the
    continuing reproduction of the inequalities and a-morality
    of anachronistic forms of class relation in that society).
    The 'nihilism' of Punk is economic only in the final
    instance; and clearly constitutes at one level a deep
    attack on the double-standards and the pretence of British
    middle class society.

24. Hunter Davies' account of The Glory Game, and, even more impressively, Arthur Hopcraft"s The Football Man, were not written by professional sociologists, but they each provide an account of the social significance of soccer at the side of which the psychological accounts of Harrington and others appear merely uninformed and even simply wrong. (Davies 1972); Hopcraft 1970).

25. The authors of the Harrington Report of 1967 were apparently convinced that soccer hooligans were possessed by a psychological syndrome produced by contagion in crowd situations, and evidenced by a glazed expression on the faces. They later were to witness the same expression on the faces of anti-American demonstrators in Grosvenor Square in 1968. In one move, they were able to invalidate the social or political meaning of soccer violence and the Grosvenor Square demonstrations of the late 1960's. ("Did the Football Fury Syndrome Hit Park Lane?", Sunday Times 28 June 1968). In 1972, Derek Bryce Smith, in the British Medical Journal, wrote that there was a serious possibility that "abnormal behaviour" (like soccer violence) was associated with "elevated levels of neurotoxic compounds picked up in the normal course of life" (lead, and other forms of environmental pollution). ("Could Pollution Send Fans Wild?" Guardian 29 May 1972).

26. Cf. in particular the critique of the work of Belson on the alleged relation between television and delinquency by Murdock and McCron (1979).

27. The critique of the Right-wing criminology of the Tory Party and the Press has been undertaken largely by liberal criminologists like Radzinowicz, Jones and Morris, usually in terms of the Right's refusal to consider the whole range of social factors entering into criminality. In the period of consensus politics, now at an end, this liberal critique has been reasonably telling: but the gist of the concluding remarks in this paper is that it cannot remain a very powerful critique. There is an attempt at a more fundamental critique of the criminology of the Right in Taylor (1980b, c.5).

28. Some of these concerns were specified in the Wheatley Report, in 1972, and later in the McElhone Report of 1977.

29. This next section is drawn from a recent review article in the British Journal of Criminology. (Taylor, 1979).

30. For a frightening analysis of racial violence, and its press reportage, in the East End of London, see Bethnal Green and Stepney Trades Council (1978).

31. Policing the Crisis is certainly surprisingly thin on the description and analysis of institutional apparatus of the State and is almost silent on the detailed description of the personnel of "the State", and their social and economic origins. This places the authors of that text in a very different tradition of State theory to those that are currently dominant in Canada.

32. North American audiences may not have heard the famous "Barrier of Steel" speech of Mrs. Margaret Thatcher, on 19 April 1979, in which inter alia she averred that

   "in their muddled but different ways the vandals on the picket lines and the muggers on the streets have got the same message - 'we want our demands met, or else', and 'get out of our way, give us your handbag, or else!'"

REFERENCES

Alt, J. (1976)   "Beyond Class: the decline of industrial
    labor and leisure"   Telos 28 (summer)

Bethnal Green and Stepney Trades Council (1978) Blood on
    the Streets   A report by Bethnal Green and Stepney
    Trades council on Racial Attacks in East London.

Clarke, J. (1973)   "Football Hooliganism and the Skinheads"
    Occasional paper, Centre for Contemporary Cultural
    Studies, University of Birmingham.

Clarke, J., Hall, S., Jefferson, T. and Roberts, B. (1975)
    "Subcultures, Cultures and Class" in Hall S. and
    Jefferson T. (eds) Resistance through Rituals: Youth
    Subcultures in Post War Britain. London: Hutchinson

Clarke, J. (1975)   "The Skinheads and the Magical Recovery
    of Community"   in Hall S. and Jefferson T. eds. op.cit.

Clarke, J. (1978)   "Football and Working Class Fans:
    Tradition and Change"   in R. Ingham (ed) Football
    Hooliganism: the Wider Context   London: Inter-Action
    Imprint.

Cohen, P. (1976)   "Cognitive Styles, Spectator Roles and
    the Social Organization of the Football End"   Aspects
    of the Youth Question (318a Mare St., London E.2):
    Working Paper No.6.

Cohen, S. (1972)   Folk Devils and Moral Panics: the
    Creation of the Mods and Rockers. London: McGibbon and
    Kee.

Davies, H. (1972)   The Glory Game   London: Weidenfeld
    and Nicholson

Frith, S. (1978)   The Sociology of Rock   London: Constable

Gittlin, T. (1979   "Prime Time Ideology: The Hegemonic
    Process in Television Entertainment"   Social Problems
    26(3) (February)

Greenberg, P.S. and Whelton, C. (1977)   "Wild in the Stands"
    New Times 9(10) 11 November

Hall, S., Connell, I. and Curti, L. (1976)   "The 'Unity' of
    Current Affairs Television"   Cultural Studies 9 pp.51-94

Hall, S. (1978)   "The treatment of 'football hooliganism' in the press"   in Ingham R. ed., op.cit.

Hall, S., Crichter, C. Jefferson, T., Clarke, J. and Roberts, B. (1978)   Policing the Crisis: Mugging, the State and Law and Order   London: Macmillan

Hopcraft, A. (1970)   The Football Man   London: Penguin

Hoyland, J. (1969)   "The Skinheads: a Youth Group for the National Front?"   Black Dwarf (30 August)

Ingham, R. (1978)   "A Critique of Some Previous Recommendations" in Ingham R., ed., op.cit.

Jones, M.N. (1969,1970)   "Soccer Hooliganism in the Metropolitan Police District"   Management Services Department Reports 8/9 and 19/70.   (Unpublished)

Lang (1969)   Report of the Working Party on Crowd Behaviour at Football Matches (Chairman: Sir John Lang). London: HMSO

Lang, K. and Lang, G.E.   (1961)   Collective Dynamics New York: Crowell

Lemert, E.M. (1950)   Social Pathology   New York: McGraw-Hill

Lever, J. (1969)   "Soccer as a Brazilian Way of Life" Trans-Action (December), reprinted in G.P. Stone ed. Games, Sport and Power New Brunswick, N.J.: Trans-Action Inc.

Marsh, P., Rosser, E. and Harré, R. (1978)   The Rules of Disorder   London: Routledge and Kegan Paul

Marsh, P. (1978a)   Aggro: The Illusion of Violence London: Dent

Marsh, P. (1978b)   "A Critique of the Sports Council/SSRC Report 'Public Disorder and Sporting Events'" in Ingham R. ed., op.cit.

Morgan, P. (1978)   Delinquent Fantasies   London: Temple Smith

Murdock, G. and McCron, R. (1979)   "The Broadcasting and Delinquency Debate"   Screen Education 30 (Spring)

Robins, D. and Cohen, P. (1978) Knuckle Sandwich: Growing
    Up in the Working Class City London: Penguin

Schwendinger, H. and Schwendinger, J. (1976) "Marginal
    Youth and Social Policy" Social Problems 24(2) (December)

Smith, M.D., (1975) "Sport and Collective Violence" in
    D.W. Ball and J.W. Loy eds Sport and Social Order:
    Contributions to the Sociology of Sport Reading, Mass:
    Addison-Wesley

Social Science Research Council (1978) Public Disorder
    and Sporting Events: a report by a joint council of
    the Sports Council and the Social Science Research
    Council London: Sports Council/SSRC

Taylor, I. (1971a) "Soccer Consciousness and Soccer
    Hooliganism" in S. Cohen ed. Images of Deviance
    London: Penguin

Taylor, I. (1971b) "'Football Mad'- a Speculative Sociology
    of Soccer Hooliganism" in E. Dunning ed. The Sociology
    of Sport London: Cass

Taylor, I. (1976) "Spectator Violence around Football:
    the rise and fall of the 'Working Class Weekend'"
    Research Papers in Physical Education 3(2)

Taylor, I. (1979) "Two New Departures in the Analysis of
    Youth Violence" British Journal of Criminology (July)

Taylor, I. (1980a) "The Law and Issue in the British and
    Canadian General Elections of 1979" Canadian Journal
    of Sociology (January)

Taylor, I. (1980b) Crime at the End of the Welfare State
    London: Macmillan

Wilson, J.Q. (1975) Thinking about Crime New York:
    Vintage

3

Sport, Sports Violence and the State

Response to Gruneau and Taylor

Wallace Clement

The basic question, the question common to all
social sciences is a question of how a society reproduces
itself. In other words how do the relationships in any
society continue to persist and be reproduced over time.
As I see it this is a core mystery after which all social
scientists quest. Many have approached the question
primarily from the economic perspective; how does a society
reproduce its material means of existence and distribute its
resources. It is, of course, a central but limited question
and needs to be supplemented by questions concerning the
ideological reproduction society; that is how does a society
legitimate its economic structure. It necessarily leads to
the questions of the political and cultural domain and it is
these two spheres of the political and cultural domains
which constitute the theme of this conference. Sport is of
course in the domain of the cultural, yet it is determined
by its relationships to the political and the economic.
The study of sport can be used as these two papers illustrate
as a key to addressing how it is that a society reproduces
itself ideologically and how this intersects with our daily
lives.

In my reading of the two papers, both Gruneau and
Taylor are arguing essentially the same things, although
they develop their analyses through somewhat different
data. They are arguing that sports, and the violence
associated with sports, are expressions of concrete social
relations, that they are inherently bound up with broader
social processes and dramatize these processes. They are
not innocently independent, autonomous, or separate from
society. It is the nexus between sports, and sports
violence, and what is going on in society that they are
addressing. To that extent both papers are making the
same argument. I am not so much interested in either the

98

history of various treatments of violence or histories of
theories of the state (and much of the two papers concentrate
on those histories) as I am on the outcome of the performing
of analyses each of the authors suggest is possible within
their proposed frameworks. I argue that in both of the
papers too much is left to the imagination. I would like to
give them each a framework within which they might concretely
fill out their analyses and, in aid of this task, I would offer
a series of questions that I would pose to them both. I shall
follow this with some specific but brief comments on each of
the papers.

First of all to what extent are the phenomena that
they are examining reflective of a cultural class response
to domination? Secondly, what relative weights do they
assign to the containment elements of sports culture and
the solidarity element? This is extremely important and I
will return to this momentarily as the main thrust of my
comments. Are we any further ahead as a result of their
analyses in understanding how society reproduces itself?
If as I suspect we are, then can they specify how conflict
manifested in sports relates to the formation of class?
Concretely, I would see the manifestation of these questions
in the two papers and I'll go through first Taylor and
then Gruneau.

Taylor, as I suggested, stops too soon. He does not
really perform the analysis that he contends needs to be
done, taken up instead with critiques of other perspectives.
Anyone who has read Hall's et al. book on Policing the
Crisis[1] can imagine the analysis that Taylor has in mind
if not fill in the requisite data which certainly I do not
have the capacity to do. I agree that we need to locate
the expressions such as violence within a political

economy context of the state and class forces. It is
behaviour that can indeed be explained by the structure of
the economy which generates youth unemployment, youth
underemployment and increasingly the coercive role of the
state to contain the resultant conflict. I still do not
know why it is that violence becomes centred in sporting
events. It still leaves much more to be learned particularly
about the formation of ideology and what leads people to
political action and this is essentially what I would like
Ian to attempt to address his remarks to.

In terms of Rick's paper, I would like him to address
much more concretely what he sees and what he argues are
the transformative aspects of sport rather than only the
reproductive aspects of sport. Rick argues that sports
represent a powerful affirmation of the legitimacy of the
existing social conditions and therefore tend to reinforce
these conditions. The question is how sport does this, but
more importantly from my perspective, is how does sport
constitute a resistance to existing arrangements? In other
words, how is he concretely going to make his argument that
sports are not only an expression of the dominant ideology,
but in some way can be used as a transformative element
that is to consolidate the transformative aspects of class?

In some work that I have been doing recently, and it
comes from a different literature in terms of the work place
and the work place struggles, I find the use of the concepts
of coordination of work and control over work to be
extremely useful.[2] Under the capitalist stage of production
coordination and control become synonomous with one another.
I think that if we examine these processes in sport we may
have a very powerful beginning to analyses that examine the
relationships of sports to class reproduction and transformation. An obvious starting point would be to examine

100

historically the coordination and control of athletic labour and how they become married together obviously for professional sports and coaching activities, etc. I would like to see Rick address this question in terms of the transformative aspects of class. He makes an exceedingly important suggestion that he doesn't pick up again in terms of the notion of reproduction, and that is, how an over-emphasis on the homogeniety of dominant values and ruling interests leads to a possibility of denying the creative role that cultural forms take. So I would like to see some confrontation with the problem of the resistance of working class culture around the issue of sports. And I guess I would like to see him address the question that Ian raised at the end of his paper. This is a question that comes out of the Hall et al. work and the important cultural work being done at the Birmingham University Centre for Contemporary Cultural Studies. How can sports break through the hegemony of the ruling class? Specifically how does Rick Gruneau propose to test his proposition that when a subordinate group is in a position to challenge a dominant group as a result of some change in historical circumstances there is a tendency for the forms of cultural expression of the subordinate to take on a transformative rather than a reproductive character.[3] In other words, I would like both Ian and Rick to address fundamentally the question about how a society reproduces itself, and how social change takes place, and what the role of culture is (specifically sport) within this reproduction.

NOTES AND REFERENCES

1. See S. Hall et al., <u>Policing The Crisis</u>: <u>Mugging,</u>
    <u>the State and Law and Order.</u> London: Macmillan, 1978

2. An important discussion of these concepts is provided
    in Harry Braverman, <u>Labor and Monopoly Capital</u>.
    New York: Monthly Review Press, 1974. Also see
    Richard C. Edwards, <u>Contested Terrain: The Trans-</u>
    <u>formation of the Workplace in the Twentieth Century</u>.
    New York: Basic Books, 1979

3. Gruneau states this notion more specifically in "Power
    and Play in Canadian Social Development". <u>Working</u>
    <u>Papers in the Sociological Study of Sports and Leisure</u>,
    Volume 2 (No.1), 1979. Kingston: Sport Studies Research
    Group, Queen's University.

4
Sport and Hegemony

Some Theoretical Problems

John Hargreaves

The subject of this paper forms part of a larger work concerned with the problem of the association between sports and patterns of hegemony in Britain.[1] Here I want to examine the theoretical problems involved in constructing a Marxist framework for an approach to the problem. Within the scope of this paper I cannot hope to deal in detail with the various Marxist contributions to this topic or to the study of sport in general, but some very brief general remarks are apposite to begin with. The strength of the Marxist tradition in general, and of the particular contribution it has made already to the study of sport as a social phenomenon, is its willingness to give due attention to and the insights it provides into, processes of domination in society and in particular, of course, to the impingement of class relationships and of economic processes on cultural life. This is in marked contrast to the Sociology of Sport, which has tended to grossly neglect this aspect.[2]

Leaving aside the pragmatic, 'official Marxist' treatment of sport,[3] three types of approach within the Marxist tradition can be identified, namely, correspondence theory, reproduction theory and hegemony theory.[4] Because of the weaknesses of the first two I shall concentrate on the third type of approach.

Correspondence theory characterizes sport as a simple reflection of capitalism: its structure and its cultural ethos are completely determined and dominated by capitalist forces and the interests of the ruling class, so that it is a totally alienating activity.[5] Reproduction theory, on the other hand, claims that culture and sport are related to the capitalist mode of production and the dominant social relations in terms of their specificity, that is, their differences and their autonomy; and that it is precisely because of their autonomy that they are enabled to function to reproduce the dominant social relations.[6]

The faults of these approaches have been demonstrated in detail elsewhere, but the fundamental weakness they both share is a one-sided, deterministic and static model of capitalist society.[7] Sport is viewed as a totally ideological phenomenon, totally controlled by, and working in the interests of, the dominant class without limit. There is little or no conception of a dialectic between dominant groups attempting to control and use sport, and subordinate groups with their own responses to such attempts, so there is no real explanation of conflict surrounding sports, of their differentiated nature, and little sense either of sport and culture as material processes. Correspondence and reproduction theory, however, by no means exhaust the possibilities offered by the Marxist tradition, and it is to hegemony theory therefore that we now turn.

In order to show how sport may be encompassed within this third type of approach, it is necessary to show precisely how it is grounded in Marx's theory and also, of course, to discuss to what extent Marx's theory itself presents problems for this project. Though this takes the discussion somewhat away from a concrete consideration of the character of sport it is absolutely necessary in order to avoid misunderstandings.

Marx's historical materialism can be, and indeed, has been interpreted as being fundamentally anti-determinist, anti-idealist, and anti-dualist. The familiar dichotomies of traditional theory - mind/matter, mind/body, subject/object, theory/practice, fact/value, individual/society, etc. - are treated as important and interesting only up to a point, for their limitation is that they pose problems of social

105

existence ultimately in metaphysical terms. The polarity
between thought and existence is treated instead by Marx
in dialectical terms, as two aspects of a single, material
reality, and the polarity is resolved through the concept of
practice.[8] Men are part of nature and they are obliged to
interchange with and act on it in order to exist and satisfy
their needs, which is accomplished through the labour process.
The human body is a force of nature, but men are not only able
to overcome nature in the labour process simply because they
are themselves part of nature but also because they possess
the capacity to reflect on their circumstances and to
formulate and pursue purposes in relation to them.[9] Thought
then, has no separate existence outside the material world -
it is an integral part of the process whereby men produce
their world through their labour and their power to reflect,
and in doing so they transform nature and themselves. Since
there can be no human existence or consciousness outside
social relationships, what we are describing is a historical
reality.[10]Nature, the labour process, technology and thought
are necessarily mediated by culture and social relations -
relations which are no less material than nature and the
forces of production. Labour then, is not merely a physical
capacity, and the labour process is not just a physical
process - in labour the mental and the physical, nature and
culture, theory and practice, are united in one continuous
movement.

Note that such a conception of social relations
methodologically rules out explanation of the relations
between different aspects of the totality, between say, the
mode of production and sport, in terms of a unidirectional
causation process whereby the former determines the latter.
Instead, it is a refutation and a rejection of positivist

conceptions of causation processes in human affairs as such, whether uni or multi-casual, since they cannot encompass active human agency that is, practice in history. It enables the oversimplistic notion of sport as 'located' in some space labelled the 'superstructure' to be avoided, and for sport to be treated as a social relation which is internally related to the mode of production, politics and culture. Sport, like any other form of social relation can thus be seen to possess economic, political, cultural and ideological aspects, the relative importance of which, varies with the character of social conditions pertaining at a given time.

But Marx also theorizes within the framework of a second polarity, the model of base and superstructure, and there is a discrepancy between the two frameworks.[11] The superstructure cannot be equated with consciousness, since in Marx's usage it evidently subsumes material institutions like the state; and the base, or economic relations cannot be equated with social being because the latter encompasses all social relations, including the economic. If the two frameworks are taken in isolation from one another certain problems arise. It appears that from the point of view of the base-superstructure polarity consciousness and non-economic institutions are directly determined by external economic structures. This is the orthodox Marxist stand; it is also the predominant interpretation in anti-Marxist circles; and it is ultimately the Althusserian School's position. On the other hand, if we take the being-consciousness or theory-practice polarity in isolation, practice appears as undetermined, as a product purely of men's free will.

Ideology, culture and politics - and consequently sport and hegemony - assume different connotations depending upon which polarity serves as the context. Within the base-superstructure framework they appear as secondary institutions directly determined by the economic structure. Within the theory-practice polarity they appear as free, as conscious products of subjects. As Williams has cogently argued, the distinction between base and superstructure may instead of a metaphorical and relational meaning acquire a descriptive and conceptual meaning, which purports to indicate the existence of separate observable areas of social life.[12] The danger of reductionism is bad enough, but it is also the reproduction in an altered form of the separation of culture from material social life typical of idealism, which it is supposed to counteract, that is so crippling. The sense of culture as a constitutive process is thus compromised: instead of making cultural history material and social, it is made dependent and instrumental.

Marx himself does not fully integrate this double perspective in his work, but it can be integrated if his work is taken as a unity.[13] The base-superstructure polarity can then be seen as an attempt to show culture and consciousness cannot be analysed on their own - they have a foundation in material reality. It is also an attempt to give a sense of the primacy of economic relations in social being without reducing the latter to the former. The theory-practice polarity emphasizes the foundation of all institutions in practice and that material reality is not a given objective world separated from the subject. Yet this practice is itself determined by crystallizations of past practice. If this integration is not made then two kinds of error result: the superstructure is considered subordinate to the base, and sport seen as completely dependent upon it, or conversely, as autonomous from it and sport is severed from the economy. Neither autonomy nor sub-ordination solves the problem.

Marx argues there is a contradiction in the capitalist

mode of production: it is driven by historical laws of accumulation that generate recurrent economic crises and its dynamic depends upon class exploitation, which creates social conflict between classes and produces the potential for its overthrow. Yet the collapse of capitalism is not seen as an inevitable event, but rather as an ever present tendency, which may be offset in various ways: by a restructuring of capital, by expansion into new areas of exploitation, by political action through the agency of the state - but crucially, it is dependent upon men making their own history.[14] If it can be said to have causal primacy in any sense the economy is presented as exerting crucial but highly specific kinds of limits and pressures on social life, rather than as the only real material force upon which everything else is dependent.[15]

The great merit of Marx's political economy for the study of culture and sport lies in the way the spread of capitalist rationality is specified as a feature of capitalism, per se, rather than as an abstract rationalizing tendency. The pursuit of efficiency which tends to permeate all aspects of society including sport has its roots in the quest for profit and Marx reveals the inherently contradictory nature of capitalist society which is thereby produced. This is a valuable corrective to the tendency in modern sociology, derived in the main from Weber, to confuse capitalist rationality with rationality as such, and to attribute rationalization to 'industrial society' - a view which has bedevilled the sociology of sport.[16]

For example, it is postulated that organized sport exhibits substantially the same features in State capitalist societies like Russia, and it is argued that therefore sport can only be explained with reference to features which both

109

types of society share in common, namely features of 'industrial society', such as rationalization, certain patterns of stratification, nationalism, and so on. A number of objections can be raised against this view. Firstly, the category 'industrial society' is analytically rather weak and somewhat misleading, since it encourages a characterization of societies primarily according to the type of technology and level of economic development, rather than according to the specific types of social relationship, which renders it just as deterministic and reified a view of social life as the orthodox Marxist theorization in terms of base and superstructure it seeks to displace. Furthermore, it allows radically different kinds of society, from the point of view of their modes of production, politics and culture, to be assimilated to one undifferentiated category.[17]

But the really fundamental objection is to the logic of the argument, as opposed to the substantive claims about industrial society. Rationalization, competition, chauvinism, etc. which often characterize sport are treated as abstract universals, or as if they possessed the character of physical objects, which can be plucked out of their social contexts and compared with each other across national boundaries as if they were things in themselves. Whereas these phenomena are socially produced: they take their meaning and function from their particular context, where they denote specific social practices, processes and relationships; and they therefore possess a specific content derived from the nature of the totality of which they form part. There is really no argument over whether rationalization, ruthless competition, chauvinism, or whatever, work to cement structures of inequality - that observation is in itself uninformative - the real issue is what is the concrete character of the social order these

features help to support. In a capitalist society, for
example, rationalization processes work in a particular
direction, one which tends to favour and support the existence
of a capitalist class, whereas in a different type of social
order, such as the Soviet Union, it serves a different
pattern of domination. Therefore, even though on superficial
examination rationalization, etc., in sport may appear to be
the same phenomena in contrasting societies, they cannot be
said to be the same at all. Logically it does not follow
that such phenomena must be attributed to the same causal set
of circumstances in each case. Their presence in different
types of society is determined by radically different kinds of
context. Lest it be said that the principle of relating
social phenomena to their social context robs us of the chance
of comparative analysis, it must be said that of course, such
comparisons between societies can be made, provided that
whatever is compared is seen in its context, which logically
means the contexts themselves must be also compared. It is
worth noting in passing that, so far, there does not seem to
be a single case of a successful explanation of a social
phenomenon along the lines prescribed by the point of view
against which we are arguing.

Lastly, the method of abstracting elements for comparison
and treating them as universals neglects the reality that we
are not comparing independent phenomena. The reality is
that international competition between the two superpowers in
particular has meant the rationalization of social life,
including sport, in these two types of society is mutually
determining, and nowhere perhaps is this more evident than in
sport. In order to compete with the west Russia emulated the
west's sporting achievements by rationalizing the whole
structure of its sport. Her success in international
competition in turn stimulated the further rationalization of

sport in the west, and so on. This seems to be a telling vindication of Marx's dialectical method outlined here, which analyses elements in relation to the contradictory totality of social relationships, for his analysis of capitalism was never restricted to the national context alone - for him it is a system on a world scale.

Marx's theory culminates in a critique of political economy and though he certainly managed to transcend his antagonists' level of conceptualization, his mature work does concentrate on political economy more than any other single aspect of capitalist society. It may be, as Thompson suggests, that he became more entangled in its thickets than he realized, in a way to the detriment, perhaps, of his treatment of other important problems.[17] For example, he never produced anything like the equivalent of his work on the mode of production, in his work on the State, or in his work on specific features of civil society, such as the class structure.

Though the theory goes some considerable way towards integrating the mode of production with other aspects of society, especially with political processes, we cannot move without problems from what is given in Capital to a theory which would satisfactorily encompass a theory of sport and hegemony. It is clearly necessary to relate sport very closely to the mode of production, but by itself it is insufficient. While it probably cannot be reiterated enough in some quarters that capitalist society is inherently unstable - an insight which makes pluralist 'end of ideology' and 'post-capitalist society' theses, together with Marcuse's notion of the total incorporation of the western working class, rather ludicrous - the insight was never by itself adequate.[19] The best indication of this is the fact that capitalism has survived successive economic traumas (the inter-war period and, so far, the seventies), so the really pressing theoretical problem would seem to be to pinpoint the social processes that are responsible for its survival which extend beyond the mode of production.[20]

In this connection the theory of ideology in Marx would appear to be potentially immensely fruitful, for example, in showing how ideas and beliefs may be linked to the interests of classes, for its insights into the way ruling groups are able to set limits to the propagation of ideas opposed to their interests, and into the way ruling groups attempt to put forward their interests as the general interest.

The problem with his theory of ideology for an analysis of modern capitalist society is that as it was left by Marx, it tends to be restricted to certain ideological forms and processes only - coherently articulated religious, philosophical, social and political ideas, and to the inverted, distorted representations of reality of the capitalist and the 'common man', which arise as a matter of course through the workings of the capitalist mode of production. Important as knowledge of these is, they by no means exhaust the field of ideological production in a modern capitalist society. The complex mediations whereby specific sets of ideas become dominant and conceal contradicitions remains to be fully worked out. The Marxist tradition as a whole has been rather slow to develop his insights in this area, having taken some wrong turnings in a positivist direction since his time with the result that Marxist attempts to characterize sport as a material force have not advanced very far. The tendency to treat ideology as a mere reflection of material circumstances, as pure illusion, rather than as an active material process; the complete assimilation of cultural forms like sport to ideology; the tendency to imply a unidirectional process whereby ideology is always invented and imposed on subordinates by a homogeneous ruling class; and the assumption that ideology consists of a uniform set of beliefs, is too simplistic.

It is to these kinds of problems that Gramsci's theory of hegemony was addressed and for which it would seem possesses great utility, for it complements the detailed attention Marx gives to economic and political aspects and sets out to elaborate the way culture and ideology connect with them as part of the totality. The concept of hegemony in Gramsci is consequently at once more inclusive, extending beyond and reworking the concepts of culture and ideology examined so far.[21] Coming out of the anti-determinist, anti-positivist 'Hegelian Marxist' tradition, Gramsci's theory allows sport to be related to society in a way which does not reduce it to a mere appendage of the mode of production or a servant of the ruling class.[22]

By hegemony Gramsci meant the ability of a dominant class, or class fraction, to exercise a special kind of leadership over a society, a leadership not simply based on ownership and control of the means of production, a monopoly of state power and the ability to impose its ideas willy nilly on the population, but which is also founded on 'moral' leadership, the ability to obtain the consent of the dominated, which amounts to something more than acquiescence, and unites the whole society positively behind it in a 'historic bloc'. A hegemonic class manages in a variety of ways to suffuse every level or pore of the society, from the most formal institutions down to the informal practices and meanings of everyday life with its version of reality: "it is a lived system of meanings and values - constitutive and constituting - which as they are experienced as practices appear as reciprocally confirming. It thus constitutes a sense of reality for most people in society, a sense of absolute because experienced reality .... It is, that is to say, in the strongest sense a 'culture' which has also to be seen as the lived dominance and subordination of particular classes."[23] What Gramsci stresses above all is the way a specific historical form of domination becomes sedimented and naturalized as 'commonsense' in practical consciousness, that is, in and through everyday living, so that the seemingly most innocuous values, meanings and practices reproduce a particular class's hegemony. It is easy to see how from this point of view, popular culture, and specifically sport, could be given their proper share of attention alongside other cultural constituents of civil society, like language usage, formal and informal education, the media, habits and customs, etc., as resources out of which a class fashions its hegemony.

One of the most vital points heavily emphasized in the theory is how problematic it is for a class or group to establish and maintain its hegemony. This is always dependent upon the specific features of the national context, and so patterns of hegemony do not only vary from country to country according to their history and social structure, but also according to the particular set of circumstances pertaining in a given society at different times. Hegemony is never guaranteed to a class and it must work hard for it: by making genuine concessions to other classes and groups; by accommodating imaginatively and positively to opposing pressures; by forming alliances with potential enemies; by being able to forsee and pre-empt alternatives to its hegemony; and by assessing accurately what combination of coercion and persuasion to use. Most of the time a hegemonic class manages to incorporate potential opposition by negotiation, concessions, threats and pressures before opposition can reach serious proportions, which would bring its legitimacy into question, but this tends to be a labour of Sisyphus, and at times, particularly when consent breaks down and opposition results in a crisis situation, the balance between the use of force and persuasion may shift in favour of the former, but exclusive reliance upon force in the long term renders hegemony inherently unstable.

There are certain problems to be dealt with in Gramsci's theory if it is to be used in the study of sport. In certain places his ambiguity can open the way to an interpretation which could make the analysis of sport just as abstract, static and totalizing as correspondence and reproduction theory. It is a common misconception that the theory is concerned purely with ideological hegemony exercised in civil society and not with coercion exercised by the state, but this is based upon a highly selective reading of Gramsci, which ignores much else of what he has to say. Anderson does show convincingly, however, that although this interpretation is incorrect, there is a 'slippage' in Gramsci's conception of hegemony, the state and civil society and the relationship between them.[25] In fact, Gramsci at times oscillates between three different versions of the relationship: in one, hegemony pertains to civil society and coercion to the state; in another, hegemony is divided into its civil and political components, so that the state becomes an apparatus of hegemony as well; and a third conception assimilates civil society to the state, so that any distinction between them disappears. There is then at least some tendency to neglect the role of coercion and to overemphasize the role of consent and consciousness and culture. As Anderson points out in correction, the role of the state and civil society in the west is asymmetrical - coercion is located in the state, and consent is located both in civil society and in the state, so hegemony is founded on a combination of both. But in addition, one should also take account of the increasing role of the state in obtaining consent as well as employing coercion. For example, with respect to sport, the state promotes it with campaigns designed to persuade adults to participate, but it also coerces children into participation in sport through schooling. It is the state, however, rather than civil society that is the ultimate guarantor of bourgeois hegemony.

Secondly, Gramsci departs from Marx in locating civil society in the 'superstructure', so separating it in a sense from the mode of production. With the exception of his essay on 'Americanism and Fordism', Gramsci in practice paid relatively little attention to the mode of production in his theory, treating hegemony, in the main, as a political and ideological process pertaining to the 'superstructure'.[26] This may account for a tendency to underestimate the coercive function and ideological influence of labour process itself, which gives the employer an opportunity to exert influence over the worker. For example, it is well known that historically, employers have provided sports facilities to enhance their control over the workforce.[27] Provided these defects are corrected and the meaning of the concept thus made clear, it should prove extremely useful when applied to the study of sport.

At the outset the sense in which sport can be conceived of as autonomous in terms of hegemony theory must be clarified. The problem with other Marxist approaches is that there is no real room for a conception of sporting activity as autonomous at all. In hegemony theory, on the other hand, the autonomy of sporting activity can be given a concrete grounding in identifiable social relations, if we ask the questions autonomy for what?, and autonomy to do what? In other words, the autonomy of an activity must be considered

117

with respect to specific social processes. Gramsci's theory
sees the character of capitalist society in terms of class
relations and opposition between classes, so the relevant
social processes are precisely those through which classes
are constituted and through which they are related to each
other. What is relevant as far as the autonomy of sport is
concerned is the extent to which dominant classes and groups
are able to use it to impose their views and interests on
others, and the extent to which subordinate classes and groups
are able to resist and overcome those attempts.

The extent to which sports as a whole, or individual
sports are autonomous in this sense is a matter of empirical
(as opposed to empiricist) investigation.[28] The theory of
hegemony thus places sport, in so far as it is related to
hegemony, firmly in the context of struggles between classes
and groups, but in a manner which allows for negotiation,
compromises and accommodation between them, as well as
straightforward domination, to be taken into account in the
analysis. For example, just as Marx argued that the
specificity of the 19th century British State was the outcome
of conflicts within the ruling class and of the attempts by
the contending parties to resolve them, so the specificity of
sport in Britain can be attributed to some extent to conflicts
between dominant groups and their attempts to resolve these
conflicts.[29] Thus participation in sport in the public schools
was one way in which the interests of different fractions of
the ruling class were accommodated. Indeed, it is probably
necessary to view the development of sport in the context of
conflict between a range of different groups, for example,
old versus new capital (the amateur gentleman tradition versus
Kerry Packer), big business versus small and medium business
(growth of sponsorship in sport), in addition to the conflict

118

between bourgeoisie and proletariat.

If the extent to which any given institution is incorporative and the manner in which it is so varies with the specific hegemonic pattern, the question as to where sport stands in a particular hegemony remains open to empirical investigation. We know, for example, that certain institutions and formations in British Society tend to be more firmly incorporative than others - work, education, the media, law and the major political parties come into this category - while in contrast certain other institutions, such as shop stewards' committees, radical political groupings, certain forms of artistic activity, the women's movement, ethnic organizations, etc., tend to encourage opposition of one kind or another. Where sport figures in this continuum is problematic.

It is fairly clear also that the strategies of incorporation pursued by dominant groups vary according to the type of institution in question and the moment in time: they may vary from compulsion and manipulation, through various forms of persuasion, to negotiation, concession and compromise. Also the mode of compliance worked out by subordinate groups in response, varies with the institutional type and the strategies ruling groups employ - from positive allegiance, through tacit acquiescence, to a pragmatic or instrumental mode of participation, in the absence of any perceived alternative to it.

The characterization of sport in terms of these three dimensions of hegemony - the extent of incorporation, the strategic mode of incorporation, and the mode of compliance - is difficult also, given the great variety of sports in existence, the great variation of social settings in which they take place, and the paucity of good, reliable and detailed information. It would be dangerous therefore to assume that sport can be treated as an undifferentiated whole, and there are much more likely to be wide variations between sports, and in individual sports at different times, along each of the dimensions of hegemony. Some types of sport may be strongly incorporative: sport in the English public schools of the late 19th and early 20th century was so for the middle and upper classes. Other sports may exert a rather weak effect, for example, the race track meeting and certain other spectator sports. Some may be performed under compulsion, with acquiescence of under protest like a good proportion of school sport still; other types through persuasion, like YMCA and some forms of mass spectator sport; in yet others compliance may be spontaneous and very positive, like playing in the local team. A given sport may thus manifest quite startling variations along the different dimensions according to social and historical context. For example, the F.A. Cup Final is plainly in a different category to and has a different social significance from the local match on the common, the kickabout in the street, or village football in the 18th century. Eventually it should be possible to classify different sports in terms of the three dimensions, but in doing so it should always be born in mind that the place of particular sports, and indeed of sport as a whole, in hegemony varies with historical and social circumstance, so there is no question of a fixed, formalistic classificatory scheme.

Since sport is inserted into and partakes of a whole range of institutions, formations, relationships and processes - the mode of production, education, political institutions, the media, youth culture, class formations, ethnic groups, sexual patterns, cultural traditions, and so on, the theory of hegemony demands the investigation of precisely how sport is related to the major features of the totality. The most important task in this project is to identify those features specific to sports which may enable them to contribute to the process whereby class rule and class power are translated into 'commonsense' and legitimated.

One potentially useful way of tackling this is to consider sports in their ritual and dramatic aspects, that is to say, sports can be categorized in certain key respects as a species of political ritual and as a kind of popular theatre.[30] Probably more than any other area of social life, with the exception of religion, sports are replete with ritual activity and powerful symbolism - which is, no doubt, why the idea that sport has replaced religion as the opium of the people is appealing to some theorists. Regretably, Marx attached no great significance to ritual activity and its associated symbolism, and surprisingly, in view of his interest in culture, neither did Gramsci, or indeed the Marxist tradition as a whole. The theory of hegemony could be enormously enriched, it would seem, if this kind of material were incorporated. It is a pity that the field has been left mainly to explorers in the Durkheimian tradition, who to their credit, have given it a good deal of attention.[31]

Neo-Durkheimian structural-functionalist sociology has emphasized the non-instrumental, expressive functions of ritual in reinforcing and recreating "value-consensus' in societies, and a number of writers have argued, for example, that certain official rituals or ceremonies, like the coronation of the British monarch and the inauguration of the American President function in this way.[32] The drawbacks of tying the analysis of ritual to such a framework hardly need emphasizing once again. The primacy given to value-consensus as a necessary condition of social integration is in any case unwarranted, since it is clear social integration can exist without it, and there is little evidence for its existence in western democracies.[33] Neo-Durkheimians have concentrated their attentions too narrowly on a small range of official ceremonies heavily pervaded by the hegemonic ideology, while ignoring others which are not. If the concept of ritual is defined so that it is applicable to aspects of other forms of activity, such as demonstrations, strikes and sports, it can readily be seen that ritual activity can also express alternatives to hegemony or counter-hegemonies, and be at the centre of conflict. Most importantly, however, there is a key element in ritual activity central to Durkheim's own theory of ritual, which is omitted by Neo-Durkheimians - the cognitive component.[34]

If we understand by ritual, activity that is: "Rule-governed ... of a symbolic character which draws the attention of its participants to objects of thought and feeling which they hold to be of special significance"[35], and if we abstract it from the functionalist framework, placing it within the context of a theory of hegemony instead, ritual activity can then be seen as a crucial strategic factor in class relations and in the construction of hegemony. The objects of thought and feeling to which ritual activity draws attention may be multiple and occur at different levels of meaning. Ritual symbols "...condense many references uniting them in a single cognitive and affective field."[36], that is to say, they stand for many things at once: "Each has a 'fan' or 'spectrum' of reference which tend to be interlinked by what is usually a simple mode of association, its very simplicity enabling it to interconnect a wide variety of signification.[37] Lukes'

definition of ritual, strictly speaking, does not very clearly
differentiate ritual activity from other forms of social
activity, since all social relations are rule-governed and
symbolically mediated, but it does at least allow the
recognition that some forms or aspects of social relations
have a much more ritualistic character than others, and also
that some are much more directly representative of key social
relations than others.

Plainly, many official ceremonies reinforce hegemony in
the way they draw people's attention and invoke their
loyalties towards certain powerfully evoked representations
of the social and political order. But, as Lukes points out,
many other institutionalized activities that may not be
primarily identified by their participants as rituals play
an exactly similar role. The ritual surrounding the British
legal and educational systems are only two of the more obvious
examples that have been studied and there are many others,
including sports.[38] Such ritual activities can play a
significant part in hegemony, legitimating and perpetuating
the predominant conceptions by helping define the nature of
society and defining away alternatives. In Lukes' lucid
formulation: "....political ritual should be seen as
reinforcing, recreating and organizing representations
collectives (to use Durkheim's term) .... the symbolism of
political ritual represents, inter alia, particular models
or political paradigms of society and how it functions. In
this sense, such ritual plays, as Durkheim argued, a cognitive
role, rendering intelligible society and social relationships,
serving to organize people's knowledge of the past and present
and their capacity to imagine the future. In other words, it
helps to define as authoritative certain ways of seeing
society: it serves to specify what in society is of special
significance, it draws people's attention to certain forms

of relationships and activity - and at the same time therefore, it deflects their attention from other forms, since every way of seeing is also a way of not seeing".[39]

What has to be added to this in relation to sport as a form of political ritual, is that ritual activity, of course, possesses a powerful dramatic element and it is this element which is particularly compelling in sports. The drama in sport is often interpreted simply in terms of its entertainment effect, that is, as a performance and a spectacle which serves as an escape from reality. There is no doubt that sports are entertaining, but the dramatic element and its effects cannot be understood merely in these terms: it is the associated element in ritual which makes it such a powerful form of communication in drawing people's attention to and making statements about objects of thought and feeling. There is a crucial difference, however, between sport as drama on the one hand, and the drama of official rituals and ceremonies and the formalized drama of the theatre on the other. Compared with the latter the dramatic element in sport makes it the quintessential form of popular theatre. In marked contrast, the theatre in Britain is in no sense a popular institution. On the other hand also, the great occasions of state tend to be managed, staged and acted almost exclusively by dominant groups and active popular participation tends to be minimal. Considered as a dramatic form, as popular theatre, sport offers far more opportunity for people to play a significant part, to actively participate, to communicate common experiences and shared meanings, because it is embedded in a popular tradition, which connects more directly and organically with people's lives. It also has a strong localism - loyalty to neighbourhood, town, country, through identification with and participation in the team.

Sport as a form of popular theatre lies in the same tradition as the great festivals of mediaeval Europe, which were only finally snuffed out in Britain in the 19th century.[40] As a form of popular theatre it gives people a part to play, or involves them meaningfully in performances that express and communicate, in organized form, collective experiences and meanings concerning the major themes of life. In an essentially well-worked and understood way, they rehearse what is taken for granted already by participants and observers, in familiar language gesture and style.

The modern theatre, or even the cinema, in some instances, is quite different in this respect, in that new areas of experience are often consciously explored, or new ways of exploring familiar experiences are developed in a deliberately didactic way. Sport, in contrast, as a form of popular theatre is very much part of a tradition which is strongly plebian, but whose elements are largely residual rather than emergent.[41]

Tradition, whether popular or otherwise, is always contested and selective, a version of the past which is intended to connect with and ratify the present, and within a particular hegemony it is usually in the interests of dominant classes to see as far as possible that this selection is passed off as 'the tradition', defined and constructed so as to offer as little challenge as possible in the form of an alternative tradition. There is nearly always therefore, a sustained attempt to exert control over, or even to wrest control from the majority, and only when it is relatively safe to do so will it be left unattended.

The advantage of seeing sport from this point of view, as ritual and drama which is part of a popular tradition, is that it obviates the necessity of accounting for the possible effects of sport in such crude terms as 'brainwashing' or 'drugging' or 'catharsis' and returns the analysis to the cognitive level, that is, to people's rationalities that are grounded in material practices. The conception allows us to analyze the meanings and practices involved in sport as a 'hidden curriculum', embedded in ritual and dramatic form, which is firmly rooted also in a particular cultural tradition. As a way of making statements about the nature of society ritual activity is highly resistive to 'rational' argument and is therefore admirably suited as an ideologically closed form of communication. In order to assess the extent to which sporting practices as a form of political ritual play a part in hegemony, it is necessary, as Lukes cogently suggests, to seek answers to a number of relevant and related questions: "Who (i.e. which social groups) have prescribed their performance and specified the rules which govern them? Who (which social groups) specify the objects of thought and feeling they symbolize - specifically, certain forms of social relationship and activity - as of special significance? Who exactly holds them to be specially significant, and significant in what ways? In the interests of which social groups does the acceptance of these ways of seeing operate? And what forms of social relationship and activity are in consequence ignored as of less or no significance? Under what conditions are political rituals most effective in getting participants and observers to internalize the political paradigms they represent? How are such rituals used strategically by different groups, exerting or seeking power in society?"[42]

Patterson, in his analysis of a Test Match riot in Jamaica shows how sporting ritual and symbol can be related to hegemony and illustrates how these elements might be incorporated in a theory of hegemony.[43] Cricket symbolizes

126

the social character of West Indian society - the deep
divisions, the tensions and the uneasy hegemony of the white-
oriented 'elite' over the black lower classes. For the former,
as for the departed white colonial masters, cricket is a
symbol of the perfectly ordered society, with its complex
rules and the ideology of obedience and authority personified
by the figure of the umpire. For the latter, however, it is
one of the few sources of solidarity and pride uniting 'us'
against the hated 'them', so victory becomes immensely
important. In a Test Match, so long as the home side is
winning, the elite's claim to share the opposition to the
former colonial masters, whom they have replaced and whose
culture they share, is accepted by the mass. But when they
are losing the make-believe is shattered and the symbol of
the ordered society is transformed into Jamaican society as
it is, as rioters battle with police amidst the tear gas
enveloping the cricket ground.

In modern capitalist societies it is the media who are
primarily responsible for the dramatization and construction
of sports as a species of political ritual and for its
transmission to the population at large. In their working
assumptions and practices - the type of commentary, the use
of verbal and visual imagery - the media re-dramatize and
re-present what are already potent dramatic spectacles within
a framework of interpretation, which facilitates the passing
of ideologically encoded messages, that is, preferred ways
of seeing sport and society.

Sports tend to be presented in the media as symbolic
representations of a particular kind of social order, so that
in effect they become modern morality plays, serving to
justify and uphold dominant values and ideas. The model of
the social order encoded in media practices and assumptions

is a pluralist and basically harmonious one, but threatened by deviations from established procedures and the outbreak of conflict. The figure of the judge, referee or umpire symbolizes legitimate authority, whose duty it is to punish infringements of the norms, and whose decisions are beyond challenge. A good game/society is one conducted according to the established rules; a problematic game/society is one where infringements of the established rules occur.

In the media's treatment of sport the concern with rule adherence and infringement extends beyond the actual sporting events themselves to comment and judgement on the participants' private lives and increasingly to the spectators' conduct also. The players become personifications of certain kinds of values and the interpretation of performances and of the conduct of spectators becomes part of a wider process whereby particular kinds of life styles, values and ideas are 'sold'. Modern British football, for example, which because of its great popularity - especially with the working class - attracts very high media coverage, has become the focus for the expression of concern, not only with rule infringement on the field, but with the potential breakdown of law and order and of society.[44] Although most professional footballers are almost entirely working class in social origin, compared with other sections of the labour force their conditions of employment are significantly different: their union is relatively weak, wages range from a minority of highly paid 'stars' to the level of the semi-skilled worker, with the majority clustered at the middle and lower levels, compensation for injury is low and pensions non-existent, there is virtually no job protection, and the employer can interfere with, and rigidly control, the players' private lives, especially the younger ones.[45] In other words, the relation

128

between employer and employee in British football (and also
in many other sports) is a concrete fulfillment of the
bourgeois ideal of how the labour force should be governed
and rewarded: the individual has to continually prove himself
in competition with others to obtain his livelihood, and
success is judged according to individual ability and
achievement, under the conditions set by the market. In
this context control over players' lives by employers and
control over them on the field by the referee, becomes a
symbol **for** the control which employers in general exercise
over the labour force and which dominant groups exercise over
society. In the terms in which the media present the game,
in effect it becomes a dramatic symbol encoded with preferred
ways of seeing the relation between capital and labour. The
game is commented on in terms similar to those in which the
media also comments on the performance of the labour force.
Players and teams are praised and commended for their
successful achievements, for obeying the rules, for fitting
in with the team, as examples of manhood. etc.. Or
conversely, they are condemned for failure, for rule infringements on or off the field, for adopting deviant life styles,
'letting down the country', and so on. There is, in fact, in
Britain a remarkable parallel between the framework of
assumptions within which the media interpret social and
political questions - especially with respect to industrial
relations - and the framework within which sport is presented.[46]
Football, and probably other sports as well thus come to serve
as exemplifications of the bourgeois ideal of the individualistic
competitive, 'meritocratic' society.

Where international competition in sporting events is
involved, they also come to function as symbols of national
unity, that is, they tend to serve as vehicles for the

celebration of supposed national virtues and as a way of expressing chauvinistic ideas and sentiments about other nations in stereotypical form. In Britain, for example, the media's presentation tends to be homologous with the way her imperial past and involvement in war is conventionally presented. In both, the John Bull image is brought into play, whereby the British nation is depicted as the plucky, little, unprepared underdog, who always plays fair, up against the ruthless, professional, bully, who possesses all the advantages.

In any pattern of hegemony there is necessarily a discrepancy between the dominant ideological modes of understanding society and the way society is concretely experienced by individuals in different and opposed class positions, so that organized ways of managing the gap are created. Unlike education, with which sport is closely associated, and which is controlled by dominant groups in a well articulated, formally organized attempt to define away the gap, sport is a far more 'spontaneous' way the working class possesses to close it. To opposed classes and groups sport in different ways is a metaphor for the ideal society: it provides a model of how society should operate if it were actually to function in accordance with the promises held out in ideology. In Britain, for example, there is supposed to be equality of opportunity, or at least a progressive diminution of inequalities of that kind, yet they remain in practice; rewards should be commensurate with merit and effort, but the maldistribution of wealth, income and power makes this impossible beyond a certain point; market competition is supposed to be free and between equals, but to a great extent it is restricted and is between units of very unequal weight; rules should apply equally to everyone, but realistically they cannot where social and economic inequality is rampant;

there are supposed to be agreed values and rules of conduct, but the existing rules are contested; and the outcome of action is supposed to be rationally predictable, but in most people's experience fate commonly plays a major part in social existence.[47]

Working class existence especially is still very much determined by chance or luck, and by what must seem to be the same thing - decisions made by 'them'. In sports chance is also a vital ingredient, but the difference between the structuring of working class people's life chances through economic and political processes and the working out of chance in sports, is that whereas in the former chance is structured unequally against one, in the latter realm, in marked contrast, chance is randomly distributed and therefore operates equally and justly. It is no accident then, that gambling has been found to be much more popular among subordinate groups generally, and that it is traditionally so strongly associated with sports: the very point of sport is that the outcome is never certain, no one controls, no one has a superior chance of winning, and therefore in this sense everyone is equal. The stark difference between the experience of ordinary life in a capitalist society and the experience of sport is that though fate and chance play a central part in both, it is in sports that justice and equality prevail and that fate rules dispassionately. What has proved problematic, if not impossible, to construct within the dominant social relations has been constructed in sports: there are relatively simple, clear criteria for establishing merit, reward and achievement, that is, in sport and nowhere else success depends on the 'objective' assessment of ability and achievement.

To be sure, all this is relative and sports cannot be

divorced from the major pressures of social existence, and obviously, in practice, it is often difficult to decide on where merit and achievement lies - who should be selected for the team, who wins the points decision in a boxing match, how to resolve the continual arguments over football referee's decisions - but the presumption tends to be that a decision can always in principle be reached, and matters are relatively clear-cut compared with, say, how to decide on pay differentials, or on who should receive certain kinds of education. Sport perhaps has a meaning therefore to those who are relatively deprived of wealth and power, because through it valued qualities, which cannot normally be experienced very easily in the ordinary course of events, since they are systematically devalued, undermined and their realization in life blocked, can be experienced and demonstrated. Sports, are therefore not simply attractive and compelling because they compensate for deprivations by being enjoyable, exciting, associated with play and recreation. They are compelling and deeply meaningful because they are part of a culture whereby opportunities are provided for recognizing in others, experiencing oneself and demonstrating to others basic human qualities: merited achievement, skill, grace, cunning, endurance, initiative, risk-taking and decision-making, courage, strength, imagination, dignity, comradeship, contact with nature, and more qualities. A great many sports probably demand more in terms of such qualities and give more satisfaction than the majority of jobs.

To recognize that sports provide a kind of utopia or approximation to a world in which the promises held out, but denied by capitalism, are realized and everything functions as it should do ideally, is not to say that sports are simply spurious or a form of escapism: if they did not genuinely satisfy deeply held needs they would fail to attract people;

and in saying they provide genuine satisfactions we are not
claiming either that they can compensate people for their
deprivations to the point of eradicating them from
consciousness and making them content with their lot. If this
is so, how can sports be said to buttress hegemony in any
sense at all? The answer to this is that they do so in
principle in the way any process of class accommodation,
such as economism does: just as labour in pursuing economism
made valuable gains, but at the same time had to concede
influence to dominant groups in the shape of control over
production, politics and the means of communication, so
sports too represent real material gains for working class
people, which could not be achieved without conceding influence
to dominant groups in the cultural sphere. Dominant groups
do associate themselves with the voluntary organization of
popular sports, sports are commercialized, they do figure in
school curricula, they are mediated by the press and broadcasting, and the state does intervene in them, and thus,
dominant groups have many opportunities for intervening in
and using sports in their own interests. But just as
economism does not necessarily lead to the total incorporation
of the working class, as we have seen, neither does the
intervention of dominant groups in popular culture lead to it
either, significant though it undoubtedly is. If sports
are a metaphor for British capitalism and society it is
unlikely that the metaphor will mean the same to both
dominant and subordinate classes. As far as the former is
concerned sport is a striking metaphor for an idealized
capitalism, which asserts that it works, and in doing so
draws attention to bourgeois values and norms; whereas for
the latter, sport is more a metaphor for how life should be -
an implicit condemnation of a society that does not work so

133

well for them.

Changes in the mode of production, communications and decision-making processes in the advanced capitalist societies mean that the dominant social order and culture reaches much further than previously into areas of social life hitherto defined as private, with a consequent pressure on the capacity of popular cultural tradition to serve as a repository of common experiences and meanings.[48] We can hypothesize that sport, especially in its more organized forms, has played and will continue to play a part in hegemony in societies like Britain. The efficacy of such attempts by dominant groups to trade off popular culture is bound to be uneven, some degree or other of tension and contradiction is bound to exist in sport, even those institutional contexts where sport is more firmly hegemonic, such as the media, education, and some of the more commercialized sports. Sports form one of a number of arenas in which classes accommodate to each other. The basis of accommodation may involve manipulation and even coercion, but it usually also works through concession and compromise, and thus on the basis of a pragmatic acceptance of hegemony on the part of subordinate groups.

CONCLUSION

I have argued that the sport-hegemony relation cannot be understood simply as a means of maintaining or reproducing the dominant pattern of social relations, and against the view that it simply reflects, and is determined by, the mode of production. I have also argued that equally, sport cannot be dissociated from the context of class relations and specific hegemonic patterns. In order to understand how sport forms part of the totality, the relevant processes must be analysed in dialectical terms - as characterized by conflict and consent, coercion and struggle, the outcome of

134

which is always problematic to some degree for all parties concerned. Sport must also be conceived and characterized in its own specific terms, namely as a central component in popular cultural tradition, with its own meanings, which, though they may be ideologically significant, are not merely reducible to expressions of ruling class ideology. Further, if the role that sport plays in hegemony is to be properly understood, the relevant processes have to be elucidated in their concrete detail.

NOTES AND REFERENCES

1.   Hargreaves, J., _Sport and Hegemony in Britain_,
     Macmillan, forthcoming.

2.   Loy, J.W. and Kenyon, G.S., eds., _Sport, Culture and_
     Society, 1969; Dunning, E., ed., _The Sociology of_
     Sport, 1971; Talamini, J.T., and Page, C.H., eds.,
     Sport and Society; An Anthology, 1973; Sage, G.H. ed.,
     Sport and American Society, 1973; Albonico, R. and
     Pfister-Binz, K., eds., _Sociology of Sport_, 1971;
     Mangan, J.A., ed., _Physical Education and Sport:_
     Sociological and Cultural Perspectives, 1973; Guttman,
     A., _From Ritual to Record_, 1978; Jokl E., and Simons, E.,
     International Research in Sport and Physical Education,
     1964; Luschen, G., "The Sociology of Sport", _Current_
     Sociology, 1967; Snyder E., and Spreitzer, E.,
     "Sociology of Sport: An Overview", in Yiannakis, A.,
     et al, eds., _Sport Sociology_, 1976; Nixon, H.L.,
     Sport and Social Organization, 1976. As a contrast to
     the consensus view see also: Cohen, P. and Robbins, D.,
     Knuckle Sandwich, 1978;, Taylor, I., "Social Control
     Through Sport", unpublished paper, University of
     Sheffield, 1971; Taylor, I., "Soccer Violence and
     Soccer Hooliganism", in Cohen, S., ed., _Images of_
     Deviance, 1971; Patterson, O., "The Cricket Ritual in
     the West Indies", _New Society_, No. 352, 26th June, 1969;
     Scott, J., _The Athletic Revolution_, 1971; Edwards, H.
     The Revolt of the Black Athlete, 1970; Edwards, H.,
     The Sociology of Sport; Listiak, A., "Legitimate
     Deviance and Social Class", in Gruneau, R.S. and
     Albinson, J.G., eds., _Canadian Sport_, 1976; Critcher, C.,
     and Willis, P., "Women in Sport", _Cultural Studies, 5_
     Spring, 1974; Hargreaves, J.E., "The Political Economy
     of Mass Sport", in Parker, S.R., et al, eds., _Sport and_
     Leisure in Contemporary Society, 1975.

3.   For an account of "official" Marxism's view and treat-
     ment of sport see: Riordan, J., _Sport in Soviet Society_,
     1977; Riordan, J. ed., _Sport Under Communism_, 1978.
     Wohl, A., "Fifty Years of Physical Culture in the USSR",
     International Review of Sport Sociology, Vol. 3, 1968;
     Mao Tse Tung, "A Study of Physical Education", in
     Schram, S.R., _The Political Thought of Mao Tse Tung_,
     1969, p. 152-160.

4.   Hall, S., _Schooling and Society_, Open University Unit
     32, E202, "A Review of the Course", 1977.

5. Brohm, J.M., _Sport: A Prison of Measured Time_, 1978;
    Hoch, P., _Rip Off The Big Game_, 1972; Vinnai, G.,
    Football Mania, 1973.

6. Althusser, L., "Ideology and Ideological State
    Apparatuses", _Lenin and Philosophy_, 1971. Bourdieu,P.,
    "Sport and Social Class", _Social Science Information_,
    17, 6, 1978, pp. 819-840; Bourdieu, P., and Passeron, J.C.
    Reproduction in Education, Society and Culture, 1977.

7. Amongst the mounting volume of critical work on
    Althusser, the most recent and comprehensive is
    Thompson, E.P., "The Poverty of Theory", _The Poverty
    of Theory and Other Essays_, 1978; see also Geras, N.,
    "Louis Althusser: An Assessment" _New Left Review,_
    1971; Hargreaves, _op cit_, chap. 2.

8. Marx, K., "Theses on Feuerbach", Easton, L.D., and
    Guddat, K.H., eds., _Writings of the Young Marx on
    Philosophy and Society_, 1967; Schmidt, A., _The Concept
    of Nature in Marx_, 1971.

9. Marx, K. _Capital_, Vol. 1, p. 177-8.

10. See Marx's "Sixth Thesis on Feurbach". Marx states:
    "Feurbach resolves the religious essence into the human
    essence. But the human essence is no abstraction
    inherent in each single individual. In its reality it
    is the ensemble of the social relations". _Marx/Engels
    Selected Works_ in three volumes. Moscow: Progress
    Publishers, 1969, (I) p. 114.

11. Larrain, J., _The Concept of Ideology_, 1979.

12. Williams, R., _Marxism and Literature_, 1977, Part II,
    Chap. 1., Marx uses the base-superstructure model a
    good deal more carefully than his critics and the
    orthodox Marxist tradition allow for. In the 1859
    Preface to the Critique of Political Economy, for
    example, he refers to relations of production as:
    "... _appropriate_ to a given stage in the development of
    their material forces of production" - not as determined
    by the latter. The superstructure, as such, is not
    referred to as determined, but instead he refers to
    "... the economic structure of society, the real
    foundation, on which _arises a legal and political
    superstructure_ and to which _correspond_ definite forms
    of social consciousness." Marx refers to "The mode of
    production of material life conditions the general
    processes of social, political and economic life."-
    and does not claim it directly determines the latter.

See Coulter, J., "Marxism and The Engels Paradox", *Socialist Register*, 1971.

13. Larrain, *op cit*.

14. Marx, *Capital*, Vol. III, Part 3.

15. Williams, R., *op cit*; Williams, R., *Politics and Letters*, p. 137-151; Thompson, E.P., *op cit*.

16. For a critique of Weber's concept see Mommsen, W., *The Age of Bureaucracy*; Marcuse, H., "Industrialization and Capitalism in the Thought of Max Weber", *Negations*. For various usages of the concept of rationalization to explain the structure and development of sport see: Guttman, *op cit*.; Page C., "Introduction", in J.T. Talamini and Page, *Sport and Society: An Anthology*, 1973; Dunning, E., and Sheard, K., *Barbarians., Gentlemen and Players*, 1979.

17. The literature on the question is voluminous: for writers who stress the differences see esp. Deutscher, I., *The Unfinished Revolution*, 1967; Mandel, E., *Marxist Economic Theory*, Chap. 15, 1974; Parkin, F., *Class Inequality and Political Order*, 1973; Giddens, A., *The Class Structure of the Advanced Societies*, 1973. For differences in sport see: Riordan, J., *op cit*; Riordan, ed., *op cit*. For an account of sport under the Nazis see Mandell, R., *The Nazi Olympics*, 1974; Grunberger, R., *A Social History of the Third Reich*, 1971.

18. Thompson, op. cit.

19. Marcuse, *One Dimensional Man*, op cit.; Bell, D., *The End of Ideology*.

20. A recent British work, Gamble, A., and Walton, P., *Capitalism in Crisis*, 1977, illustrates the problem: it offers an incisive analysis of contraditions in the mode of production, but no adequate explanation of capitalism's ability to survive economic crises and culminates in a set of conclusions compatible with both a 'reformist' and a revolutionary political solution.

21. Gramsci, A., *The Prison Notebooks*, ed. Hoare, Q., and Smith, P. Nowell, 1971.

22. Some of the major theorists in this tradition exhibit defects not shared by Gramsci. The early Lukacs treats the mode of production in too abstract a fashion and there is little or no attempt to trace the complex

mediations of class domination - Lukacs, G., <u>History</u>
<u>and Class Consciousness</u>, 1971. In the case of the
Frankfurt School, this task is attempted, but in terms
of 'total alienation' and the incorporation of the working class and thus despite intentions to the contrary
there is a determinism quite foreign to Marx. This
school also carries over into the analysis of culture
and ideology an implicit, and unMarxist distinction
between 'high' and 'mass' culture, which results in a
denigration and dismissal of popular culture and which
blocks the way to paying sport any serious attention.
Anderson, P., <u>Considerations on Western Marxism</u>.

23. Williams, op cit., p. 110.

24. Boggs, C., Gramsci's Marxism, 1976; Anderson, P.,
"Origins of the Present Crisis", <u>New Left Review</u> 23;
Hall, S., et al, "Politics and Ideology: Gramsci",
<u>Cultural Studies</u> 10, 1977.

25. Anderson, P., "The Antinomies of Antonio Gramsci",
<u>New Left Review</u>, 100, 1976/77.

26. Gramsci, op cit.

27. Bailey, P., <u>Leisure and Class in Victorian England</u>,
1978.

28. Thompson, op cit., distinguishes 'empiricist' from
'empirical mode of investigation.

29. Marx, <u>Political Writings</u>, ed., Fernback, D., Vol 2,
p. 250-298.

30. Lukes, S., "Political Ritual and Social Integration",
<u>Sociology</u>, Vol. 9, No. 2, May, 1975; Edelman, M., <u>The</u>
<u>Symbolic Uses of Politics</u>, 1967.

31. Durkheim, E., <u>Elementary Forms of the Religious Life</u>,
1915. The most interesting work has been done by
social anthropologists, see for example, Gluckman, M.,
<u>Politics, Law and Ritual in Tribal Society</u>, 1965;
Douglas, M., <u>Purity and Danger</u>, 1966; Turner, V.W.,
"Symbols in Ndembu Ritual", in Emmet, D., and McIntyre,
A., eds. <u>Sociological Theory and Philosophical Analysis</u>
and Turner, <u>The Ritual Process</u>, 1969, and <u>Dramas, Fields</u>
<u>and Metaphors</u>, 1974.

32. Shils, E., and Young, M., "The Meaning of the Coronation",
<u>Sociological Review</u>, 1, 1953; Bellah, R., <u>Civil Religion</u>
<u>in America</u>, 1968.

33. Mann, M., "Social Cohesion in Liberal Democracy", *American Sociological Review*, 35, 1970.

34. Lukes, op cit.

35. Ibid. p. 301.

36. Turner cited in ibid. p. 305, note 2.

37. Ibid.

38. Bernstein, B., *Class, Codes and Control*, Vol. 3 "Ritual in Education"; Hay, D. "Property, Authority and the Criminal Law", in Hay, D., et al, eds., *Albion's Fatal Tree*, 1977.

39. Lukes, op cit., p. 301.

40. Burke, P., *Popular Culture in Early Modern Europe*, 1978; Malcolmson, R., *Popular Recreations in English Society*, 1973; Bailey, op cit.

41. Williams, op cit., chap. 8.

42. Lukes, op cit., p.302.

43. Patterson, op cit.

44. Hall, S., "The Treatment of Football Hooliganism in the Press", in Ingham, R., et al, *Football Hooliganism*, 1978.

45. Dabscheck, B., "Defensive Manchester: A History of The Professional Footballers' Association", unpub., Department of Industrial Relations, London School of Economics, 1978.

46. Glasgow University Media Group, *Bad News*, Vol. I, 1977.

47. Westergaard, J., and Ressler, H., *Class in a Capitalist Society*, 1976

48. Habermas, J., *Legitimation Crisis*, 1977.

5

Sport and the
Logic of Capitalism

Rob Beamish

Introduction

The general question posed in this volume concerns
the relation of sport to the state. The book illustrates
that there are many ways to address that problem but at the
same time it can be observed that irrespective of each
presentation's unique content, the form of approach is
constant. Each paper examines the sport/state relation
predominantly at the level of social and cultural relations.
The interconnections of sport and the state to the relations
of production have been left largely unexplored. In the
following analysis, I will redress that situation by
investigating what is often termed the "infrastructural"
dimension of social history and subsequently examine its
relation to institutionalized sport in capitalist society.
This undertaking may appear out of place in this particular
conference but there are a number of reasons why it merits
attention in this context. These reasons range from some
fairly "pragmatic" concerns to fundamental questions of
epistemology and ontology. In the order of what I see to be
their increasing importance, the following considerations
substantiate why the society/labour question needs to be
addressed.

Within what has been widely designated as "the state
debate" the society/labour question was broached only
recently.[1] A number of German sociologists, economists and
political scientists responded to positions comparable to the
"relative autonomy of the state" argument explored by Ralph
Miliband (1969), Nicos Poulantzas (1973), Leo Panitch (1977),
Dennis Olsen (1977) and others. In effect, the question
posed by the Germans was; if the qualifier "relative" has any
semantic significance, irrespective of its syntactic misuse,
then where do the constraints to state "autonomy" lie?[2]

Studying that problem, the "state derivation debate" material deals with the relation of the state to forms of social labour in industrial capitalist society (that is, the society/labour issue). The ideas generated in those exchanges, while not completely satisfying,[3] helped balance a previously one-sided study of the state and introduced specific aspects of the social dialectic that are required for a full comprehension of the state's form and content.

The papers presented in this volume, and studies of sport and the state already available in the literature, readily interact with discussions of the state/society relation but they only impinge indirectly, if at all, with the state/labour one. In terms of purely "pragmatic" research interests, a discussion of the sport/labour relation is needed at this time so that a fully comprehensive analysis of the sport/state relation within both moments of the social dialectic - that is, social relations and production relations - can be established. If the sport/labour relation is not studied systematically, then the interlocks it shares with the state/labour relation discussed recently in the "derivation debate" will not be made.

This "pragmatic" concern leads to a general and more fundamental issue in the study of sport. The majority of work done on sport and the state totally neglects the relation of labour to society because the analytic frameworks employed most often in those studies exclude its investigation a priori.[4] The omission of the society/labour relation is not surprising in the case of most theories used by sport sociologists in their research, but one would expect that Marxist studies of sport, with their concerns centred in the relations of production, would have addressed the issue in detail.[5] Unfortunately, a survey of Marxist and Marxist-inspired studies of sport currently available in English shows that this is not the case. As a result, while Richard Gruneau (1979:14) is correct in his assessment that "in actuality, Marxist and Marxist-inspired cultural radicals have tended to think more seriously about these things (that is, modern sport and related issues) than most;" his statement is not intended to be, nor should it be misunderstood as, an affirmation of the theoretical frameworks currently informing those investigations.[6] With regard to the implementation of a complete analysis of the social dialectic and its relation to sport, Ralph Miliband's challenge for a Marxist sociology of sport must still be taken seriously (cf. Miliband 1977:51-2).

The question of theoretical comprehensiveness, however, is not simply a sectarian matter. It involves key epistemologic and methodological issues pertinent to the study of sport in particular and society in general. Human society is tremendously complex and to comprehend it, or any of its parts, the totality cannot be ignored. Hegel's notion that the truth is the whole strikes the mark directly. Hegel's work in the Phenomenology of Mind (Geist) and the Logic addresses the heart of the matter as well. The kernel of his insights can be encapsulated in the following points. (i) The complexity of reality cannot be comprehended with mere formal logic which analytically divides the social totality into separate concepts and rigidly holds them apart (cf. Hegel 1969:793-4). To do so is merely to elevate our natural prejudices, presuppositions and understandings to a scientific status. (ii) Reality can only be known in its actuality - that is, in its full variation and complexity - when the essential connectedness of all aspects of reality are drawn together into a synthetic whole (see Hegel 1969:794, 834-5). (iii) This can only be done by beginning with a synthetically logical epistemological position. (iv) Nevertheless, such an approach does not, and

cannot, begin with the whole. It is initiated with an
analysis of the most essential, simple, abstract relation of
reality as it immediately appears (see Hegel 1969:827-8).
Analysis proceeds to develop a comprehension of the relation
of that part to the totality by "unfolding" the multitude of
connections (or mediate relations) that relates the part to
other parts and all parts into a totality.

As a logical process this is an imperative procedure,
but in following it, Hegel reduced the history of man to the
epistemological process of discovering the logical character
of the social and natural worlds (cf. Marx 1973:101). Critics
have now demonstrated his error and have gone beyond Hegel's
abstract construction of history. The task of developing
Hegel's work required the establishment of the historically
concrete point of departure in human history rather than
locating its abstract logical form alone. The correct
material, empirical point of departure for social history
relates to the universal condition of mankind - productive
activity. Man is part of nature in many ways. He has a
distinct biological make-up, requires certain foods to meet
his caloric needs, etc., but this is all part of man's
relation to the history of nature and as such falls outside
of the purview of social science. Man's social history, the
subject matter of social science, is dependent upon his
mediate relation to nature. Man must interact with nature to
realize himself physically and potentially. His productive
activity mediates man with nature and changes his own being
and his social formations. It is, therefore, the point of
departure for comprehending social history.

Productive activity is comprised of two sets of relations
that have to be addressed synthetically; they are the society/
labour relation and the culture/society relation. To ignore

either, or to treat them separately, will render an analysis that cannot comprehensively deal with the totality of social history. There is more to be said about this synthetic method, but I will address those points when they become directly pertinent to the ensuing discussion.

I   Sport and the Economy

Karl Marx was one of many German intellectuals who confronted the logical restrictions of the Hegalian system. He resolved the abstract/concrete relation in a study of Hegel's analysis of the state - appropriately enough - in 1843. After that breakthrough, he began to use a material dialectical framework to study society as a totality. For the next decade and a half, Marx studied a specific historically determinate social formation - industrial capitalist society. In 1859, he began to publish the results of that work and introduced it with an aphoristic outline of the "anatomy of civil society". He (1964 v. 13, p.8-9) wrote,

> In the social production of their life,
> men enter into determinate, indispensible
> relations, (that are) independent of their
> will; relations of production which accord
> with a determinate stage of development of
> their material forces of production. The
> sum total of these relations of production
> constitute the economic structure of society,
> the real foundation on which rises a legal
> and political superstructure and which
> accords with determinate forms of social
> consciousness (cf. Marx 1970:20).

A hasty connection of the above statement by Marx, my previous methodological outline and my introductory comments that the sport/labour relation has been neglected in the past, might encourage the conclusion that there is indeed a large body of economic literature studying sport within the

society/labour relation. After all, if social production is
the point of departure for the analysis of society and social
production is made up of specific relations of production
which in turn constitute "the economic structure of society,
the real foundation on which rises a legal and political
superstructure" then sport sociologists have an abounding
supply of such information at their access. Studies by Noll
(1974), Jones (1969, 1976), Neal (1964) or Burman (1974)
might be pointed to.[7] A modest critic may claim that my
argument concerning neglect in the sport literature is
overstated while a more strident one would argue that it is
inaccurate. Nevertheless, despite the surprising volume of
economic literature accorded sport, both critical assessments
would be wrong. A close examination of the premises and
objectives informing these economic studies of institutionalized
sport will show they are problematic regarding a thorough
comprehension of the relation of sport to the social and
production relations of capitalism.

J.C. Jones'(1969, 1976) study of the National Hockey
League is a good representative example of the economic
perspective adopted in the sport literature. Among other
things, it lucidly demonstrates that professional hockey
management's actual interest is the pursuit of individual
club profits through joint profit maximization and not
necessarily icing a winning team. Jones also indicates how
inter- and intra-league arrangements, which structure
monopoly conditions in the product market and monopsony
conditions in the factor market, aid the profit maximizing
objective. It is noteworthy that, symptomatic of the neo-
classical approach, one change Jones suggests to improve
hockey is an alteration of the cartel controls over the
factor and product markets. In other words, he advocates

tinkering with the circulation processes to solve the problems he uncovers. Finally, Jones shows how equilibrium can be re-established and maintained even when a rival league exists.

The criticisms of the Jones' study, and similarly inspired neo-classical investigations of sport, are not that their results have no redeeming value. These studies do advance the understanding of sport in certain areas. Nevertheless, the limitations they contain raise serious doubt concerning their ability to represent the "economic foundation" Marx mentioned (and they do not) or yielding comprehensive knowledge about sport as an institutionalized sphere of social life.

The Jones study, like all neo-classical analyses, attempts to present economic activity within a systematic framework of alleged universal applicability.[8] This positivist[9] feature may be more implicit than explicit in studies of sport, but it exists nonetheless. Neo-classical macro-economic theory begins by accepting the following assumptions as universal. (i) All actors are utility maximizers by nature. (ii) the interests of all economic groups are at least reconcilable if not perfectly harmonious. (iii) There is a long range tendency to equilibrium in the system. (iv) Any change which occurs is gradual (cf. Sweezy 1972:57, Heilbroner 1970:168-75, Nell 1973:77-89). An additional inclusion is the positivist methodological imperative that the surface appearance of economic movement is the exclusive universe for data collection. The conception that more essential relations than the directly observable social facts of exchange processes exist and that they can be investigated is rejected as metaphysical and unscientific.

The existence and pervasiveness of such assumptions is the result of a complex set of subjective and objective, internal and external relations. They cannot be explored fully at this time, but certain fundamental aspects of those relations and their limitations can be overviewed. The foremost internal factor contributing to the systematic, positivist nature of neo-classical economics concerns the objective of any positivist undertaking. A positivist science strives to transcend the limits of ideographic analysis and construct nomothetic laws. These laws are founded on the basis of observable patterns of collectable empirical data which can be ordered and utilized to falsify hypotheses and propositions. Neo-classical economics was, in this sense, the pinnacle of early political economists' attempts to nurture the natural scientific dimension of their Enlightenment heritage. It is interesting to note here that political economy became the "science" of economics when it was felt that it had attained, or was close to attaining, such a universal character. As economics, it was above the fray of political life (cf. Jevons 1970:48-9).

James Mill's attempt to systematize David Ricardo's economic principles is likely the earliest serious contribution to the nomothetic nature of economics, although Adam Smith (1937) had previously subsumed all economic activity under the auspices of the unseen hand in 1776 (cf. Marx 1971, v. 3, p. 84-5). Mill's endeavours were continued by Samuel Bailey, received considerable support from German political economists such as Adolf Wagner, Rodbertus, Schaffle and others, and experienced a watershed point in John Stuart Mill's 1848 edition of Principles of Political Economy.

Mill's work is pivotal for two reasons. First, confronted by certain objective features of the economy, namely its

depression or recession tendency, and various theoretical
formulations of crisis and decline that had begun with
Malthus and been continued by Ricardo, Mill accepted the
notion that the industrial economy would move through a
dynamic growth phase into a static one. This static state,
Mill (1893:334ff) perceived, would be the "mature" (or normal)
form of industrial society. Mill (1893:41, 275-8) argued
that since production was a realm of economic life that was
beyond human control and only exchange and distribution
could be regulated by man, it was the dynamics of distribution
political economy had to understand.[10] As a result, Mill's
work continued the goal of a systematic scientific form of
political economy because he saw that as the form of knowledge
needed to control distribution. In addition, his ideas
underscored a tendency that had begun to gain ascendency
since 1832. This trend was the movement away from the study
of production to a study of distribution.

William Stanley Jevons'marginal utility "revolution"
completed the paths laid by Mill. Jevons' "somewhat novel
opinion, that value depends entirely upon utility" (Jevons
1970:77) removed all questions of value from the objective
relations of the production process and placed them squarely
in the exchange processes of economic life. This climaxed
the growing attention the exchange realm had received since
Mill. It should also be noted that this is the realm of
economic life that continues to dominate neo-classical study.
In addition, the mathematical nature of the utility curves
that could be produced from Jevon's conception of value
accentuated the positivist nature of economic study and
crowned the work of the elder Mill. The "Jevons revolution"
meant that economic life, irrespective of the type of labour
producing social goods, could (apparently) be explained by a

set of empirical observations and mathematical formulae pertaining to the exchange processes. Now economists, more than political economists before them, could (and still do) approach "the specific, historical form of social labour, which is exemplified in capitalist production (as) the absolutely, (not historically) necessary, natural and reasonable relations of social labour" (Marx 1977:   cf. 174-5, 175 note 35). The differentia specifica of productive activity under capitalism cannot be detected in the form of analysis they adopted - nor was it a central concern. Once the form of analysis was established and its problem sphere carefully demarcated, the results it yielded confirmed many of its assumptions.

The phenomena studied by economists present a particular content to the form of analysis they employ. In addition, the positivist approach employed supports and fosters the neoclassical world view evident in Jones and other studies of sport. This is a problem and therefore merits some attention. Marx (1977:125) pointed out that "the wealth of societies in which the capitalist mode of production dominates appears as an immense collection of commodities". As a result, "the commodity appears as the elementary form (of wealth)". Neoclassical economists extensively monitor the movement of wealth and commodities, and do this well. At one level this constitutes a significant contribution to our knowledge. The "fetish character" of the commodity world is, after all, not merely a false conscious misunderstanding in which a definite relation between men assumes "the fantastic form of a relation between things" (Marx 1977:169). Commodity fetishism is both subjective and objective. Marx noted, "(the) fetishism of the world of commodities arises from the peculiar social character of the labour which produces them" (Marx 1977: 165). The social relations between producers "appear as what they are; that is, as thingly relations between persons and social relations between things" (Marx 1977:166 emphasis added). "The objective conditions essential to the realization of labour are alienated from the worker and become manifest as fetishes endowed with a will and soul of their own" (Marx 1977b:1003). In short, commodity society is, "a social formation in which the process of production has mastery over man, instead of the opposite" (Marx 1977:175, cf. 163-77, especially 164, 174-5 and notes 34 and 35). Nevertheless, sophisticated studies of commodity movement yields only partial knowledge and neo-classical economics is limited because this circumscribed dimension of economic life subsumes all of its attention. Further, the methodological approach employed in that monitoring process has serious inherent limitations itself. Since contemporary economics has adopted a positivist mode of analysis, it concentrates on the observable relations of the society. As a positivist enterprise it strives for universality and is concerned with the generalizable character of these relations. These are significantly problematic means and ends.

Using the commodity as an example, the limitations of attention to appearance alone can be demonstrated. It is evident upon a close examination that the relations involved in a commodity's creation and those of its exchange and circulation are not fully revealed by attending only to its immediately observable form. I will not pursue this in any extended detail but will make the point by looking at some basic issues. Some forms of athletic activity are commodities in capitalist society. As such, they have both use-value and exchange-value. As use-value, athletics has the universal character of satisfying human health needs and wants either directly or indirectly (see Marx 1977:125-6). In this sense, sport is the subject of physics, chemistry, kinesiology, physiology, anatomy and medicine. Sport as a use-value also has a specific bearing in political economy regarding the valorization process of the abstract social labour contained in it as a spectacle. Athletic labour that is congealed into a use-value that is not socially necessary (and lacrosse would be an example), or is above the average social labour time (Rogie Vachon's performance for the Detroit Red Wings in 1978-79, for instance) will either not be marketable (lacrosse failed as a professional sport three times) or is sold at a decreased profit margin (thus Detroit tried to release Vachon through waivers). With regard to the exchange-value aspect of sport, it should be noted that as a commodity it represents the value contained in the good. The value component in capitalist society is of two types - necessary value and surplus-value. Without the profit component (surplus-value) which is directly or indirectly contained in sport, many professional sport leagues in North America would cease to operate. If sport had no value component, then players would not be drawing salaries and making sport a means of livelihood. Finally, these moments of value, exchange-value, use-value and surplus-value impinge upon the labour process.[11] I will not unfold those relations now, but the above clearly substantiates that even a "thing" as apparently simple as the commodity cannot be adequately comprehended unless its internal dimensions are explored. Neo-classical economic theory, due to its positivist orientation, leaves these inner dimensions untouched because they fall outside its methodological purview.

It is, I think, safe to conclude that neglecting a detailed analysis of specific elements comprising a social

framework, which is characteristic of the neo-classical
positivist approach, is not just bad history; it is of
limited use for fully comprehending the present as well.
The weight of available historical and anthropological
evidence substantiates that every concrete social formation -
primitive communal, capitalist, slave, etc., - has a set of
specific relations and historically bound laws which
constitute its existing form and its changing form and
content. A universalistic, nomological science fails to
draw out the specific features of any of those social
formations, past or present. This means that the unique
forces of the present social structure which give it its
particular dynamism are glossed over. C. Wright Mills'
methodological comment that "No study that does not come
back to the problems of biography, of history and their
intersection within a society has completed its intellectual
journey" (Mills 1959:6, cf. 3-24) is a salient point.
Study of economic relations in the neo-classical economic
mode does not make this journey with sufficient sensitivity
to the unique conditions comprising the relation of sport
to the capitalist social formation.

The a-historical bias of marginal utility theory is
not its sole weakness. A second problem is the emphasis
accorded the exchange and circulation processes.
Circulation is exclusively a social relation, which may or
may not manifest itself as a relation among things. Whatever
its form, circulation is a determinate moment of economic
relations and not the point of origin. I pointed out above
that production is the universal condition of man, due to
his primary state of alienation from nature (cf. Krader
1976:1-3, 186, Beamish 1979:23-4, Marx 1977:290, 1977b:980-2,
998, 1020, Marx and Engels 1975, v. 3, p.336, Meszaros
1975:79-80, Giddens 1976:15-16). Man does not immediately

possess goods to be consumed or circulated. He must interact
with nature to acquire or produce those goods which are
subsequently circulated via distribution processes and under
specific historical conditions, exchange processes. Production
directly involves both the society/labour and the culture/
society moments of the dialectic as a whole and it is from
this initial comprehension that more complex and determinate
forms of the social totality can be comprehended. To
virtually ignore the production process, or to emphasize the
exchange/circulation realm unduly is a problematic position
vis-à-vis the generation of a comprehensive analysis of
social processes and formations.

II   Sport and Social Labour

(i) A rather pedestrian example can make an important point
clearly. "A chair with four legs and a velvet covering may
be used as a throne. But this chair, a thing for sitting on,
does not become a throne by virtue of its use-value"
(Marx 1977b:997). A chair serves as a throne because it is
located in a specific set of concrete historical circumstances.
It is constructed from elements "which form an integral part
of the labour process independently of any particular social
formation"as well as "the specific social characteristics
peculiar to them in a given historical phase" (Marx 1977b:998,
cf. 998-9, 1022, Marx 1977:290, Marx 1973:503). [12] As
different as sport and thrones may be, they are similar in
this last respect. Sport may be used as a means of livelihood, or impell an individual to train at 10,000 feet
above sea level because it is a form of mediate human
activity comprised of a determinate form of historical
labour. Stated abstractly, and in general terms, sport is a
determinate form of human activity conditioned by specific

155

material and historical features of the society/labour and culture/society moments of the dialectic of social history. Therefore, comprehension of sport begins in the same way that Marx began his analysis of political economy in 1857. "The object (Gegenstand) before us, to begin with (is) material production. ...(S)ocially determined, individual production - is, of course, the point of departure" (Marx 1973:83).

There is a precision to this conception that must be noted. The departure point is not merely human activity - a very broad category of mediate human action. It is precisely "socially determined individual production" which is of a specific nature. Marx (1973:106-7) noted later in the 1857 introduction that,

> In all forms of society there is one specific kind of production which predominates over the rest, whose relations thus assign rank and influence to the others. It is a general illumination which bathes all the other colours and modifies their particularity (cf. Marx 1973: 500, 496, 486).

He continued on to observe that in pastoral society it is a certain form of tillage, or landed property that dominates, whereas bourgeois society landed property is "entirely dominated by capital". The point of departure Marx had in mind in his opening sentence to the 1857 Grundrisse introduction is the dominant productive activity that structures the way human consumption wants are met and in capitalist society that means the wage-labour/capital relation. Thus it follows that to develop a full comprehension of modern institutionalized sport, one that allows the systematic comparing and contrasting of a New York Ranger/New York Islander semi-final hockey series, a ten point uneven bar gymnastics routine at the

Olympics and a National Pee Wee Lacrosse final, sport must
be located within the context of the wage-labour/capital
production process.

Locating sport within the production process is a
complex undertaking, so I will proceed in three stages.
The initial section will raise certain comparative features
of human labour within two general categories of social
formations - the primitive communal form and the civil-
social form.[13] The primitive communal form of society and
its concomitant production relations offers a helpful
heuristic contrast to those forms that constitute societies
of a civil nature (of which capitalism is a specific instance).
The content of productive labour in all forms of civil society
is the same, although the form of labour differs. By
contrast, both form and content of the labour process in
communal forms differs from that of civil forms. Through
the construction of a communal/civil society contrast, the
basic characteristics of productive labour in civil society
are easily seen and how they are determined by specific
civil formations may then be tackled.

The communal/civil contrast is followed by an analysis
of the specific features of capitalist socially productive
labour which differentiates it from all other forms of social
labour in civil societies. Finally, the relation of
professional sport to capitalist social labour is discussed
in connection with problems of social change. The analysis
in the final section is not exhaustive. It considers
theoretical issues for the most part and the empirical,
concrete dimension is not developed. The conclusions
reached remain more suggestive than authoritative because
this approach to the study of sport is still in the

preliminary stages of elaboration. Nevertheless, the ideas developed substantiate the need for studying sport in its relation to productive activity of a specifically determinate historical nature, via the synthetic approach, so that sport's complexity can be fully addressed in a comparative fashion.

II   A Contrast of Communal Society and Civil Society

(ii) The structure of a primitive communal (or collective, cf. Krader 1978) form of society is such that the activity of production and consumption as well as the work of production required to maintain, or reproduce, the community, is undertaken by it as a self contained unity with all of the tasks shared by the full membership of the group. These tasks are not separated, nor are they carried out by independent fractions of the community. In addition, labour in primitive communal society is communal in form and concrete in content. Labour is concrete in content because it is undertaken to produce goods that meet concrete utility wants of the community. Goods are produced for their physical characteristics and the time of labour is not abstractly estimated beforehand nor calculated in process or post festum. This does not mean that there is no awareness of time; as Marx noted in Capital, a hunter making arrows is aware that the time spent in arrow production is consumed at the expense of time that could be spent hunting. Nevertheless, the abstract calculation of production time is not discerned in a precise manner so that the activity can be differentiated from others on the basis of such abstract criteria. That change only develops as exchange begins to dominate productive activity and abstract value must be considered. Labour's form is communal since the results of productive labour are used to meet all - or virtually all - of the consumption and reproduction wants of the communal unit exclusively. Products meet communal wants either directly through the product's consumption or indirectly by the use of the product in subsequent productive activity (cf. Marx 1977:290, 125). The goods produced by the concrete work of the unit's members are distributed throughout the unit to meet the wants of all. It is important to observe that this mode of dispersal bears no exchange character; it is purely a distributive process. In the same manner that parents today distribute goods to their children, or raw material and capital goods are distributed throughout a factory without any exchange relation involved in that mediation, goods are similarly dispersed within the communal unit (see Marx 1977:171-2, Krader 1976:195-7).

Man's mastery over nature, in the primitive communal condition, is mediated by simple technological forces and as a result, there is little objective cause for the separation of hand and head labour. The concrete nature of work also determines an objective and subjective environment conducive to maintaining that unity. Labour, as an active process, is always influenced by both the culture/society and society/ labour moments of the social dialectic. In the primitive communal form, the degree to which abstract considerations enter into the divison of labour is considerably less than in social forms dominated by exchange and value. As a result, while not wholly determined by concrete geographical and physiological factors, there is a more pronounced concrete use-value bias to the division of labour in the community than in any other social formation.(Krader 1976:197).

Within the primitive communal form, because of the exclusively concrete nature of the productive process, the impetus for change is closely related to the concrete conditions of existence and not abstract ones. This means that the society/labour and culture/society moments of the social dialectic have a particular form of expression that contrasts markedly with later civil forms of society. Since man's relation to nature, under all historical circumstances, is a mediate one, he must interact with nature. In that process the stamp of man's social arrangements, tools, culturally refined skills, lore etc., are employed in the creation of a collection of goods to fulfill individual and social wants. Both society/labour and culture/society moments of the dialectic of social history are influential, but in the primitive condition, work is only concrete - no abstract value is produced. As a result, all change, or resistance to change, in the productive activity of those workers is related to the concrete and not the abstract. The culture/ society moment of the dialectic does not contain the social pressure of abstract relations that emerges later in civil forms. The society/labour moment, as a concrete problem of work and human mediation, is the more likely locus of productive change (cf. Marx 1973:475, 494, 496).[14]

Historically, the destruction of the primitive communal form has entailed two major processes. Neither of them are logically necessary for the advancement of human productive capacities, nor must they both occur within the same group. When they do both take place in the same community, either may precede the other or they may develop simultaneously.

One change is the separation of the unit of production from the unit of consumption. Such a change introduces the dimension of social labour into the work process. The community no longer meets its consumption wants exclusively through its own productive activity. Some wants (old or new)

160

are now met through the exchange of goods produced within the group for goods fabricated outside of it. Labour is determinately negated as a concrete form to become a composite of concrete and abstract moments.[15] Productive activity becomes both private and social. As private labour it remains concrete work and provides products employed within the private distributive network of the community. As social labour, labour is both concrete and abstract because it creates products for both use and exchange.

This second form of labour is social because its product is not solely consumption oriented. The product is made to enter a set of exchange relations between social groups - hence its social character (Krader 1976:196-7). As an exchangeable product, its content is at once concrete and abstract; it is made up of qualitatively unique concrete labour and quantitatively comparative abstract labour. The concrete content of a produced commodity is its physically useful nature. Social labour's abstract moment is the specific quantity of socially necessary, simple, abstract labour. This is its value. The labour must be socially necessary to meet the wants of the recipient trading group (or individual). Social labour is abstract because it is the common nature it shares with all other qualitatively distinct use-values that underlies the exchange process. This allows quantitative equivalents to be traded. Finally, social labour is simple insofar as it represents a basic level of labour and the various gradients pertinent to superior skill, quality of work, quality of material, training, etc., have been reduced to a lowest common denominator (see Marx 1977:126-31).

Social labour which is simultaneously abstract and concrete is a historically determinate productive activity

161

of a far different type than communal labour which is
concrete only. Social labour is the result of a division
of labour originally obtaining between communities and
begins as the separation of production and consumption units
for specific goods only. However, once the production and
consumption units are separated, they become increasingly
independent and are linked solely by exchange processes
(Krader 1976:197, Marx 1977:132-3). Labour is now aimed to
"produce not only a use-value, but a commodity; not only
use-value, but value;" (Marx 1977:293). The social
character of the society/labour and culture/society aspects
of human society become increasingly dominant over the
concrete - although neither is separable. Social change
is increasingly related to the abstract dimension of
production as the law of value becomes the dominant productive
moment "bath(ing) all other colours and modify(ing) their
particularity." The fetish character of commodities, as a
subjective and objective dimension of social life in
capitalist society, is a development of the ascendence of
the law of value to dominate all social relations.

The other major change that significantly alters the
communal form is the separation of the social whole into two
groups, one of which produces all the commodities that are
consumed directly by the community or are exchanged for other
consumable goods. This production enables the community to
meet all of the wants needed to maintain the community at
its current level and/or allow expansion and growth. This
productive labour meets what may be termed the reproductive
needs and wants of the community. The second group does not
engage in productive activity needed to reproduce the
community. As a result, the unit of communal production and
reproduction is no longer one. The productive/reproductive

labour is performed by a portion of the community, while the
other portion lives off of the labour of that productive
segment. Naturally the production/reproduction change is a
historically viable possibility only after the surplus yield
of a community's labour is sufficiently large that it can be
appropriated by a group - or class - of non-producers. The
surplus, or some part of it, is then employed by the non-
producing group to meet its specific consumption and
reproduction wants. However, just as the separation of the
production/consumption unit, via exchange processes, has no
logical necessity, the production/reproduction change is
historically created and not logically ontological. The
appropriation of the surplus by a non-producing segment of the
society constitutes the origin of the political economy in
opposition to the communal one. It is the movement to class
society, of which the communal-social is the least complex
form (cf. Krader 1978). These class formations often lead to
legal codification of class domination, thus requiring the
formation of a state. Class society then becomes civil
society.

The major consideration to be noted here is that
previously existing communal goals and interests are broken
apart by the production/reproduction division. The class of
producers and class of non-producers hold separate, and in
many fundamental ways, opposing sets of goals and interests.
The separation is institutionalized and legitimized through
the introduction of a legal code which is enforced by either
a private group or a state formation. The separation of the
state from civil society is the product of the legal
codification of the extraction of the surplus. Because the
state is linked to the appropriation of surplus by a non-
producing group, the same powers which enable that group to
make that material change, are used to structure the state.

163

Control of the state, to a more or less extensive degree, remains with the class holding the dominant power. The state's existence is objectively located in the production/reproduction class cleavage although its full character involves a complex series of subjective and objective determinations.

II   The Wage-labour/Capital Relation

(iii) The objective changes in the production/consumption and production/reproduction relations of the society/labour and culture/society moments of the social dialectic which create a social form of labour and a political economy are the common underlying content of many forms of civil society - for example, communal-social, slave, feudal, or capitalist. The form of this content, however, changes in each case. The specific civil form of concern here is industrial capitalism. Within its production relations two particular features distinguish it from all forms of social labour in other civil societies. First, the worker has the formal legal freedom to sell his ability to do work. Through a series of social changes, primarily related to the separation and independence of the production and consumption units and the creation of a powerful class of non-producers, the worker lost access to the means of production (cf. Marx 1977:873-940, 169, Marx 1973: 503-8, Moore 1966:3-40, Hobson 1926:1-25, Dobb 1963, Hilton 1978). [16] The worker freed from social and traditional ties to the land was simultaneously separated from all means of realizing his labour and reproducing his life through productive activity.

This relates to the second distinctive feature of industrial capitalist society. The commodity - that is, labour-power - that the worker may sell in the market is unique.

> If you call labour a commodity, it is not
> a commodity which is produced in order to
> exchange and then brought to the market
> where it must exchange with other
> commodities according to the respective
> quantities of each which there may be
> in the market at that time; nay, it is
> brought to the market before it is
> created (cited by Marx 1977:675, note 2).

In other words, since the worker has no access to the means of production, workers cannot bring a finished product to market. Their only saleable commodity is the ability to do work (Marx 1977:675). "What in this transaction is directly sold is not a commodity in which labour has already realized itself, but the use of labour-power itself (Marx 1971:v.1, p.397, cf. 72 Marx 1973:464-5, Marx 1977:300, 677, Marx 1977b:984, Rosdolsky 1977:212). The most important fact of this historical condition is that labour-power is the single commodity that can, in an exchange of equivalents, be purchased for use over a specified period of time to create surplus-value. Marx emphasized this distinctive feature of capitalist production by noting,

> As the unity of the labour process and
> the process of creating value, the
> production process is the process of
> commodity production; as the unity of
> the labour process and the process of
> valorization, it is the capitalist
> process of production, the capitalist
> form of commodities production.
> (Marx 1977:304).

The dominant productive process in capitalist society may be encapsulated in the following way. It is social labour. Therefore it is abstract and concrete. It occurs in a civil - therefore class - society in which the worker has no direct access to the means of production and consequently can only realize his productive potential to meet all of his socially determined productive wants through the sale of the only commodity he owns - his labour-power. The purchase of labour-power by capital is unique insofar as its primary objective is the augmentation - or valorization - of the capital which purchased the labour-power, raw material, and capital equipment that it brings together.

II   Sport and Capitalist Production Relations

(iv) Using the specific form and content of capitalist labour processes as the point of departure, a comprehensive analysis of sport as either an identifiable whole or as part of a social totality may be developed. This analytic procedure leads, naturally, to many issues of varying scope and importance but at this point I will use it to address one broad theme that is central to pivotal concerns in sport study. That issue is social change.

Recently, Richard Gruneau (1979) addressed this basic issue in a working paper "Power and Play in Canadian Social Development." Although this piece is preliminary in nature, representing an early formulation of work that is currently in progress (Gruneau 1979:60-1), it stands as one of the few pieces in sport study that addresses the question of change in sport with the sophistication required to develop our understanding of the process. "Power and Play" also contributes a refreshing historical analysis in terms of content per se and the challenge it carries for others to discard the purely descriptive procedures that currently dominate sport study and replace them with theoretically informed analytic research. The paper is germane to my presentation because its discussion of social change presents a useful foundation for elaborating upon certain seminal dimensions of that process. I find certain aspects of Gruneau's paper extremely suggestive and

166

will critically examine his work in order to draw out specific features I feel need further development and emphasis.

Gruneau (1979:1-7, 12-15) begins by identifying and criticizing two competing interpretations of sport activity. Concerning the idealist thesis, which portrays sport as an autonomous realm of human activity, he (1979:2) concludes that the argument may make "moving theology (see Michael Novak's The Joy of Sport) but it is bad sociology" (cf. Gruneau 1980:4-8). The alternative perspective, a mechanistic and deterministic approach, depicts institutionalized sport as virtually an epiphenomenal by-product of the society in which it exists. Gruneau (1979:13-14, cf. 3-4) maintains that,

> ...to argue, as Paul Hoch (1972) has, that modern institutionalized established games and sports effectively socialize their participants with reactionary elitist, racist, sexist, and consumatory attitudes, and thereby function directly as instruments of class rule, does more to mystify the relationship between power and play in modern times than to explain it. [17]

To overcome the idealist fallacy of sport's absolute autonomy and the rigid determinism of the neo-18th century materialists (often masquerading as Marxist analysists, Gruneau introduces the transformative/reproductive couplet as a conceptual tool for the study of social life. This conception is useful insofar as it draws attention to complexities that are often overlooked in sport study. In essence, the couplet has been culled by Gruneau from Anthony Giddens' discussions of social structure and the structuration process (see Giddens 1973, 1976, 1977). The idea emphasizes the two-fold nature of the structuration process. Structure, Giddens argues, constrains action within certain limits and, at the same time, facilitates action. Rational agents can only act through structure. Through their action social agents (re)make and reform--or (re)produce and transform-- social structure. Since structure is the social product of human agents, it can never be reproduced in an identical form through all moments of history (or, indeed, individual life span). Assuming that structure would be (or could be) duplicated ignores the active role of agency. History is the result of human action and even though structure weighs heavily upon all agents, this burden is socially mediate and not directly instrumental.

Gruneau indicates the transformative/reproductive nature of sport by examining three instances of its existence. He describes the transformative potential of sport by examining, (i) sport's play component, (ii) sport's cultural nature and (iii) sport as part of the class dynamic in civil society. His discussion implicitly builds upon a progressive integration of each of these factors to produce an image of sport as structured agency.

Probably the most controversial facet of sport's agency component developed by Gruneau is the play--or unregulated, spontaneous, boundary straining--component of sport. "Power and Play's" introductory theoretical section examines the play process. Gruneau does not romaticize play. He (1979:6) acknowledges that the "nominal freedom of early children's play almost immediately becomes subject to the 'contents' of culture and the logic of social structural arrangements." Nevertheless, Gruneau warns, to think of play as simply a mirror of a specific social structure "leaves unanswered some important questions about the degree to which the self-generated, expressive features of play may also contain transformative potential." Play is not a "nonreflexive arena for assimilating existing structure and accommodating ourselves to our surround- ings." Play is more. It contains an "assertive expressive"

character (Gruneau's term) which allows players to seek the
boundaries of their activities and push against and alter
those bounds. This is the transformative moment of play.[18]
This idea has certain far reaching implications for Gruneau's
argument.

The role of the playful moment is an important one for
Gruneau, at least at the personal level--although, since all
structuration stems from individual action, this personal
level ripples into the social fabric as a whole. Gruneau
(1979:48) notes that it is the play component of sport which
plays a significant role in challenging given institutionalized
structural sport forms.

> (W)e should recognize that at the private
> personal level, the meanings of games and sports
> do not always align with the reproductive
> features of their public counterparts. An
> appreciation of the essential drama of the
> contest and the attempt to realize the promise
> of play in our private lives helps individuals
> cope with the injustices of a society that
> correlates dignity and personal worth with
> abstract notions of skill acquisition, efficiency
> and productive capacity.

We are not always--indeed, seldom--successful in using the
play moment of sport to alter the bounds and structures of
institutionalized sport but, Gruneau (1979:48) maintains, the
(potential) movement of these transformative drives out of
private spheres of meaning into the public domain presents
"the promise of realizing our playful capacities to create
new games in a new society." What is required for the
realization of that potential is "the social force that will
give it substance."

Gruneau also presents the transformative potential of
the play moment in an indirect, almost negative, manner. He
(1979:13) argues that mechanistic theories of sports and games

which emphasize the reproductive nature of such activity are not completely wrong. Sport is reproductive to a great extent in capitalist society (or civil-socialist society, for that matter). While games and sports provide "the illusion of an escape from alienating social conditions because they offer the drama of play," all too often it is only the promise that one is left with and not an expression of the play component itself. The play moment is severely constrained. Nevertheless, it should be noted that by making this point, "Power and Play" recognizes the play moment's continued existence--however constrained it may be within sport. It is on this bases that Gruneau delivers a solid blow to the mechanistic reproductive thesis.

Gruneau's struggle with the complex nature of sport and its relation to social formations is a long overdue study of play, sport and social change. Nevertheless, I think that his essay is best seen as a set of base line arguments that have to be expanded upon further before a full comprehension of sport in capitalist society will be approachable. First, the play dimension of mediate human activity requires further elaboration and specification. One may wish to pursue that development through the structuration thesis and thus follow and emendate the course charted by Giddens. Or, one may wish to wrestle with the issue within Marx's negative ontology (to use Alfred Schmidt's description) and thus draw upon Karl Korsch (1970), Georg Lukacs (1971, 1978), Alfred Schmidt (1971) and, more recently, Lawrence Krader (1976, 1979). In either case, one would recognize that mediate activity is part of our natural history which qualitatively separates us from nature. It is, in short, a large part of what makes us human. Further, it must be realized that the very nature of mediate activity means that social history can never be either wholly reproductive nor autonomously transformative--the relation of knowledge and practice makes either extreme impossible (see Krader 1979:59-64). However, once this has been developed as a cornerstone to our analyses of social history and elaborated upon as an ontological moment of sport study, then researchers must realize that the questions requiring answers are related to the specific social characteristics of mediate processes within a given historical phase. The transformative potential of the play component of sport leads us into those questions but it does not confront the particularity of change under specific historical conditions. Certainly humankind makes and transforms its social conditions but this change process is not carried out exactly as human agents choose. The dimension of specificity within an historical phase needs careful and sensitive elucidation.

Gruneau moves us toward the concerns of specificity that I have just mentioned by discussing sport as a cultural form. This is a significant aspect of sporting activity that too few have addressed.[19] Gruneau (1979:4-5) argues that simple reproductive arguments about sport emphasize "the homogeniety of dominant values and ruling interests," thereby tending to "deny a creative role in the development of cultural forms." He (1979:4) states that a mechanistic view "does not satis-factorally grasp the complexity of meanings associated with play and related game activities." These oversights, he stresses, are highly problematic because the cultural sphere is an extremely complex and fragmented realm of social life. I endorse Gruneau's analysis here but would add that closer examination of the cultural process is required so that our comprehension of sport as a cultural form and the transform-ative/reproductive potential inherent to it, can be fully appreciated.[20]

171

Sport as a cultural process has two moments to it. The first is directly tied to the concrete labour of the athlete per se and the second is the relation of that concrete activity to the context in which it occurs. Naturally, the separation I have introduced here is somewhat forced and artificial, but is heuristically necessary to clarify certain points concerning the study of sport as a cultural process.

Culture is not an autonomous realm of social reality. Generically, its creation, transformation, and persistent existence is rooted in practical human activity. It is humankind's primary alienation from nature and the particular mediate relation that we share with nature because of our unique natural capacities that gives rise to culture. The mediate labour process undertaken by a reflective, language bearing human is the ultimate source of all culture (see Krader 1979:59-64).[21] As a result, culture's existence is rooted in concrete labour which produces an object. Through the production of that object, however, not only are ideas formulated concerning the teleology of the labour process, but man's tested knowledge of certain ideas is also established. Thus, labour produces a concrete object and a subjective comprehension of the object and knowledge of the specific mediate processes that created that object. Culture, then, is the created object and the ideational constructs associated with an object's production. Culture is changed and developed by the reflective linking of a created concrete object, with ideational constructs and further mental or concrete labour.

Now let us turn to sport. Gruneau (1979:5) points out, "subordinate groups in a society develop their own character-istic forms of cultural expression that dramatize the contra-dictory nature of their experiences." Does sport, as a cultural form, allow for the dramatic expression of underclass

172

groups? In terms of a strictly generic analysis of culture, I would say no. To fully appreciate this total denial, it is helpful to consider some comparisons. Some forms of human labour can, and do, generically act as very dramatic vehicles for the expression of contradiction, conflict, protest, or any combination thereof. In the case of writing, the concrete labour process per se can produce a concrete object that will contribute significantly to the transformative consciousness of an underclass group. Gaskell's Mary Barton, Dickens' Hard Times, Zola's Germinal, or Solzhenitsyn's One Day in the Life of Ivan Denisovich are all examples. The labour of writing generically produces an object that can, for the writer and reader, foment anger and conflict. A writer may accomplish this by nakedly portraying the dominant classes disdainful view of the subjected class. An author may--as Machiavelli did in The Prince and Gramsci tried to do in The Modern Prince --demystify the mechanisms used by upper classes to dominate society. Finally, a writer's labour might be used to develop various scenarios through suggestion (or in detail) concerning how existing conditions might be transcended. Live theatre-- Brecht's Three Penny Opera or the Acadian based plays of Antonine Maillet, for example--may, through the labour of writing or the labour of acting, contribute transformative commentary because of the very nature of the concrete work that is always involved in either activity. Television, photography, painting and sculpture are all cultural products that possess critical dimensions through the very nature of their concrete use-value form. Can the same be said of sport?

From the generic perspective, I would maintain that sporting labour per se does not contain a critical dimension. The labour involved in producing the game or contest produces an object that is continually reflected upon, altered and developed. There is no doubt about this. The process of skill

acquisition is dependent upon this very process. Indeed, a
major internal source for the thrust of rationalization in
sport stems from the actor's creation of both an object (the
contest) and an ideational realm which is reflectively incorporated into all-ensuing game creating labour. Nevertheless, generically speaking, the athletic labour process does
not contain a transformative character equivalent to that
found in other cultural practices. Change is constrained,
almost wholly, to content and does not affect form when the
generic labour process is considered in abstraction. Understanding this aspect of sport labour in the cultural process
is helpful in many respects. Nevertheless, it has certain
fundamental problems.

When the subject/object relation of sport is focussed
upon in such a starkly abstract form, there is an inducement
to fall into a position that accords sport a sui generis
reality. Clearly this would be incorrect. The reflective
actors in sports and games are bearers of other social
relations and ideas. This point is seminal, not only because
it emphasizes the imbeddedness of sport in social relations
but because it forces every analyst to identify exactly how
the relation of sport and society is constructed. In
fulfilling this task one is forced to deal with the problem
in a manner that leads somewhat further than the analysis
presented in "Power and Play."

How can the potentially transformative dramatization of
a lacrosse title won by the North Shore Native community, or
the significance of a tradesman's victory over Sir Henry
Pellat in a mile run at the turn of the century be fully
understood? Players' strikes, boycotts, or the use of sport
as an ideological conveyance present other instances in which
the potential (and reality) of sport as class dramatization

may be illustrated and must be comprehended. To grasp the critical and transformative potential of sport in these instances requires the integration of sport within the cultural process as a whole and this means, first and foremost, the study of the relations and relationships existing between sport labour and the social labour process of a particular historical form and substance.

Gruneau's work once again provides a foundation and comparative backdrop for this analysis, by overviewing some of these relations. He looks at sport as part of the larger cultural process and illustrates its expressive nature for various class interests in early industrial Britain prior to 1830, in Canada during the same period and progresses through the period of Canadian industrialization to the present time. His analysis covers amateur and professional sport and their relationship in Canada from the 1800's to the 1970's. I cannot deal with all the phases of sport development examined by Gruneau but by looking at the emergence of sport as a business venture I can tentatively sketch some of the relations I think need to be developed for a comprehensive grasp of sport and the cultural process.

Gruneau's discussion of the emergence of corporate games and sport details the ascendence of capitalist class interests to dominate sport as a business venture. The analysis is clear, informative and stresses, for the most part, objective relations involved in that process. Nonetheless, it does not explain what it is in the historically determinate logic of capital that impells it to expand its domination over various spheres of private labour and turn them into social forms of labour - sport being one example of this "take over". There are objective dimensions of the capitalist mode of production which accord with this type of expansion.

175

One such impetus was addressed by Marx in his analysis
of the impact that the increased extraction of relative
surplus-value, as opposed to absolute surplus-value, had on
the realization of surplus-value valorized in production.
Marx (1973:402-9) argued that barriers to the realization of
valorized capital arose on the basis of capital's unique logic
and its manifestation in concrete social formations. While
such barriers are easily transcendable in the ideal, they
require specific concrete material change to be overcome in
actuality. The concrete changes involved included the
following; (i) "quantitative expansion of existing consumption", (ii) "creation of new wants by propogating existing
ones in a wider circle", and (iii) "production of new wants
and discovery and creation of new use-values" (Marx 1973:408,
cf. 287). The third solution is an important objective
impetus behind capital's movement into the athletic world.

The domination of sport by capital involves a second
objective dimension - that is the original formal subsumption
of labour by capital, followed by its real subsumption
(cf. Marx 1977b:1023-37). Early entrepreneurial activity in
sport is a movement toward the formal subsumption of athletic
labour as a productive labour process. Instead of sport
falling outside of the realm of social labour, and existing
solely as private labour, it is transferred - or determinately
negated - into productive labour. Betts (1953) and Nixon
(1974) supply discussions of some of the social and technological changes that facilitated the establishment of the
formal subsumption of sport to capital in the United States.
Similar conditions could be enumerated for the Canadian case.
As formally subsumed labour, the athletic activity is no
longer a form of concrete mediate human action - it becomes a
commodity of abstract and concrete value. This transformation
has virtually nothing to do with the concrete nature of the

athlete's labour per se. Therefore the emergence of sport as
a commodity is not intrinsically related to the generic nature
of sport labour. Sport as a commodity is not a necessary
logical outcome of games that have a competitive, winner/loser
structure. It is due to their domination by a particular set
of social relations and in this instance the dominating
relations are capitalist ones.

Gruneau (1979:35-6) discusses some of the manifestations
associated with that change. Athletic labour, as an abstract
and concrete commodity, requires the formation of formally
incorporated clubs and sports businesses of limited liability
to successfully market sport as a saleable good. Secondly,
as formally subsumed labour, the degree to which it is
regulated is left largely to "market forces" - to the extent
they exist in the product market under such circumstances -
and there is considerable fluctuation in entrepreneurial
success. However, once labour is formally subsumed then "on
this foundation there now arises a technologically and otherwise specific mode of production - capitalist production -
which transforms the nature of the labour process and its
actual condition" (Marx 1977b:1034-5). While the formal
subsumption of labour is akin to the original accumulation of
the capital process, its expansion to the real subsumption of
labour places it fully under the domination of capital.
Professional sport, as a real form of social labour, has been
thus incorporated into the Canadian economy.

As a form of activity that is completely subsumed under
capitalist relations, professional athletes in North America
work under a historically specific set of production relations.
Athletes do not own or control the means of producing their
athletic labour-power. They have no access to professional
leagues other than through the sale of their labour-power to

existing franchise owners. Through this sale and purchase
process, athletes engage in productive labour that creates
exchange-value, use-value and surplus-value. The capitaliza-
tion of professional sport and the realization of the surplus
portion of the activity by capital creates an edifice of
secondary alienated production relations which confronts the
athlete/worker and dominates his activity to an increasing
degree (cf. Marx 1973:453, 455, 307-10, 295-7, 343-6, Marx
1977b:1003-5). This factor within sport, plus the parallel
situation in other production processes in society as a whole,
has historically created a concentration of capital into large
finance and industrial capital portfolios. Within the sphere
of professional sport, this renders the possibility of
establishing a player owned and controlled league, which would
permit athletes to reproduce themselves and their families
through their own productive activity, a potential in logic
and theory alone - not in practice. The financial struggles
undergone by extremely wealthy private capitalists, corporate
capital and community capital to keep the World Hockey
Association afloat long enough to force a merger with the
National Hockey League is evidence of that reality.

At the micro-level, the sale and purchase of professional
athletic labour-power also reveals the specific nature of the
process in question. Professional sport owners (and managers)
purchase labour-power that produces a commodity. As a
commodity, sport is no longer a mere process of utility that
is enjoyed by the player for his own health, welfare, amuse-
ment, distraction or whatever. Nor is it solely a concrete
use-value to be watched by bystanders. Sport is a commodity
of abstract and concrete value. Its concrete nature, as the
single contest and the league (or series) standings of which
the game is one part, now falls within the realm of the

political economy. It is located there because sport, as a commodity, is determinately negated to form abstract and concrete value. Any discussion of change or status in professional sport, therefore, must address this unity because that unity is its actuality. Studying one side (or moment) or the other as separate facets fails to grasp the reality completely.

Given that this is the current state of professional sport, what factors are involved in either maintaining that form and substance or in fundamentally altering it? Power is clearly one central dimension of change or stability. The ability of a dominant group to organize itself, have access to and control of normative and material resources, permits it to control the political agenda, political decisions and maintain a given set of social relations. An ascendent group, in accruing power, must marshal similar factors to oppose the dominant group and social structure. This dimension of change is determined by the particular social relations in which sport is located.

Power, which is a necessary dimension of change, is general and specific. It is a general aspect of change but its concrete expression is also specifically determined by historical circumstances. That specificity is two dimensional. It concerns what specific factors may be mobilized to create power and it also entails the object that power is directed against. To create change, specific aspects of a social system must be altered. In the case of the capitalist domination of professional sport, this involves a number of historically specific features which have little, if anything, to do with the generic character of sport labour. The aspects in question are related completely to the commodity nature of sport and athletic labour. These relations of the objective dimension of professional sport, which have been determined by historical factors, are the fundamental relations that change, or the maintenance of the status quo, must be related to. To be precise, change is related to sport's existence as a unity of exchange-value, value, and surplus-value.

To change the surplus-value relation, which results in the domination of sport by a group of non-producers, requires the removal of sport from the civil-social dimension of productive activity. Within the microcosm of sport this would first entail workers' control of the entire administration and structuring of the product. Once such control was obtained, the surplus revenue which currently goes to corporate profit, management salaries, and other capital costs related to the maintenance of a non-productive strata could be either eliminated or redistributed. It could be objectively eliminated because the concrete power structures requiring it would have been changed. The class formerly appropriating the surplus would no longer control the means of production to the degree that would allow them to continue the appropriation of the surplus. In addition, with the removal of a non-productive segment of the sport structure, surplus would not have to be generated to meet that sector's wants. The mechanics of eliminating the surplus could be accomplished for example, by reducing the length of schedules or decreasing the number of games played per week. Alternately, it could be reduced by lowering the admission prices to games or the costs to networks for television rights. Another scenario could see a re-distribution of the surplus by channeling it into minor pro or amateur leagues to a greater extent than is currently done. Finally, the redistribution option might take the form of major and minor league expansion to create more jobs for athletes. The totality of the problem is, of course, much broader than this, but some of the essential questions are tapped through these relations.

Elimination of the surplus component in the microcosm is only one aspect of change. The value moment of sport would still exist, even though no surplus was produced. As value, sport in capitalist society could still be a commodity of social labour. Meeting the demands of the "market" would mean that the commodity would continue to dominate the producers--that is, the objective nature of the fetishism of commodities would persist. As a saleable value, sport must provide entertainment. It must compete in the "market" for spectator revenue, or else establish structures which allow it to control such competition. A single example will high-light the problems inherent to the continued existence of the value relation. The rationalization of sport as a commodity is not based exclusively on player wants or the logic of the game as a use-value--it simultaneously involves market considerations. The need for competitive teams in order to provide the uncertain outcome which makes sport appealing would continue to restrict player movement to some degree. That form of value oriented bureaucratic rationality would persist. The technological changes which make sport faster, less subject to the conditions of nature, and demand tremendous human subjugation to "scientific training" would not necessarily be eliminated if sport remained as a factor in the social economy. Because sport is still value based in a capitalist economy, workers/athletes would be using it as a means of livelihood. To endure the physical demands of the game as a spectacle, plus compete for labour positions, would demand a certain continuation of such training procedures.

Finally, sport as a microcosm is not the least bit autonomous from the whole of society. It is totally tied, as

a form of social labour and a form of surplus-value to the
social framework of which it is a part. Removing the civil
or surplus aspect from sport does not affect the conditions
of sport in the social whole. One example is the continued
persistence of class differences in the social whole.
Inequality of condition would continue to leave sport a
selective representational aspect of society. This would have
less impact on the athletes themselves however than concerns
related to the social-labour dimension.

Were sport to attempt to eliminate its social labour
character it would leave athletes with no way of living within
the social economy per se. If sport was returned to the sphere
of private labour then the athletes who do not own the means
of production would still have to labour elsewhere to live.
In other words, unless the conditions of social labour as a
whole are dealt with, then the alteration of social labour
relations in sport (or any part of society) merely returns it
to the realm of private labour. Athlete/workers would still
have to find a source of revenue from which they could
reproduce themselves and their families.

My concern here is not to address these problems in a
thorough fashion--indeed, I have only broached a small portion
of the historically determinate logical issues involved. I
want merely to indicate here, through these examples, some of
the essential relations that are involved in social change in
sport in capitalist society and the interrelations that exist
between the part and the social whole. However, in spite of
the adumbrated nature of this last section, some salient
conclusions can still be drawn. First, a part of society--
sport in this case--is clearly related to the social whole.
Change within the part is not only dependent upon power
relations within the part, but power relations between the

part and the whole and within the whole itself. Additionally, where change in the part does occur, it is still determined by the whole--the "unintended" consequences of change in the part are determined to a large degree by the whole. The second conclusion that may be made is that change in sport in capitalist society is fundamentally tied to the production relations which dominate the whole and the part. Gruneau's discussion of transformation and reproduction in "Power and Play" leads analysis in the correct direction, but this general orienting framework must be made more specific and precise. The nature of change in a capitalist industrial society is determined by a number of specific concrete material factors. To comprehend those features one must begin to address their determinately variegated form and relation with the production process which creates exchange-value, use-value and surplus-value. This is by no means the end of the analysis, it is only the beginning. As Krader (1978) aptly comments, understanding the mode of production is not the same as understanding the society as a whole. The mode of production "is not the whole of the economic formation of society, but it is the sensitive indicator of the relations of the economy and the society." To comprehend sport, and fully grasp its complexity, one must begin study with the dominant production process in the social formation under study. Once the labour/society relation has been established then the relation of sport to the dominant form of labour must follow. In a capitalist society the society/labour relation involves the production of exchange-value, use-value and surplus-value. These three moments, as a unity, must be related to the sport form. Then, on that basis, a synthetic analysis, moving from the simple abstract to the concrete may follow to develop a full and comprehensive analysis of sport under the conditions of capitalist production.

NOTES

Before beginning to write this paper I discussed certain
aspects of its content with a number of people. I would like
to thank Hart Cantelon, Richard Gruneau, Charles Jenkins,
Kevin Whitaker, and members of the "Krader circle" for posing
questions and problems that helped me clarify some of the
ideas I have presented in this paper. Nada Beamish, Richard
Helmes and Cyril Levitt read a draft of this paper and their
commentary was extremely helpful both in terms of the form
and the content of this paper.

1. The "state debate" is much broader than the contrasting
position Poulantzas (1973) offers in Political Power and
Social Classes to Miliband's (1965) discussion of Marx's
theory of the state or the ideas put forward in The State and
Capitalist Society (Miliband 1969). It extends beyond their
exchanges as well (see Miliband 1970, 1973, 1977: 67-90,
Poulantzas 1969, 1976). One would have to at least include
O'Connor (1973), Gough (1975), Offe (1972), Habermas (1976),
the contributions made in the "derivation debate" by Muller,
Heususs, Altvater, Reichelt, Hirsch and others (Holloway and
Picciotto 1978), contributions like Olsen's, Panitch's,
Wolfe's, Armstrong's and others in the Canadian State
discussions (cf. Panitch 1977) and Macpherson's (1977) to
have a well rounded conception of the issues involved in this
particular set of questions.

2. The German debate, in essence, was not a response to
Miliband and Poulantzas - but more directly to Offe and
Habermas. This, however, is only the internal moment of the
debate. Externally it was a response to practical political
concerns within the Federal Republic of Germany in the late
1960's. The three major factors involved were, (i) the
recession of 1966-7, (ii) the coming to power of the social
democratic party in 1969 and (iii) the failure of the student
movement to "link" with any worker movements (cf. Holloway and
Picciotto 1978:4, 15-16).

3. Holloway and Picciotto (1978:21-9) raise several limitations to the debate but I would add the following as well.
The German debate began because it was realized that "to
understand the limits to state action it was necessary to
analyse the relation between state and society; to understand
this relation, it was seen to be necessary to analyse the
source of the relation, the source of the particularization
of capitalist society into apparently autonomous spheres of
state and society" (Holloway and Picciotto 1978:16). The

problem is that this relation did not begin with capitalist society - but with the first forms of civil society. Even though the work of Pashukanis (1979) was brought into the debate once it was underway, the historical origin of the state, and thus its immediate relation to civil society, was not thoroughly examined. A second problem is the abstract nature of the discussion. The state is a concrete relation which is best approached in its concrete form and not via theoretical abstraction per se. The relation of form and content, at the level of the state must emphasize concrete content to a greater degree than what is supplied by the contributions to the derivation debate.

4.   The society/labour relation is excluded in many theoretical approaches used in social research. Some examples are, structural functionalism (cf. Therborn 1976), social linguistics (cf. Habermas 1972, 1975, 1976b), phenomenological analysis, symbolic interactionism (cf. Lichtman 1970), and, oddly enough, exchange theory. There has not yet been a thorough and detailed analysis of the implementation of various theoretical frameworks to the study of sport, although general reviews are available. Gruneau (1976) explicitly, and Ingham (1975:339-44) more implicitly, have made some critical commentary on the use of various theoretical frameworks to study sport. Loy, McPherson and Kenyon (1972) and Snyder (1974) are more comfortable with the potpourri currently employed and make no evaluative commentary.

5.   Although the list is not exhaustive, I have in mind studies like those by Hoch (1972), Vinnai (1973), Beamish (1978), Helmes (1978), Gruneau (1975, 1976), Kidd (1979), Brohm (1978), Hargreaves (1976) and Riordan (1976). The critical study of sport which "spun off" the 1960's "new left" movement and "counter cultural" interests also neglects a thorough analysis of the society/labour moment. See, for example, studies by Barnes (1973), Meggyesy (1971), Parrish (1971), Shaw (1973), Scott (1971), Flood (1970), Conacher (1971), or Kidd and Macfarlane (1972). Many of the studies listed above broach the problem, but none deal with it systematically.

6.   Gruneau (1979:14) continues his statement, "Further, while such (Marxist and Marxist-inspired) critiques may have been of limited applicability they are infinitely preferable to the growing liberal orthodoxy in state and corporate sponsored games and sports that avoids encounters with critical evaluation altogether" (emphasis added).

7.   This list is not exhaustive by any means. Michener
(1976:337-74) and Loy, McPherson and Kenyon (1978:256-90,
see especially 263-79) provide reviews of some of the
major studies of the "economics" of sport. Other individual
studies of particular note are, Meyers (1975), El Hodiri
and Quirk (1971) and Quirk (1973).

8.   In a comparison of classical political economy and
contemporary economics, Dobb (1972:42) pointed this out
quite clearly. He emphasized that political economists
"focussed on what was peculiar to a particular system of
economic relations, even at the expense of a wider, but
perhaps more barren generality". Since that time, Dobb adds,
"I think it is not incorrect to say that the efforts of
economic analysis have been predominantly directed along (a)
second road. In abstracting phenomena of exchange from the
productive relations and the property institutions of which
they are a part, an attempt has been made to arrive at
generalizations which hold for any type of exchange economy".

9.   The term "positivism", like that of "bourgeois", writes
Giddens (1974:ix), has become "a derogatory epithet" and is
used less as a classificatory concept. I am not using the
term as a pejorative ad hominem, although I certainly have
criticisms concerning its usefulness as a mode of social
inquiry. My discussion of the positivist features of
economic analysis is directed at the analytic framework
per se. As a positivist mode of analysis, contemporary
economic theory subscribes to the following premises. (i)
The rule of phenomenalism; i.e. there is no real difference
between "essence" and "phenomenon". (ii) The rule of
nominalism; i.e. that we can only acknowledge the existence
of a thing when experience obliges us to. (iii) There is a
separation of facts from values. (iv) The belief in the
unity of the scientific method for the study of the natural
and social worlds (cf. Kolakowski 1969, Giddens 1974:1-22,
1976:11-16, 131-44).

10.   Marx (1973:86-7) argued that it was customary for
political economists to preface their work with a general
discussion of production as it relates to the general
conditions of all production, exclusive of historical location.
The aim of this procedure, Marx continued, was "to present
production - see e.g. Mill - as distinct from distribution
etc., as encased in eternal natural laws independent of
history, at which opportunity bourgeois relations are then
quietly smuggled in as the inviolable natural laws on which
society in the abstract is founded... In distribution, by
contrast, humanity has allegedly permitted itself to be
considerably more arbitrary".

11. The study of appearances has implications concerning work processes as well. Sport is, after all, a process as much as it is a product. Jones and others who adopt the neo-classical perspective have little distinctive to say about the particularity of sport as a mediate society/labour, culture/society process because their perspective assumes that capitalist processes of production are of a universal character (although the technology may be more advanced). Because work is universal, the product of all labour is treated as a mere article - a product of human activity. This is a simplification. Marx pointed out that, "The product of capitalist production is neither a mere product (a use-value), nor just a commodity, i.e. a product with an exchange-value, but a product specific to itself, namely surplus-value. Its product is commodities that represent more labour than was invested for their production in the shape of money or commodities" (Marx 1977b:1001, cf. 1006-7).

12. The specificity of Marx's analysis is all too often ignored and surprisingly so since it is an essential aspect of his work in general and of Capital in particular. I will not attempt to elaborate on this concern here in a note, but direct attention to the excellent discussions of Korsch (1971:16-25, 40-1, 50, 53) and Rosdolsky (1977:25-35, 1974: 65-70).

13. The material used in this section is based upon Lawrence Krader's recent work concerning the law of value and the dialectic of civil society. Most influential have been his essays "The Asiatic Mode of Production", "The Early History of the Theory of Value" and "On Value" (Krader 1976). Throughout the section, I have cited Krader's work specifically and that of Marx to make it easier for the reader to locate some specific points I feel may be challenging or worthy of further consideration.

14. Marx (1973:494) pointed out that, "...the preservation of the old community includes the destruction of the conditions on which it rests, turns into its opposite. If it were thought that productivity on the same land could be increased by developing the forces of production etc. (this precisely the slowest of all in traditional agriculture), then the new order would include combinations of labour, a large part of the day spent in agriculture etc., and thereby again suspend the old economic conditions of the community. Not only do the objective conditions change in the act of reproduction, e.g. the village becomes a town, the winderness a cleared field etc., but the producers change too, in that they bring out new

qualities in themselves, develop themselves in production, transfer themselves, develop new powers and ideas, new modes of intercourse, new wants, and new language."

15.   Marx (1867:16) described this process as a dialectical process in the first edition of Capital.   "In that it (i.e. one commodity) compares the other commodity to itself as value, it relates itself to itself as value. In that it relates itself to itself as value, it at the same time differentiates itself from itself as use value. In that this is its value magnitude expressed in the coat - and value magnitude is both, value in general and quantiatively the same value - it gives its value-being a different value form from its immediate being (Dasein)."

16.   "Capital does not create the objective conditions of labour, Rather, its original formation is that, through the historic process of the dissolution of the old mode of production, value existing as money-wealth is enabled, on the one side, to buy the objective conditions of labour; on the other side, to exchange money for the living labour of the workers who have been set free. All these moments are present; their divorce is itself a historic process, a process of dissolution, and it is the latter which enables money to transform itself into capital" (Marx 1973:506-7).

17.   Gruneau does not argue that "Marxists" are the only culprits. He (1979:10-13) displays the same features in the analysis of the "liberal" historian Arthur Lower as well.

18.   Gruneau (1979:6) argues "(a)s John Shotter (1973) points out, play is an assertive expressive act through which individuals attempt to expand their personal "powers" and exercise a degree of control over their immediate environments. It is an essential statement of our human capacities, not only to transform ourselves in interaction with our surroundings, but also to exert an influence on these surroundings." Given Gruneau's further work on the structure/agency problem, I am certain that his argument would be more ontologically rooted in agency per se than it was in his working paper. Play is just one form of human agency and is thus ontologically mediate and possesses a transformative/reproductive character--though some spheres of agency have (or appear to have) fewer reproductive constraints to their activity than others. Schmidt (1971) terms this aspect of agency (or practice) as a "negative ontology". If Gruneau made this step to ontology he and I

would be identifiably on identical ontological grounds.

19. Some important exceptions to this statement would
include the work of Alan Ingham (1975, 1979), Clifford Geertz
(1972), Thorstein Veblen (1953), and George Herbert Mead
(1934).

20. In these passages I have revised my original conference
presentation to some degree. I am less rigid in acknowledging
any transformative potential to sport, but I allow for this
softening by recognizing that the dynamics of sport's cultural
nature which are (potentially) transformative can only really
be handled adequately by linking sport to the social labour
process as a whole -- a central concern in my conference
presentation. My changed position stems largely from the work
I undertook following the conference when I tried to outline a
materialist methodology for sport study. That work was prompted
by Alan Ingham's "Methodology in the Sociology of Sport: From
Symptoms of Malaise to Weber for a Cure", Quest, 31 (2), 1979.
I am indebted to Ingham for the many hours he spent with me at
the conference, over the telephone and through the mail debating
various points concerning our respective positions. That
dialogue was a significant catalyst in helping me grasp what I
feel is a deeper and more comprehensive conception of cultural
processes. The work of Lawrence Krader (1979) has also been
tremendously influential in the development of these ideas.

21. This paragraph is a highly adumbrated summary statement
of the position I have developed at some length in, "The
Materialist Approach to Sport Study: An Alternative
Prescription to the Methodological Malaise", (Beamish 1980,
see also Beamish 1981 and 1982).

REFERENCES

Barnes, Lavern. The Plastic Orgasm. Richmond Hill,
   1973   Ontario: Simon and Schuster of Canada Ltd.

Beamish, Rob. "Socioeconomic and Demographic Characteristics
   1978   of the National Executives of Selected Amateur
          Sports in Canada (1975)", Working Papers in the
          Sociological Study of Sports and Leisure, Kingston
          Ontario: Sport Studies Research Group.

_____ "Re-establishing the Radical Form of the
   1979   Materialist Conceptualization of Alienation", a
          paper presented at the annual meetings of the
          Canadian Sociology and Anthropology Association,
          University of Saskatchewan, Saskatoon, Saskatchewan,
          June 1-4.

_____ "Central Issues in the Materialist Study of
   1980   Sport as a Cultural Practice". A paper presented
          at the first annual conference for the North American
          Society for the Sociology of Sport, Denver, Colorado,
          October 16-19, 1980.

_____ "The Materialist Approach to Sport Study: An
   1981   Alternative Prescription to the Discipline's
          Methodological Malaise", Quest, 33(1).

_____ "The Use of a Materialist Method for Comparative
   1982   Sport Study". Proceedings of the Second Annual
          ICCPES Meetings, Dalhousie University, Nova Scotia,
          September 23-27, 1980.

Brohm, Jean-Marie. Sport: A Prison of Measured Time.
   1978   London: Inks Links.

Burman, George. Proceedings of the Conference of the Economics
   1974   of Professional Sports. Washington: National
          Football League Players Association.

Flood, Curt. The Way It Is. New York: Trident Press
   1970

Gold, David, Lo, Clarence and Wright, Erik O. "Recent
   1975   Developments in Marxist Theories of the Capitalist
          State". Monthly Review, v. 27, no. 5   6.

Conacher, Brian. Hockey in Canada: The Way It Is. Toronto:
   1971   Simon and Schuster.

Dobb, Maurice. Studies in the Development of Capitalism,
   1963   New York: International Publishers.

_____. "The Trend of Modern Economics." in A Critique
1972   of Economic Theory, E. Hunt and J. Schwartz, editors.
        Baltimore: Penguin Books Ltd.

El Hodiri, M. and Quirk, J. "An Economic Model of a
    1971   Professional Sports League." Journal of Political
            Economy. v. 79, p. 1032-

Goertz, Clifford. "Deep Play: Notes on the Balinese Cockfight."
    1972   Daedalus (Winter)

Giddens, Anthony. The Class Structure of the Advanced
    1973   Societies. London: Hutchinson & Co. Ltd.

_____   (editor) Positivism and Sociology. London:
    1974   Heineman Educational Books Ltd.

_____   New Rules of Sociological Method. London:
    1976   Hutchinson and Co., Ltd.

_____   Studies in Social and Political Theory.
    1977   New York: Basic Books

Gough, Ian. "State Expenditure in Advanced Capitalism." New
        Left Review, v. 92 p. 53-92.

Gruneau, Richard. "Sport, Social Differentiation and Social
    1975   Inequality." Sport and the Social Order, J. Loy
            and D. Ball editors. Don Mills: Addison-Wesley
            Publishing Company.

_____   "Class or Mass: Notes on the Democratization
    1976   of Canadian Amateur Sport." Canadian Sport:
            Sociological Perspectives, R.S. Gruneau and
            J. Albinson editors. Don Mills: Addison-Wesley
            Publishing Co.

_____   "Sport as an Area of Sociological Study,"
    1976   Canadian Sport: Sociological Perspectives, R.S.
            Gruneau and J. Albinson editors. Don Mills:
            Addison-Wesley Publishing Co.,

_____   "Power and Play in Canadian Social
    1979   Development." Working Papers in the Sociological
            Study of Sports and Leisure, Kingston, Ontario:
            Sport Studies Research Group.

_____   "Freedom and Constraint: The Paradoxes of
    1980   Play, Games and Sports." A typescript of the article
            that is forthcoming in The Journal of Sport History,
            Winter.

Habermas, Jurgen. "Toward a Theory of Communicative
1972   Competence." Recent Sociology No. 2, P. Dreitzel
        editor. New York: The Macmillan Co.

_____ "Towards a Reconstruction of Historical
1975   Materialism." Theory and Society, v. 2. p. 287-300.

_____ Legitimation Crisis. London: Heineman
1976   Educational Books.

_____ "Some Distinctions in Universal Pragmatics."
1976   Theory and Society, v. 3, p. 155-67.

Hargreaves, John. "The Political Economy of Mass Sport."
1976   Sport and Leisure in Contemporary Society, S. Parker
        Editor. London: School of the Environment,
        Polytechnic of London.

Hegel, G.W.F. The Phenomenology of Mind. Translated by
1967   J.B. Baillie. New York: Harper Torchbooks.

_____ Hegel's Science of Logic. Translated by
1969   A.V. Miller. London: George Allen and Unwin Ltd.

Heilbroner, Robert. "Is Economic Theory Possible? Between
1970   Capitalism and Socialism. New York: Vintage Books
        p. 165-92.

Helmes, Richard. "Ideology and Social Control in Canadian
1978   Sport." Working Papers in the Sociological Study of
        Sport and Leisure. Kingston, Ontario. Sports Studies
        Research Group.

Hilton, Rodney (editor). The Transition from Feudalism to
1978   Capitalism. London: Verso Books.

Hobson, J.A. The Evolution of Modern Capitalism. London:
1926   George Allen and Unwin Ltd.

Hoch, Paul. Rip Off the Big Game. New York: Doubleday &
1973   Company Inc.

Holloway, John and Picciotto, Sol (editors). State and Capital:
1978   A Marxist Debate. London: Edward Arnold Ltd.

Ingham, Alan. "Occupational Subcultures in the Work World of
1975   Sport." Sport and the Social Order, D. Ball and J.
        Loy editors. Toronto: Addison-Wesley, p. 333-90.

_____. "Methodology in the Sociology of Sport: From
1979   Symptoms of Malaise to Weber for a Cure." Quest,
          31 (2), p. 187-215.

_____. John Loy and Richard Swetman. "Heroes, Sport
1980   and Society: Issues of Transformation and Reproduc-
          tion." A paper presented at the symposium, "The
          Athlete and the Emergence of Modern Spirit." Centre
          for Medieval and Renaissance Study, U.C.L.A., Los
          Angeles, June. A revised version of this paper has
          been printed by the Sport Studies Research Group,
          Queen's University, Working Papers in the Sociological
          Study of Sport and Leisure, Volume 2, November 4, 1979.

Jevons, W.S. The Theory of Political Economy. Middlesex:
1970   Penguin Books.

Jones, J.C. "The Economy of the National Hockey League."
1969   Canadian Journal of Economics. v. 2, p. 1-20.

_____. "The Economics of the N.H.L. Revisited: Post-
1976   script on Structural Change, Behaviour and Government
          Policy." Canadian Sport: Sociological Perspectives.
          R.S. Gruneau and J. Albinson editors. Don Mills:
          Addison-Wesley Publishing Co.

Kidd, Bruce. The Political Economy of Sport: CAHPER Sociology
1979   of Sport Monograph series.

Kidd, Bruce, and Macfarlane, John. The Death of Hockey. Toronto:
1972   New Press.

Kolakowski, Leszek. The Alienation of Reason. Translated by
1969   N. Guterman. Garden City, N.Y.: Anchor Books

Korsch, Karl. Three Essays on Marxism. Translated by T.M.
1971   Holmes. London: Pluto Press.

_____. Marxism and Philosophy (1923). Translated by
1970   F. Halliday. London: New Left Books.

Krader, Lawrence. The Dialectic of Civil Society. The
1976   Netherlands: Van Gorcum Press.

_____. "Die asiatische Produktionsweise" Anworten
1978   auf Bahros Herausforderung des "realm Sociolismus."
          W. Wolter editor. Berlin: Olle and Wolter.

_____. A Treatise on Social Labour. Assen: Van
1979   Gorcum Press.

Lichtman, Richard. "Symbolic Interactionism and Social
1970   Reality: Some Marxist Queries." Berkeley Journal
          of Sociology, v. 15, p. 75-94.

Loy, John, McPherson, Barry and Kenyon Gerold. Sport and Social
   1978   Systems. Don Mills, Ontario: Addison-Wesley
          Publishing Co.

Lukacs, Georg. The Social Ontology of Being: Marx.
   1978   Translated by David Fernbach. London: Merlin Press.

_____. History and Class Consciousness. Translated
   1971   by R. Livingston. London: Merlin Press.

Macpherson, C.B. The Life and Times of Liberal Democracy.
   1977   London: Oxford University Press.

Marx, Karl. Das Kapital Hamburg: Otto Meisner Publisher.
   1867

_____. A Contribution to the Critique of Political
   1970   Economy. Translated by S.W. Ryazanskaya. New York:
          International Publishers, Inc.

Marx, Karl. Theories of Surplus-value (3 volumes). Edited by
   1971   K. Kautsky and translated by Emile Burns. Moscow:
          Progress Publishers.

_____. Grundrisse. Translated by Martin Nicholaus.
   1973   England: Penguin Books.

_____. Capital (volume 1) Translated by Ben Fowkes.
   1977   Vintage Books.

_____. "The Result of the Immediate Production Process."
   1977b Translated by R. Livingstone. New York: Vintage
          Books.

_____. Capital (volume 2). Translated by David Fernbach.
   1978   Middlesex, England, Penguin Books Ltd.

_____. and F. Engels. Werke Berlin: Dietz Verlag.
   1964

_____. Collected Works. New York:
   1975   International Publishers.

Mead, George Herbert. Mind, Self and Society. Chicago:
   1934   University of Chicago Press.

Meggyesy, Dave. Out of Their League. New York: Ramparts
   1971   Press.

Meszaros, Istvan. *Marx's Theory of Alienation*. London:
1975   Merlin Press.

Meyers, J.A. "Background and History of Sports." *Sports*
1975   *Business and Finance*. New York: D.E. Hellerman and
         Company.

Michener, James A. *Sports in America* New York: Random House.
1976

Miliband, Ralph. "Marx and the State." *The Socialist Register*.
1965   London: The Merlin Press.

_____. *The State and Capitalist Society*. London:
1969   Weidenfield and Nicolson Co.

_____. "The Capitalist State: A Reply to
1970   Poulantzas." *New Left Review* no. 59, p. 53-60

_____. "Poulantzas and the Capitalist State."
1973   *New Left Review* no. 82.

_____. Marxism and Politics. Oxford: Oxford
1977   University Press.

Mill, John Stuart. *Principles of Political Economy* (2 vols.).
1893   New York: Appleton and Company.

Mills, C. Wright. *The Sociological Imagination*. New York:
1959   Oxford Press.

Moore, Barrington. *Social Origin of Dictatorship and Democracy*.
1966   Boston: Beacon Press.

Neale, W.C. "The Peculiar Economics of Pro Sport." *Sport,*
1969   *Culture and Society*. J. Loy and G. Kenyon editors.
         Toronto: Macmillan Press.

Nell, Edward. "Economics: The Revival of Political Economy."
1973   *Ideology in Social Science*. R. Blackborn editor.
         Bungay, Suffolk: The Chaucer Press Ltd.

Nixon, Howard. "The Commercial and Organizational Development
1974   of Modern Sport." *International Review of Sport
         Sociology*. vol. 9, p. 107-35.

Noll, Roger. *Government and the Sporting Business*. Washington
1974   The Brookings Institution.

O'Connor, James. The Fiscal Crisis of the State. New York:
1973   St. Martins Press.

Offe, Claus. Strukturprobleme des kapitalistiche Staates.
1972   Frankfurt.

Olsen, Dennis. "The State Elite." Canadian State. L. Panitch
1977   editor Toronto: University of Toronto Press,
        p. 199-224.

Panitch, Leo (editor). The Canadian State. Toronto:
1977   University of Toronto Press.

_____. "The Role and Nature of the Canadian State."
1977   The Canadian State. Toronto: University of Toronto
        Press, p. 3-27

Parrish, Bernie. They Call it a Game. New York: Dial Press
1971

Pashukanis, Evgeny. Law and Marxism: A General Theory.
1979   London: Inks Links.

Poulantzas, Nicos. "The Problem of the Capitalist State."
1969   New Left Review. no. 58, p. 67-78.

_____. Political Power and Social Classes.
1973   London: New Left Books.

_____. "The Capitalist State: A Reply to Miliband
1976   and Laclau." New Left Review. No. 95.

Quirk, J. "An Economic Analysis of Team Movements in Profession.
1973   Sport." Law and Contemporary Problems. p. 42-66.

Riordan, J. "Marx, Lenin and Physical Culture." Journal of
1976   Sport History. vol. 3.

Rosdolsky, Roman. "Comments on the Method of Marx's Capital."
1974   New German Critique. vol. 3, p. 62-72.

_____. The Making of Marx's Capital. Translated
1977   by P. Burgess. London: Pluto Press Ltd.

Scott, Jack. The Athletic Revolution. New York: The Free
1971   Press.

Schmidt, Alfred. The Concept of Nature in Marx. Translated
1971   by Gen Fowkes. London: New Left Books.

Shaw, J.   Meat on the Hoof. New York: Dell Paperback.
    1973

Shotter, J.   "Prolegomena to an Understanding of Play."
    1973   Journal for the Theory of Social Behaviour.
              vol. 3, no. 1

Smith, Adam. The Wealth of Nations. New York: The Modern
    1937   Library.

Snyder, Eldon. "State of the Field, Sociology of Sport: An
    1974   Overview." The Sociological Quarterly. vol. 15,
              p. 467-86.

Sweezy, Paul. "Toward a Critique of Economics." Modern
    1972   Capitalism and Other Essays. New York: Monthly
              Review Press.

Therborn, Göran. Science, Class and Society. London: New
    1976   Left Books.

Vinnai, Gerhard. Football Madness. London: Ocean Books.
    1973

6

Sport, Hegemony and the Logic of Capitalism

Response To Hargreaves and Beamish

Alan Ingham

I want to deal initially with the problem of language.
Paul Piccone[1] once made a plea for the abstruse. He stated:

> The problem with clarity is that it speaks
> the language of reification.. what is clear
> to us is what somehow fits into the con-
> sumerist mentality. You want clear ideas,
> well-packaged, that can be taken home to
> enjoy, as if they were buckets of Kentucky
> Fried Chicken.... Precisely because we don't
> want (our) language to become part of that
> reification we are trying to break... you must
> make an effort in order to understand us and
> in making the effort you begin to overcome
> reification and alienation. As long as you
> insist on clarity you remain in this passive
> state: you stagnate in the mundane, the
> commonplace -- the kind of alienation that
> (our) theory is trying to overcome.

While I have a lot of sympathy for the idea that language,
like history, is enabling and constraining, emancipatory
and imprisoning, clearly I must assume that any effort to
understand the work of another, let alone construct a cogent
response, requires that one be reasonably well-versed in the
grammar used by the exponents of a particular frame of
thought. In the case of Rob Beamish and John Hargreaves, the
grammar is Marxian. And, given that my own work has not been
directly centred in this intellectual tradition, it is
difficult for me to respond in a way that does justice to the
papers. Indeed, in commenting on these papers I feel rather
like a non-denominationalist at an ecumenical council meeting.

Now by this somewhat glib remark I am not attempting
to dismiss Marxism's specialized vocabulary nor am I suggesting that Marxism is nothing more than ideology. I am only
suggesting the kinds of limits my own background must
inevitably put on my response, limits that I am presently
trying to overcome given the increased relevence of Marxian

theory to my own research. Paul Piccone's statement may be a somewhat elitist rationalization for abstruseness but it cannot be dismissed for it challenges all to transcend the "recipe knowledge" so prevalent in both bourgeois _and_ Marxian oratories. It is in this sense that I shall try to capture the essences of the positions that Beamish and Hargreaves represent.

Both Beamish and Hargreaves have moved beyond the point of appealing to Marx as a canonical authority. Yet there is, in their respective endeavors, a sense in which each attempts to restore a version of Marx as the most defensible mode of analysis. For Beamish, this involves the language of the labor theory of value; for Hargreaves it involves the language of practice and hegemony. Simplistically put, it is the logic-language of _Capital_ and the _Grundrisse_ as compared to the praxis-centred language of _The Economic and Philosophic Manuscripts_ and the "Theses on Feuerbach." I doubt that either Beamish or Hargreaves subscribes to the "young versus old Marx" dichotomy -- they probably agree that this dichotomization of Marx is undialectical. But their respective emphases lead to different interpretations concerning the determinate relation between infrastructure and superstructure. Beamish seems more ready to argue the case of homology whereas Hargreaves seems more ready to argue for cultural contradictions, the origins of which presumably lie in constitutive social process. Each of these approaches presents us with different problems in our analysis of the concrete; each enjoins the debate on how to recover totality in history from different vantage points.

Rather than challenge Beamish and Hargreaves to resolve these issues at the level of epistemology (what did Marx owe to Hegel, Spinoza, or Kant and did Marx intend to do theory or history?), I would prefer to challenge them to address each other (rather than me) at the level of the concrete. Here I do not wish to rationalize empiricism (more bits and pieces of information, we do not need) nor to rationalize a withdrawal from epistemology. I am only requesting that we do not retreat into epistemology as a means of side-stepping the necessity of empirically grasping "the social and historical meaning of the individual in society and in the period in which he has his quality and his being"[2] That is, and without wishing to encourage or create an idealization, we cannot use preclusive or dismissive epistemology and language to avoid apprehending the real links between social formation, social being, and social consciousness which, for me, is the key problematic in the context of late capitalism.

So in the spirit of grounding, can I say materializing, the respective positions of Beamish and Hargreaves, we need eventually to ask a number of empirical questions. To what extent has the internal logic of late capitalism been subsumed or, conversely, been reproduced within that realm of life-conduct called sport? To what extent is sport merely an instrument of domination in a pattern of indirect rule -- an instrument which aids in the fragmentation of subordinate groups and in the fragmentation of subordinate class consciousness (e.g., via the fractioning of the subordinate class due to willing accommodation, pragmatic acceptance, or resistance) as a real and enduring phenomenon? Or, conversely, to what extent does sport represent a component of that culture, community, communication, and political organization which Marx[3] suggests is prerequisite to class formation and out of which may emerge a revolutionary trajectory? All of these questions demand that we specify on what grounds it is possible to argue that sport is either constraining or enabling or both.

As someone whose work owes much to Max Weber, I should accuse John Hargreaves of anti-Weberian banalities, but this would detract from my overall purpose and legitimate the perennial and misguided pro-Marx contra-Weber debate. Hence, I prefer to ask John to respond to a major question which, when stated in bold terms, is: "What are the specific, relevant social processes which need to be considered in order to account for the relative autonomy of sport as a cultural formation?" On more practical grounds, one might also ask him to explain how his version of a theory of hegemony which eschews much of the "orthodox" and critical forms of Marxian theory, aids us in understanding how the working class can be both a social force capable of totalizing its own experience and a base of recruitment for reproducing the labor-capital formation in the highly rationalized and expropriative realm of certain professional sports (e.g. soccer). How does a theory of hegemony which seeks to avoid structuralism and economic determinism help us in judging, within the current historical conjunctures, the degree to which sport's intra- and inter-organizational relations of production are mani- festations of a valorization process in which the ability to assign the means of production and to allocate resources to various uses are the functions of capital and are dominated by the owners and managers of capital? How does a theory of hegemony which denies both "orthodox" Marxism and Weberian theory aid us to fully comprehend the existence and persistence of a rationalized production process in which athletic labor is often conditioned by "rational" planning, measurability,

temporal indicators, the need for reproducibility, inter-
changeability and standardization, work discipline, affective
neutrality, routine, and specificity of function. In other
words, how does John Hargreaves propose to explain those
aspects of technology's style which some would argue[4] produce
a level of performance and contest that not only attracts the
working class into consuming a form of "bourgeoisified" sport
but also into providing its labor force? How is it, if the
working class can form consensus through culture, that the
player representatives of this class are often prepared to
view each other in instrumental terms? Finally, and on the
basis of John Hargreaves' illustrations, how can he come to
grips with the aforementioned without falling back into those
very Marxian traditions he rejects?

In the case of Rob Beamish's work, I feel somewhat ill
at ease in posing a critique for, to use Friedrichs'[5] terms,
it is difficult to quarrel with a sociologist who, in this
particular paper, hesitates to draw hypotheses from the depth
of his own social being and instead falls back upon images of
man common to the larger tradition. Perhaps this is unfair
for I do not count Rob Beamish among, to use Martin Jay's[6]
terms, "those benighted Marxists who think that by recuperating
what Marx really said...(they) can resolve (the) important
theoretical questions" confronting us in contemporary social
reality. Thus, in the spirit of allowing Rob Beamish to
extend the range of his argument and, thereby, disclose the
images that move him, I would ask the following questions.

In an obverse vein to my questions to Hargreaves, Rob
Beamish might comment on the notion that if sport is subsumed
by the logic of capitalism and, thus, is not "transformative"
it would appear that the play element of sport is dead. Is

the play element, perhaps like Gouldner[7] argues about Marxism per se, thus sustained by its metaphoricality? If so, does the death of play inhibit the creation of an alternative reality that projects what might be? Here I am not arguing for romantic and culturally idealist images of spiritual freedom or for _Zeitgeist_ interpretations of cultural determination.[8] Rather, I am struck by the way that individuals attempt to _magically_ recover the freedom that they have lost by a subjective recourse to play within the objective constraints of sport. That is, is play something (akin to many unrealized standards) to which we seek elevation only to find that socially reproductive sport keeps getting in the way? Thus, with reference to Rob Beamish's specific critique of Rick Gruneau,[9] I might ask if he is accusing Gruneau (despite the latter's protestations to the contrary) of finding an ideal subject that is going to transform our world? Is there an assumption in Beamish's paper that nothing exists outside of that hierarchical, pyramidal material structure in sport we call the "feeder system" which can resist absorption? How do we interpret, then, what the Centre for Contemporary Cultural Studies group at Birmingham calls resistance rituals? And, finally, is there implicit in Rob Beamish's argument a lack of appreciation for the liberating qualities of the non-instrumental, a lack which, states Francis Hearn, [10] derives from precisely the centrality of the category of labor to the Marxian dialectic?

In sum, and if I might draw upon Max Weber's[11] metaphor of the "iron cage", the questions which I have raised derive from my feeling that Rob Beamish and John Hargreaves present us with different views of our imprisonment in history. For Beamish, sport seems yet another bar in the prison's windows, a bar which will be removed only when the buttress of the prison -- the capital/labor nexus -- is eroded, for it is the capital/labor nexus that represents the logic of historical process. For Hargreaves, there are all kinds of chinks in the prison walls, chinks (interstices) that represent in culture the ways in which the working class wins space from, [12] or warrens into,[13] the dominant particular interest. While it would be presumptuous for me to adjudicate between the positions that each author represents, I shall conclude by noting that both positions leave me a little ill at ease. On the one hand, Rob Beamish's emphasis upon the logic that under-girds the social formation seems to leave little room for empirically assessing the lived experiences of those who con-stitute and are constituted by it. Perhaps, Beamish's relative muteness concerning lived experience can be attributed to a real silence here on the part of Marx.[14] Might we not bring the knowing human subject back in? On the other hand, John Hargreaves' emphasis upon the relative autonomy of culture vis-à-vis the infrastructure and upon sport as a dramatization of contradictory social practices seems to relegate any attempt to apprehend the logic that contours (sets limits upon) the range of practical possibilities to theoretical idealism. Does this not imply that the theoretical conditions of knowledge are given secondary status to ethnographic and historical empiricism? John Hargreaves may wish to disregard certain forms of Marxian theory, but I wonder if he can, when all is said and done, do without them. This leads me to suggest that a dialectical Marxism would require both a theoretical concern for the logic of capital and an empirical concern for experience. The logic, surely, is ever present and cannot be relegated to some last instance in determination, and experience, the mediator of culture and consciousness, is not purely independent of the logic. Is not a concern for the relationships between capital's logic and lived experience integral to an adequate analysis of social formation, social being, and social consciousness? Is this concern not the crux of Gramsci's contribution?

NOTES AND REFERENCES

1. Paul Piccone (with Stanley Aronowitz, Russell Jacoby, and Trent Schroyer), "Notes and Commentary: Symposium on Class," Telos, 28 (1976), p. 163.

2. C. Wright Mills, The Sociological Imagination (New York: Oxford University Press, 1959), p. 7.

3. Karl Marx, The Eighteenth Brumaire of Louis Bonaparte (New York: International Publishers, 1963), p. 124.

4. See Peter Berger, Brigitte Berger and Hansfried Kellner, The Homeless Mind: Modernization and Consciousness (New York: Vintage Books, 1973), ch. I., and my own work, American Sport in Transition: The Maturation of Industrial Capitalism and its Impact Upon Sport (Ph.d. dissertation, University of Massachesetts, 1978).

5. Robert W. Friedrichs, A Sociology of Sociology (New York: The Free Press, 1970), p. 156.

6. Martin Jay, "Back to the Starting Line After the Theories Misfire." The Times Higher Education Supplement, 476 (December 12, 1981), pp. 11-12.

7. Alvin Gouldner, "The Metaphoricality of Marxism and the context-freeing Grammar of Socialism," Theory and Society I (1974).

8. See for examples of such images and interpretations, John Huizinga, HomoLudens, (Boston: Beacon Press, 1955), Michael Novak, The Joy of Sports (New York: Basic Books, 1976), and Allen Guttmann, From Ritual to Record (New York: Columbia University Press, 1978). A theoretically-oriented critique of Novak and Guttman can be found in Richard Gruneau, "Freedom and Constraint: The Paradoxes of Play, Games and Sports," Journal of Sport History, 7(3) (Winter, 1980).

9. Richard Gruneau, "Power and Play in Canadian Social Development," Working Papers in the Sociological Study of Sports and Leisure), 2(1) (Queen's University, Sport and Leisure Studies Research Group, 1979).

10. Francis Hearn, "Towards a Critical Theory of Play, "Telos, 30 (1976-77) p. 146.

11. Max Weber, <u>The Protestant Ethic and the Spirit of
     Capitalism</u> (New York: Scribner's, 1958).

12. See John Clarke, Stuart Hall, Tony Jefferson and Brian
     Roberts, "Subcultures, Cultures and Class." In Stuart
     Hall and Tony Jefferson (eds.), <u>Resistance Through
     Rituals</u> (London: Hutchinson, 1976), p. 42.

13. See Edward Thompson, "The Peculiarities of the English."
     In E.P. Thompson, <u>The Poverty of Theory and Other
     Essays</u> (New York: Monthly Review Press, 1978),
     pp. 245-301.

14. See Thompson, "The Poverty of Theory or An Orrery of
     Errors." In E.P. Thompson, <u>The Poverty of Theory and
     Other Essays,</u> pp. 1-205.

7
Soviet Sport Reassessed

Henry W. Morton

The success of the Soviet sport machine has been one of the Communist party leadership's great achievements. Soviet domination of international sports began with the USSR's participation in the 1952 Olympic Games and has been expanding ever since.

The aura of success and the prestige of foreign sport victories are of great importance to Soviet leaders for reasons both domestic and international. At home foreign sport triumphs, officially presented as proof of socialism's superiority over capitalism, are primarily used to stimulate feelings of national pride and Soviet patriotism to aid in preserving national unity in a polyglot society which has over 100 nationalities, and in which the ruling Russians no longer hold a majority. Abroad, USSR athletes competing frequently and winning games, medals and championships project a positive, vibrant image of success and strength which can be transferred to the Soviet Union. Athletes and coaches competing and offering clinics are valuable assets as citizen diplomats, generating good will with foreign publics who might have had no previous interaction with Soviets.

Has Soviet sport developed differently from the capitalist model, as Soviets claim, and in so doing avoided the West's exaggerated emphasis on elitism, the over-commercialization of sport and the corruption that stem from both? The answer to that is No!

Elitism became a primary characteristic of Soviet sport in the early thirty's and has remained so to this day. It has worked against providing a quality sport experience for the masses. Because of state control commercialization of sport has not developed to the extent it has in the West.

However, because of the great stress of winning, numerous corruptive practices have become institutionalized including the regular but illegal cash payments, sinecures and perquisites to star athletes; the illegal but prevalent practice of recruiting star performers from competing teams; and the illegal use of funds by communities and organizations to build sport stadia and facilities to strengthen local teams. The coddling and support of star athletes and the young who demonstrate great potential has taken place at the expense of providing sufficient facilities, equipment and coaching for those whose potential in sport is limited. This directly parallels Western practices.

Organized sport in the Soviet Union is part of the larger political, economic and social system whose values, practices and problems it reflects. In this context I wish to explore two themes: the nature of professional sport in the USSR; and systemic features of Soviet politics and society which determine and shape sport behaviour of athletes.

The Professionalization of Soviet Sport

Soviet leaders in the early Thirties decided to go "big time" in sport stressing winning and the setting of world records by Soviet sportsmen, which led to the development of professional athletes. Subsequently many similarities in sport practices developed between the USSR and the West, a reality which both sides are reluctant to recognize. In both East and West the over-emphasis on winning and the setting of world records **has** corrupted sporting principles and has led to the development of a caste system of athletes at the expense of the physical culture programs for the masses.

211

Incidentally, elitism in sport is not totally negative;
it has at least one positive value. A sport star by virtue
of his or her excellence in competition, viewed by millions
on television, can attract hordes of excited youngsters to a
sport in the hope of emulating their hero or heroine. Olga
Korbut was such an inspiration to countless numbers of
young people in the world.

Soviet sport does not admit to professionalism, and
denies that class athletes in the USSR receive salaries and
bonuses for performing. They are also the recipients of
valuable perquisites such as cars, apartments and consumer
goods that are chronically in short supply. (Outside of the
15 capital cities of republics, meats and fresh vegetables
are frequently unobtainable in stores, a wait for a separate
apartment may take more than a decade, and a car, which
costs more than four times the yearly salary of an
industrial worker is hard to buy even for those who have the
money).

Not admitting to professionalism is nothing new; it
exists in the West to this day. In the United States an
obvious example is big time collegiate sport, offering
athletic scholarships which officially pay for tuition,
room-and-board and expenses, and unofficially whatever the
alumni can afford and what the coaching staff and the
university are willing to permit.

The National Collegiate Athletic Association, the
governing body for college sports, sets limits on how much
money an athlete may receive but has difficulty in enforcing
these amounts because they fall significantly below the
market value of superior athletes who are being avidly
pursued by coaches.

Such a system of "sham-amateurism" is dramatized in
Soviet sport and is a good framework for describing professional sport in the USSR. It begins with junior athletics which are
subdivided into three age categories: 12-14, 14-16 and 16-18
year olds. As youngsters improve they will be enrolled in
special sport schools and get a chance to compete in regional,
republic and national tournaments, traveling widely throughout
the USSR with all expenses paid and receiving some spending
money besides. A special privilege is to be given better
quality warm-up suits and sport equipment frequently made
abroad, such as tennis rackets made in England or Austrian
skis. When they graduate from school and are members of a
national or republic junior team they will receive special
considerations from college admission committees. (It is very
difficult to get into Soviet universities; they frequently
have five times (or more) as many applicants as places). Once
admitted they will receive a stipend many times more than the
40 rubles a month that the average student gets and have no
worries about passing exams or graduating.

The better the athlete becomes the more lavish the
offers he will receive upon graduating from the university.
Normally he or she will choose the better endowed clubs
because they can make the best offers. They are Dynamo,
sponsored by the K.G.B. (The Committee on State Security)
with clubs in most major cities; SKA, the Central Sport Club
of the Army; Locomotive, for the railroads, Torpedo, for the
auto industry, and many others. These clubs recruit top
athletes who spend their working time at their chosen sport.

The salaries which athletes receive, as well as bonuses,
depend on how well they do in national and international

213

competition, as do their raises in pay, which are made to look
legal, by promotions to higher positions, or to higher
military rank if they play for Dynamo or the Red Army.

Jumping clubs, though officially restricted and frequently
criticized in the press is, nevertheless, a common occurrence.
Coaches use all types of incentives to snare the best athletes
from competing organizations. Clubs located in Moscow,
Leningrad and Kiev are the most attractive to players because
they are also the richest and offer the most desirable locales.
The more powerful clubs in the capitals will raid the stars
of weaker teams of their republics because it is an accepted
fact that teams located in capitals should be the best.
Those who have been raided will in turn make offers to the
best athletes playing on B league teams.

Systematic Factors. Impact of the Social and Economic System: Athletes and Black Marketeering

Because of a chronic consumer shortage with quality items
in short supply or simply not to be found in stores, the
rising young Soviet professional athlete by virtue of his
access to scarce tickets to important athletic events,
foreign sport equipment and warm-up suits (the stylish Adidas
are particularly in great demand) can augment his income by
selling these items on the black market. Another source of
revenue is talony; meal vouchers worth 3 to 5 rubles, that
an athlete receives while in training or in competition, that
can be illegally exchanged for currency while he or she
continues to eat at home or in a cafeteria.

The class athletes especially those on Soviet national
and Olympic teams who frequently travel abroad (a highly
sought after privilege) are much more heavily into black
marketeering. They even take orders for goods before leaving

214

the USSR acquiring illegal dollars from black market sources
and taking with them such Soviet goods as caviar and cameras
which can be sold profitably abroad. They return with digital
watches, stereos, leather jackets and jeans for waiting
customers at home.

The two most sought after perquisites of the professional
athlete are the assignment of a good apartment and a car.
Either one or both may be used to cause him to switch teams,
a deplored practice. "Soon after Aleksandrov's debut with
the Army club", criticized Komsomolskaia Pravda, "the newcomer
was offered a chance to buy a car without waiting his turn
and was given his own apartment. He accepted this boon as
his due ...[1].

The star soccer player or world record holder in track
and field today expects to drive if he can't get a Mercedes,
at least the best Soviet car, a Volga, which has become a
status symbol because it is expensive and almost impossible
to buy and because it is an investment with a black market
resale value of 20,000 to 30,000 rubles. (Used cars in the
Soviet Union are more expensive than new ones, because there
is no waiting period once you find a seller and can agree on
the price)[2].

Yet, despite the material rewards and perquisites which
Soviet professional athletes receive, the Soviet sport
system is more exploitative of their talents than Western
professional sports. Soviet players lack the freedom to test
the water legally to see what the market will pay for their
services in the USSR and abroad. There is no free agent
market, no official player's agent, and no athlete's union
to represent their interest against management. In this
sense the Soviet professional (who dreams of the money
Western sport stars earn) is not only illegally paid to preserve

the guise of amateurism but is also greatly underpaid by
Western standards. For a first class performance such as
might be expected from a highly paid Pete Rose or Abdul
Kareem Jabbar, the Soviet professional operating at a
comparable level receives third-rate pay. So far no Soviet
athlete has been permitted to play on Western professional teams,
to test his skill and earning capacity in the National Hockey
League (as have several Swedes) or to compete freely on the
international tennis circuit as has Ile Nastasi of Rumania or
Wojtek Fibak of Poland. Such restrictions may be eased in
years to come.

The illegal by-products of an illegal professional
sport system condoned and supported by Soviet leaders, are
many. The intent of the Soviet government was to limit the
subsidization of sport to a select group of class athletes
and to the development of young stars needed to succeed them.
But the lure of big time sports encourages B league teams to
recruit players illegally with enticing promises in the hope
of assembling a superior team that will qualify them for an A
league place. It has similarly inspired city fathers, to
build large stadia with unauthorized funds which were ear-
marked for public housing construction and new shopping
facilities - both in very short supply.

Systematic Factors II: - The Political System:
Impact of Sport Censorship

Sovetskii sport is the most popular daily in the USSR.
The policy on what type of sport news, feature stories and
editorials may appear is determined by the Sport Section of
the Propaganda Department of the Central Committee of the
Communist Party (CPSU) and the Committee of Physical Culture and
Sport under the Council of Ministers of the USSR, which function
as a sport ministry. Like any newspaper in the Soviet Union

216

it has a censor who must sign off on all stories in order for
them to be published. The censor has a thick book, nicknamed
the Talmud, which lists forbidden topics. For sport they
include the rate of pay and bonuses athletes receive, the cost
of financing sport teams and the number of weeks athletes
spend in training camps preparing for international meets.[3]
Other unmentionables are the existence of sport boarding
schools for teenagers - they are euphemistically called,
"specialized sport schools", and the mentioning by name of
the Lipetsk Central Army hockey team which plays in the A
league competing with other clubs for the USSR hockey
championship. Lipetsk cannot be mentioned because the city
has no military garrison, however its home games are played
there. Sports writers may only refer to it as the Moscow
Military Region Army Sports Club.

A striking example of sport censorship occurred at the
world Hockey Championship held in Stockholm in March, 1969.
The Soviet and Czech teams were the finalists, meeting nine
months after the Soviet invasion of Czechoslovakia. A day
before the match, Nikolai Ozerov, the Soviet television
sportscaster who was assigned to broadcast the game for the
Soviet home audience, received a telephone call from Moscow.
He was read a directive from the Central Committee of the
CPSU prohibiting him from using the following words in
describing the championship match: "attack", "defense",
"blow", "victory", "defeat", "bodycheck", "failure",
"collision", "pressure", and "struggle". Presumably such
expressions could trigger unfavorable associations in the
minds of Soviet viewers with Soviet troops occupying
Czechoslovakia.

Faced with the monumental task of describing the game,
Ozerov reported the action in the following manner: "Our

comrades have the puck;" "Nedomanski concedes the puck to
Kharlamov;" "the match is taking place in a friendly
comradely atmosphere". As that was said Glinka, the captain
of the Czech team skated by the Soviet bench and spat in the
Soviet coach Tarasov's face. Apparently Ozerov's efforts
were not appreciated since he was not permitted to broadcast
a USSR-Czech hockey match for the next six years.[4]

I would like to close with a question to which I have
no answer. The USSR has enjoyed unparalleled successes in
Olympic competition. However, it may have peaked with the
winning of 50 gold medals in the 1972 Olympic Games in
Munich and the amassing of a record point total of 788.5
in the 1976 Olympic Games in Montreal. The principle reason
for a probable future decline in Soviet sport pre-eminence
in years to come is that other countries, whose sport
programs and athletes are also heavily subsidized by the
state, are challenging Soviet dominance; today the German
Democratic Republic; tomorrow the People's Republic of China.

In the event that such a decline in Soviet sport
fortunes should take place and the USSR lose its primary
position in Olympic competition, it will be interesting to
observe the reaction of Soviet leaders and the sports public.
Both have been led to expect a steady progression of Soviet
foreign sport victories - with proclamations of the media
that this is another verification of the superiority of the
Soviet system. If this happens will the USSR undergo an
identity crisis similar to Canada's when Soviet hockey teams
beat Canada at "its game" in the Seventies? What changes
will it bring to the Soviet sport system?

NOTES AND REFERENCES

1. Komsomol'skaia pravda, December 26, 1978, translated
    in the Current Digest of the Soviet Press XXX, 52
    (Jan 1, 1979), p.10.

2. A great deal of the above information can be found
    in Aleksy Daneshkin, "The Professional/Amateur
    Athletics Structure in the USSR", a paper presented
    at the Annual Meeting of the American Association of
    Slavic Studies, October, 1979, New Haven, Conn.
    See also Henry W. Morton, Soviet Sport: Mirror of
    Soviet Society, N.Y. Collier Books, (1963), passim
    and James Riordan, Sport in Soviet Society, London,
    Cambridge University Press, (1977), passim

3. Hedrick Smith, The Russians, N.Y. Quadrangle (1976)
    pp.373-74

4. The information on Soviet sport censorship was
    reported in Evgenii Rubin, "A Former Soviet Sports
    Reporter Views the Press", a paper presented at the
    Annual Meeting of the American Association of Slavic
    Studies, October, 1979, New Haven, Conn.

8

The Rationality and Logic of Soviet Sport

Hart Cantelon

INTRODUCTION

In recent years there has been an increased scholarly interest in Soviet sport. Although it is the masterstvo (high performance sport) which has almost exclusively accounted for this interest, Soviet authorities give equal weight to the massovost' (sport-for-all) program for their phenomenal success in sport.[1] The Soviet press is rife with statistics which indicate the large number of state citizens who participate, the extent to which the program reaches the more than 100 nationalities of the 15 Republics, as well as the success of the international competitors. However, there is evidence to suggest that Soviet athletes often excell at the international level despite a dearth of facilities and no large participatory base. This paper is an attempt to address itself to the questions as to why and how the Soviet state has been as successful in international sport as it has.

The late Herbert Marcuse, in his book Soviet Marxism: A Critical Analysis introduces his argument with a discussion of the dialectic which one should keep in mind when investigating the dynamic changes (which) characterize the development of the Soviet State. He explains:

> The new society emerges within the framework of the old, through definable changes in its structure - changes which are cumulative until the essentially different structure is there. The basic form of societal reproduction, once institutionalized determines the direction of development, not only within the respective society but also beyond it.
> (Marcuse, 1958: 3-4, Emphasis added).

The Soviet state of 1979 is fundamentally different from that which characterized the State of 1917 and as an institution of that state, sport also has unquestionably been altered. However the contemporary institution has been built upon factors which characterized "the framework of the old". If one were determined to create a Marxist society, tsarist Russia would not have seemed a likely starting point.

When Lenin and the Bolsheviks, took control of the state apparatus, after the collapse of Kerensky's Provisional Government in October, 1917, they did so under appalling conditions. The population was predominately rural with over 80 percent engaged in subsistence agriculture; there was no strong entrepreneurial bourgeoisie engaged in industrial activity and that industry which had been developed was either controlled by foreign capital or the tsarist state; the state itself was organized as a highly centralized, and autocratic bureaucracy. I wish to concentrate upon the evolution from a partrimonial state bureaucracy of notables in tsarist Russia to the creation of a legal/rational state bureaucracy in the Soviet Union. This is not a fortuitous decision for the development and logic of Soviet sport parallels this evolvement. To more fully understand the rationality of Soviet sport, it is necessary to understand the historical development of the state administrative apparatus. This development, aan be built upon a discussion of some theoretical Weberian concepts, namely rationalization, authority relationships and their association with the creation of the modern administrative state apparatus. Consequently, a brief excursus into these concepts is in order.

EXCURSUS ON WEBER'S CONCEPTS OF AUTHORITY RELATIONSHIPS AND RATIONALIZATION

Authority relationships: In his discussion of authority,

Weber began with the concept of power which he considered the most fundamental form of coercion. It was "the chance of a man or a number of men to realize their own will in a communal action even against the resistance of others who are participating in that action". (Weber, 1948:180; Weber, 1947:152). In defining power in this way Weber was suggesting that any authority relationships is ultimately based upon this action. However, to infer that it is solely the utilization (or potential utilization) of power which defines authority relationships is overly simplistic. It implies no obligation on the part of the power-wielder to consider the consequences of his action or the effect it has upon the recipient of the action. Weber quite correctly noted that the most stable authority relationships were those that were legitimated and included reciprocal duties and obligations on the part of all parties in the relationship. There also is the tendency to believe that the reciprocal obligation of power to command and duty to obey is both personal and consciously understood. In reality it is the passive taken-for-granted assumptions about one's social milieu which most fully legitimates authority relationships, particularly in regards to the state. Through the routine application of unchallenged assumptions about the structure of the state and its institutions, the most discriminatory authority relationships can be justified. It is only when "the class situation has become unambiguously and openly visible to everyone as the factor determining every man's individual fate", that such legitimation is called into question. (Weber, 1968:953). Once this legitimation is challenged, i.e., it is a consciously noted relationship, it often becomes a most passionately hated object of attack. Under these circumstances the authority is either supported

223

by a reliance on coercive power or assumes a new structure.

Sport, as an institution of the state, can be a very important mechanism in either reproducing the dominant authority relationships or calling such legitimation patterns into question. In the latter circumstance, sport can aid in the transformation of former authority relationships to newer ones. Later on in the paper I will point out how sport actually served both purposes in the Soviet Union. For his part Weber clearly pointed out the importance of the game in reproducing the ascriptively-based domination patterns of traditional society. Class position predetermined whether one was a member of the ruling elite classes and the game patterns of the elite legitimated this predetermination as they were "an important power instrument for the sake of maintaining one's own dominance through mass suggestion". (Weber, 1968:1105).

The ascriptive class structure which formed the basis of traditional authority relationships Weber saw as fundamentally irrational in that they rested upon particularistic status-determined factors rather than a rationally developed legal code; a selection of authority privileges based upon technical expertise and ability, and institutionalized in the "office" rather than the individual.

Rationalization: The ideal of rationality based upon technical expertise and ability comes from Weber's long-time interest in the development of modern capitalism. Giddens (1971:179), conveniently summarizes five important features which contour Weber's modern capitalistic enterprise. They include the rational calculation of profits and losses; the existence of large numbers of contracted wage labourers; the absence of restrictions upon economic exchange on the market; the use of technology which is constructed and organized on the basis of

rational principles; and the separation of the productive
enterprise from the personal household. In order for this
modern capitalism to function, Weber believed it essential to
develop a legal/rational state administration. The one concept
which has continually reappeared in this discussion, is that
of rationalization. Rationalization suggested a "demystifying
of life", a belief that man could master all things by
calculation if he so desired[4]. Whereas the traditional state
relied upon subjectively rational action, ie., "the subjective
intention of the individual is planfully directed to the means
which are regarded as correct for a given end", the modern
industrial state implements rationally "correct" action, i.e.,
"action which uses the objectively correct means in accord
with scientific knowledge". (Weber, 1949:34).

The effect that this rationalization has had upon authority
relationships is profound. Legitimation is grounded on a
scientific basis. No longer are ascriptive characteristics
the predominant form which dictate preferential status; now
more rationalized characteristics are considered - characteristics which take into account ability, educational
credentialism and expertise. The state structure itself is
legitimated in terms of "the legality of patterns of normative
rules" (Weber, 1947:338), as a "universalistic coercive
institution". (Weber, 1968:337)[5].

The bureaucracy - the state apparatus for legitimation of
authority relationships:

Regardless of whether the authority relationships are
based upon rationally correct or rationally subjective bases
of legitimation, there is a common instrument for maintaining
the status quo authority relationships of the state. This is
the state administration - the bureaucracy. The administration
not only serves to implement the wishes of the ruling elite,

225

it also is a mechanism which serves to implicitly legitimate
the dominant authority relationships. For example, the legal/
rational administration sustains the belief in "the 'legality'
of patterns of normative rules and the right of those elevated
to authority under such rules to issue commands". The
traditional state administration supports traditional
legitimating patterns, i.e., the "established belief in the
sanctity of immemorial traditions and the legitimacy of the
status of those exercising authority under them". (Weber,
1947:338). It is readily apparent that there is a great
difference between the traditional bureaucracy and the legal/
rational administration. The former is characterized by
personal allegiance to the ruling elite, while the latter is
organized on an "impersonal selection for positions, from all
strata of the population, according to the possession of
educational qualifications". (Giddens, 1971:180). All but
the most rational actions or decisions are isolated from those
used by the administrative staff. In creating his ideal-type
concept[6], Weber listed seven characteristics upon which the
legal/rational administration is based:

  i)   continuous organization of official functions bound by
       rules;
  ii) specified sphere of competence;
  iii) organization of offices which follow the principle of
       hierarchy;
  iv) rules regulating conduct of an office may be technical
       rules or norms;
  v)   members of the administrative staff should be completely
       separated from ownership of the means of production or
       administration;
  vi) complete absence of appropriation of his official
       position by the incumbent;

vii) administrative acts, decision and rules are formulated in writing (Weber, 1947:330-353).

Although Weber saw the legal/rational state bureaucracy as a most efficient instrument for implementing the authority relationships of industrial society, he was also a product of German liberalism and as such was deeply concerned with individual freedom in many aspects of German life. The reliance on bureaucracies particularly concerned him because he believed:

> Once fully established, bureaucracy is among those social structures which are the hardest to destroy. Bureaucracy is the means of transforming social action into rationally organized action. Therefore, as an instrument of rationally organizing authority relations, bureaucracy was and is a power instrument of the first order for one who controls the bureaucratic apparatus ... Where administration has been completely bureaucratized, the resulting system of domination is practically indestructible". (Weber, 1968:987 Emphasis in original).

The development of the modern capitalist enterprise and the legal/rational state bureaucracy, Weber believed, would create the necessity of more goal-directed activity, i.e., activity which was implemented only after consideration for the most efficient means of obtaining the goals (zweckrationalität). This alliance of rational thought and action, he believed "would eventually bring about a thoroughly 'goal-oriented' type of society in which purely instrumental relationships would dominate social conduct everywhere" (Mommsen, 1974:99); and although this instrumentally-based state would be highly efficient and rational, it would eventually lead to a "new 'iron cage of serfdom', in which all forms of value-oriented social conduct would be suffocated by the almighty bureaucratic structures and by tightly knit networks of formal/

227

rational laws and regulations, against which the individual would no longer stand any chance at all" (Mommsen, 1974:57).

Weber and Socialism[7]:

This pessimistic view of the legal/rational state apparatus also influenced Weber's thoughts about socialism. He envisaged that the socialist state would need two basic requirements: some means of producing and distributing economic wealth and the necessity of legitimating authority relationships based upon proletarian domination. For Weber, the most realistic form which the distribution and production of wealth could take place in a socialist state was that of a planned economy.

> Want satisfaction by means of a planned
> economy is dependent, in ways which vary
> in kind and degree according to its
> extensiveness, on calculation in kind as
> the ultimate basis of the substantive
> orientation of economic action. Formally,
> however, the action of the producing
> individual is oriented to the instructions
> of an administrative staff, the existence
> of which is indispensible. (Weber, 1968:109
> Emphasis in the original).

The ramifications of a planned state economy were great as far as Weber was concerned. The planned economy would be such that the state itself became the capitalist entrepreneur. The state would be able to control private enterprise - if indeed any were allowed - so that the public sector would/could expand at the expense of the private one. The result would be state-controlled monopolies, a necessity if one were to rationally develop a truly planned economy. At the same time, the desire and need for a planned economy would require the utmost coordination in terms of the division of labour and the efficient and rational pursuit of goal-oriented activity, all of which could be imposed or agreed upon through legal/rational procedures. This ultimate planned economy, Weber reasoned, would be analagous to the most highly efficient industries of the market economies and therefore would follow similar legal/rational bureaucratic procedures. It is therefore logical to assume that a planned economy would also require a massive bureaucratic state and industrial apparatus to implement the short-term and long-term planning. In short, for Weber, socialism could be considered an extension of capitalist rationalization. It was a goal-oriented society that would develop more quickly than even that of the market economy. In a society which is based upon ubiquitous planning, the most rational means of dealing with this comprehensive planning is through goal-oriented activity (zweckrational activity). To achieve goal-directed activity it is necessary to create a rationally thought-out division of labour manned by individuals capable of high efficiency, productivity, and scientific calcuability. Such a system would result in great efficiency, the achievement of high productivity for the state, but Weber argued, it would also encroach on the individual freedom, personal innovation and creativity of the individual. There would be less individual freedom because the "social system would be completely dominated by purely instrumental (zweckrationale) social relationships and interaction". (Mommsen, 1974:99). Weber formulated his thoughts on socialism prior to and immediately following the October Revolution in 1917[8].

Marcuse, in analyzing the Soviet state apparatus forty years following the Revolution, made the following comments:

> Modern machinery is susceptible to capitalist as well as socialist utilization. This amounts to saying that mature capitalism and socialism have the same technical base, and the historical decision as to how this base is to be used is a political decision ... It has been noted -- how

229

> much the present "communist spirit"
> resembles the "capitalist spirit" which
> Max Weber attributed to the rising capitalist
> civilization. The Soviet state seems to
> foster the disciplinary, self-propelling,
> competitive-productive elements of this spirit
> in a streamlined and politically controlled
> form. Businesslike management, directoral
> initiative and responsibility, and scientific
> rationalization of the human and material
> resources have remained the consistently
> imposed demands through both the Stalinist
> and post-Stalinist period. (Marcuse, 1957:
> 185-186, Emphasis in original).

Weber further suggested that the bureaucracy would also be indespensible in the workers' state in order to maintain political democratization. As Giddens suggests:

> The growth of the bureaucratic state proceeds
> in close connection with the advance of
> political democratization, because the demands
> made by the democrats for political represent-
> ation and for equality before the law
> necessitate complex administrative and
> juridicial provisions to prevent the exercise
> of privilege. (Giddens, 1971:180).

In a workers' state, where political democratization has theoretically progressed the furthest, it follows that the growth of the bureaucratic state as a necessary levelling mechanism to prevent the exercise of privilege, is both necessary and rapidly implemented.

In implying the further bureaucratization of the state under socialism, Weber decisively split himself from Marx's concept of bureaucracy. Whereas Weber saw the bureaucratic state apparatus progressively expanding under socialism, for Marx, "Bureaucratic centralization is rather one particular manifestation of the bourgeois state, and consequently is as transitory a social form as is capitalism itself." (Giddens, 1971:237).

Examination of the Soviet state from its beginnings in 1917, suggests that Weber's observations were very astute concerning the virtual indestructibility of the bureaucracy as well as his prediction about the advance of the legal/ rational apparatus in relation to greater aspects of social life. Sport as an institution of the Soviet state has been utilized in a transformative role in the changing authority relationships between tsarism and socialism, as well as an agency of reproduction for the goal-oriented activity of the legal/rational bureaucratic state. Lenin and the Bolsheviks were intent on creating a highly efficient and productive industrial state in which centralized planning was to be an integral feature. The importance placed on fitness for labour productivity and military preparedness has meant that the sports apparatus is an integral part of this centralized planning. Moreover, the sports apparatus dramatizes the emphasis placed upon goal-oriented activity, particularly in regards to the discovery and training of international athletes. The historical development of the Soviet physical culture apparatus has been contoured by the logic of goal-directed activity and the quest for the most rational means of achieving these goals; but at the same time it must be remembered that this development of a goal-directed sports apparatus has taken place within the particular social-historical conditions of the Soviet state.

The growth of the rational Soviet physical culture apparatus:

Lenin took command of the tsarist state apparatus in the midst of chaos and war. In the first two years of his leadership he was faced with ending Russian participation in the First World War, fighting a Civil War against tsarist forces hostile to Communist rule, general anarchy and syndicalism

231

in rural and urban areas, and the urgent necessity of getting
the economy moving again with specialists and skilled
technicians, who by and large, did not support his Party.[9]

Capitalism in Russia had developed in two specific ways;
through direct loans from the major western industrial nations
of France, Germany, Belgium and Britain, and through state-
controlled and financed industry[10]. The pervasiveness of the
tsarist autocracy was instrumental in inhibiting the development of an entrepreneurial bourgeois class. It its stead
there was created a massive military and civil service
apparatus, appointment to which was earned through hereditary
service to the patrimonial state bureaucracy (the chin).
This system of 14 rankings had been implemented as early as
the reign of Peter I (1682-1725) and remained the "official
basis of social prestige". (Weber, 1968:1065). The historical
importance of the 14 bureaucratic ranks of the chin was that
they provided a means of access to prestigious positions for
persons other than the aristocracy. For example, it was
possible to advance through the military ranks to a position
of officer and receive the status of nobleman which then
became hereditary. Those individuals who held important
offices in the state administration had vested interests in
maintaining the tsarist bureaucratic apparatus and were both
overtly and covertly hostile to the Bolsheviks. The refusal
to carry out their responsibilities greatly disrupted economic
production which was intended to bring about the imminent
collapse of Bolshevick rule. The break-out of the Civil War
only served to further such attitudes among the civil service
and economic specialists[11]. The necessity of controlling a
hostile group of specialists essential for revitalizing
industry as well as the need to organize the general
population for military activity against the tsarist forces

232

led to the re-creation of two common instruments of institutionalized coercion: the army and secret police[12]. These organizations were called upon to legitimate the Communist right to rule in a period when the collapse of the Party, and with it the first attempt at creating a Marxist society, seemed imminent. The Army recruited former officers from the tsarist forces who, although perhaps under some duress to offer their services to the Communists were equally intrigued by Trotsky's model of military precision and discipline[13]. This military apparatus provided the first Soviet sports organization Vsevobuch (a Russian anagram for Compulsory Military Training) which carried out training of pre-military (16-18) and military (19-40) recruits. The secret police, the CHEKA, was responsible for suppressing insurrection and possible insurrection. For their part the Young Communist League (Komsomol) insured that the hostile elements were purged from the tsarist sport clubs. Thus, for example the bourgeois members and leaders of the Sokol, Maccabee, and Scouts were removed and replaced by a working class membership[14]. This purging of the old regime sports clubs began in the first years of the new Soviet state and was of major concern at the Komsomol congresses. At the 1921 Congress, for example, the Komsomol members were instructed to get rid of the bourgeois athletic clubs in several ways. They were to create new clubs and organize competitions, which would attract the youth to their organization. Legislation was to be implemented which would expropriate bourgeois facilities, ban bourgeoisie from competition or in the case of the Scout troops, liquidate them all together (Fisher, 1959:74-75).

The major dispute between the old "bourgeois" sports clubs and the new Komsomol - organized ones centered around

the ethos of the tsarist groups. They were not bourgeois in
the sense that they were the exclusive domain of the
entrepreneurial classes. In fact the Russian clubs recruited
from the gentry, the foreign bourgeoisie engaged in industrial
activity in the country, as well as selected white and blue
collar workers. They were however, bourgeois in the attitudes
toward sports, i.e.,they had assimilated the British code of
amateurism into their clubs to isolate the membership from
artisans and labourers[15]. If anything, the rigidity of the
code was greater in Russia because of its semifeudal class
relationships. In 1861, while the British code was evolving
into its particular exclusivity, the Russian tsar and nobility
were debating whether to emancipate the serfs, to view them as
human beings and not personal possessions. The presence of
such thinking within an industrializing state resulted in an
even more rigid amateur code than that of Britain. It was
this ethos that the Party leaders were committed to changing.
Sport was to be utilized as an agent of social transformation.
In the tsarist state it aided the reproduction of repressive
patrimonial authority relationships; in the new Soviet state
it was to dramatize the existence of worker (proletarian)
control. In short, the dispute centered around the Party
insistence that sport be viewed in a materialist fashion
while the leadership of the old clubs insisted on its
neutrality, as an "a-political" organization. The further
revelation that leaders of Sokol and Scout groups had
supported tsarist forces in regions under their control during
the Civil War hardened the attitudes of the new regime
against them. This was not to say that the specialists were
totally liquidated. On the contrary it was as if the Party
knew that one could control the state if one could gain
control of the bureaucracy (Weber, 1968:987). The specialists,
with knowledge of sports, the physical and emotional needs of

children and youth, were essential to the clubs. Consequently, even the "reactionary" Scout leaders "could be taken into Pioneer work (the young Pioneers being the Soviet equivalent of the Boy Scouts), provided they adopted 'sincerely and fully' the pioneer platform" (Fisher, 1959:97). The specialists did not radically change the activities they had previously taught - the Pioneers for example, engaged in nature study, practical skills, outdoor living, hygiene, athletics, community service, and crafts - but the Party officials were to dictate the atmosphere in which they were taught. Whereas during athletic competition the Komsomol were to "set aside a certain time for speeches of an agitational sort" (Fisher, 1959:75) so too the Pioneer leaders were to instruct the youth to respect the leadership of the Party and the new authority relationships. Where those attitudes were not voluntarily forthcoming, the Party could resort to the agents of coercion - the Army and Secret Police and as Ulam (1965:421) points out this did occur with increasing frequency. The Cheka (Extraordinary Commission to Combat Counter-revolution and Sabotage) the secret police apparatus had been created on December 7, 1917. In its first year of operation it executed 6300 persons for various crimes against the state such as membership in counter-revolutionary organizations, insurgency, incitement to insurgency and so on. Included in this number was a popular Moscow circus clown Bim-Bam who, made the fatal mistake of poking fun at the Bolsheviks during his performance. Party members viewing the act shot him on the spot.

What Lenin and the upper Party eschelon gradually came to accept was the fact that they, the Communist Party were not leading the state apparatus but being led. It was next to impossible to control the hostile tsarist attitudes by coercion alone and legitimation of their right to rule was

235

not forthcoming. What had to be done was to create a means by which the Party members could be trained as specialists to replace those tsarist officials that they now almost totally relied upon. This became particularly evident during the period of the New Economic Policy (1920-25) in which Lenin quite bluntly pointed out that the state apparatus was a survival from the past and had hardly changed at all. In fact he likened the bureaucracy and the Communists in charge to that of a car which was going not in the direction the driver desired but in the direction someone else desired[16]. What Lenin advocated, and what was implemented under Stalin, was the creation of a legal/rational apparatus, which among other state matters, was responsible for the training of physical culture specialists. This apparatus was to recruit individuals not on the basis of their class background but on their ability, educational credentialism and expertise. This is not to say that recruitment was totally "goal-directed". There were aspects which Weber would call wertrational (value-oriented) in that recruitment was to initially rely on recommendation by respected Communists. Once allegiance, or at least sympathy, to the Party was established, ability became the criterion for success or failure. Without the recommendation, it was (and is) unlikely that an individual can aspire to positions of authority regardless of ability[17].

By 1925, several criteria were evident regarding the future direction of the Soviet physical culture movement. It was to be developed within a materialist perspective of the state. It was to rely heavily on the resources and personnel of the Red Army and Secret Police,[18] both for providing facilities and training individuals for competition, and most important, competitive sports and games were to be an integral part of the physical culture movement. This latter criterion is an interesting development in its own right in that during the 1920-25 NEP period there was a good deal of debate as to what should actually constitute socialist physical activity. During the period immediately following the Revolution, the military authorities had been given responsibility for the sports movement. As mentioned above, in this period of War Communism, Vsevobuch had concentrated upon military training for recruits and paramilitary activities for those under the age of conscription. In this regard they were aided by the Komsomol. However with the threat of foreign intervention ended and the tsarist forces routed, the various Party and state organizations interested in the sports movement turned their attention to its development in a socialist state. All agreed to the necessity of viewing it from a materialist perspective but there was little agreement as to what concrete forms it should take. The military and secret police organizations advocated the continuation of the military/paramilitary emphasis along with some competitions under their jurisdication. The trade union leaders delegated increased responsibilities in the NEP period for revitalizing industry and creating a more efficient work force, believed they should be given authority for physical culture. From the trade unions came the Proletkul'tist movement[19] which viewed sports as remnants of the decadent tsarist past and consequently should be totally rejected. In its place, workers were to participate in newly-invented socialists workers' games, as well as labour gymnastics[20]. The labour gymnastics reflected a good deal of imagination in suggesting innovative socialist physical culture. Already in 1921, the well-known theatrical figure and producer V. Meirkhold was experimenting with his theatrical physical culture in the Tefizkul't Commission.

237

He advocated a form of Taylorized gymnastics for workers in industry in which they engaged in those movements which they used in their daily work. Labour gymnastics have been adapted into the Soviet physical culture movement as a method of keeping workers fit and more productive (Samoukov et al, 1967:49). However, the total rejection of sports tended to be unpopular among the young and Lenin's admonishment of the Proletkul'tist movement in this regard, prophetically spelled the elimination of the movement under Stalin[21].

The particular Proletkul'tist philosophy had evolved out of the earlier Education/Hygiene Department (shkol'no-sanitarnii otdel) headed by a well-known revolutionary and doctor, V.M. Bonch-Bruevich. She had been appointed director of the Department with the responsibility for education and hygiene in the new state and had gathered around her a number of respected educationalists, doctors and specialists in physical culture (Stolbov, 1977:93). It was this group which was responsible for many of the differing viewpoints concerning what should actually constitute socialist physical culture. The most popular philosophy to emerge out of the Department was that of the hygienists. This group was vitally concerned with the necessity of raising health standards, eliminating disease and epidemics. Regular participation in physical exercise was seen as one way in combating these health problems. The hygienists, although not going as far as the Proletkul'tist in rejecting all sport, were however, selective in their praise of them. Activities like "weightlifting, boxing and gymnastics were said to be irrational and dangerous, and encouraged individualist rather than collectivist attitudes and values - and, as such, were contrary to the desired socialist ethic. They frowned upon the record-breaking mania of contemporary sport in the West, and they favoured non-commercialized forms of recreation that dispensed with grandstands and spectators" (Riordan, n.d. 3)[22]. The very composition of the Educational/Hygiene Department meant that there was a good deal of dispute over the "proper" hygienic physical culture program. One group advocated "normal lessons" in which the workload and intensity was limited and strictly controlled and consisted of artistic and corrective gymnastics, as well as natural movements of running and jumping (Samoukov, 1967:51). As the Party organ responsible for specialists' training the Educational/Hygiene Department also controlled the Institutes of Physical Culture in both Moscow and Leningrad. In fact, as Riordan notes (n.d.:5), in 1924, the Moscow Institute had been renamed the Central Institute of Physical Culture and Curative Pedology. Its principal A.A. Zigmund attempted to synthesize the different philosophies arising from the hygienists and Proletkul'tists with those of the education profession. Zigmund called his method the "Soviet System of Physical Culture" and emphasized personal hygiene, natural movement in the environment, specialized motor skills necessary in industry and some "approved" sports like track and field, swimming and rowing in which the competitor competed against himself and against the clock only (Samoukov et al, 1967:53).

The hygienists of the Education/Hygiene Sanitary Department, with their several philosophies held a good deal of influence up until 1925 when several of its noteworthy members were linked with Trotsky and were subsequently purged. One legacy which has continued has been that of routinized medical supervision for all those participating in sport.

239

For their part, the Komsomol, were less than pleased with the attack on competitive sport. Evidence suggests that the alliance which had been forged between the Young Communist League and the Red Army Vsevobuch during the period of War Communism was increasingly strained during the 1920's. The youth were not content with the preoccupation with military skills at the expense of competitive games. Moreover, the labour gymnastics and hygienist/pedagogue programs did not attract the youth to the physical culture movement in any great numbers. Consequently, the Komsomol initiated their own system "Spartak", with six days training per week. They advocated participation in all sports but rejected athletic specialization. Participants were not to be sheltered from strenuous activity as "normal lessons" suggested, nor was the movement against the accomplishments of the former "bourgeois" sports. The Spartak movement, needless to say, attracted great numbers of the youth, eager to participate in sports (Samoukov et al, 1967:52).

The various attempts at creating a truly socialist physical culture movement resulted in a synthesis of the differing systems. Physical culture was seen as an essential agent of reproducing the new authority relationships in which the power of the CPSU was legitimated. Physical culture was to be established on a rational and scientific basis with fitness of workers to increase labour productivity as one goal, but competition as a means of rallying the population around the Party authority as another.

By 1925, Stalin had consolidated his claim as the heir - apparent to Lenin. It was under his direction that the physical culture movement became a more complete instrument of rationalization. The inefficiency of the bureaucracy which characterized the patrimonial tsarist apparatus and which

240

plagued Lenin in the early years of Communist Party rule was
to be rapidly changed under Stalin. The Communists themselves
were more fully in control for two main reasons. Firstly,
Lenin's admonishments to the XI and XII Party Congresses to
increase the expertise of those in positions of authority in
the bureaucracy were having some effect (Lenin, 1975:74 ff; 84 ff).
Schools and short-courses for training specialists in diverse
areas of state administration and industry had been established
and the Party administrators were better prepared for their
work as a result. Secondly, the reorganization of the Secret
Police in 1917 had ushered in a new and unique administrative
technique - terror. As Ulam points out (1965:422), "Terror
from the means of attaining and preserving power had become
an administrative technique to be used also in cases of
inefficiency, red tape, and the like" (Emphasis in the original).
This technique was to epitomize Stalin's push towards rapid
industrialization and among other things increasingly change
the bureaucracy to one which was more efficient and rationally
organized. The necessity of being more efficient at all levels
in a state organization which utilized administrative terror
is admirably pointed out by Marcuse (1958:112-113). The Soviet
state and Party bureaucracies are both organized on the premise
of democratic centralism, with lower bodies subordinate to
higher ones. Further, the centralized planned economy links
all industry and the state apparatus together in a coordinated
fashion. Therefore, inefficiency at a lower level can have
great ramifications throughout the entire system; and Stalin's
resort to terror to solve the inefficiency went much further
than the immediate source. With authority vested in the next
highest level, terror could move up the bureaucracy and across
it, drawing in not only those responsible for one specific
area of the economy but others that directly interacted with
it.

The greater rationalization of the state apparatus under Stalin was in no small part due to the fact that he was not loath to use terrorist administrative techniques and the physical culture movement was not exempt from the utilization of these techniques. The individuals in charge of the centralized organization were removed with great frequency, particularly under Stalin (See Riordan, 1977:402-406 specifically p.406). However, terror must be seen to hold an insignificant position in explaining the development of high performance athletes in the Soviet Union. I would argue that coercion has had limited use in encouraging athletes to run faster or jump higher. Terror may have made the physical culture apparatus a more efficient one but the results of this efficiency has not been terrorized athletes but highly trained and skilled individuals[23].

On July 13, 1925, steps were taken to eliminate the bickering and struggle for power between the various organizations responsible for physical culture. At the same time Party decisions were made as to the future shape and direction physical culture would take in the Soviet state.

Physical culture was to be instrumental in increasing individual health and physical fitness, to increase labour productivity, and to prepare individuals to defend the Soviet state. Implicity underlying these measures was the recognition that involvement in physical culture was an excellent means of legitimating Party control as the "Vanguard of the Proletariat".

> .... physical culture can rally the workers
> and peasants around Party, government or
> professional organizations, drawing them
> into social and political activity (Ivonina,
> 1972:19).

242

The struggle for supremacy which had been occurring between the trade unions, military and <u>Komsomol</u> organizations was to be solved by placing the All-Union Soviet of Physical Culture in charge of all aspects of physical culture. It was to:

> decide the general direction physical
> culture (would) take and (would) provide
> scientific, administrative and technical
> leadership. It (would) also develop
> proper educational attitudes and obtain
> a consensus regarding the mutual use of
> sports field, stadiums, arrange competitions
> and physical culture performances.
> (Ivonina, 1972)

The <u>Komsomol</u> and trade unions were to aid this All-Union organization in order that physical culture could be developed in the most efficient and shortest period possible. The inclusion of sports competitions suggested that those groups who did not see competition as a necessary part of the physical culture movement in a socialist state had been silenced. Competition was to aid in individual skill development, but more importantly as a vehicle to attract the masses towards physical culture. Moreover, competition was to be arranged on an international basis, initially through the Red Sports International but later through affiliation to international and Olympic organizations[24]. The Red Sports International was created to strengthen the international solidarity of workers while the Olympic movement was later to be seen as a vehicle for establishing peaceful co-existence and détente[25]. Finally, the 1925 Resolution clearly stated that the Party was to provide "political leadership to the physical culture movement". It was to insure that physical culture encompassed all age groups, that the All-Union Soviet had Party support as the highest organ of the movement, and that physical culture would develop on a scientific basis. This consolidation of competing groups into a more rational

243

and efficient apparatus still retained the <u>wertrational</u>
(value-rational) characteristics however. The Party member
was to maintain control and to organize the work of the
physical culture specialist.

With the inception of the first Five Year Plan (F.Y.P.)
in 1929, the Soviet Union embarked on a program of rapid
industrialization. Such a plan meant that a rational
bureaucratic state and industrial apparatus was not only
inevitable, it was virtually indispensable. As Marcuse so
admirably states:

> The effort to catch up in record time and
> from a state of backwardness, with the level
> of the advanced industrial countries led to
> the <u>construction and utilization of a huge</u>
> <u>productive apparatus with a system of</u>
> <u>domination and regimentation</u>. (Marcuse,
> 1958:82-83, Emphasis added)

Heavy industrial development, the development of a more
efficient transportation system, and the exploitation of
primary resources were given priority in the First R.Y.P.
The slogan "technique decides everything" pervaded this
initial plan and production was to be organized according
to the most efficient, scientific and modern methods
possible.

The introduction of the second F.Y.P. was intended to
increase the technique of the labour force to utilize the
scientifically developing means of production to the maximum.
The goal of increased labour productivity was to be achieved by
the mastering of rational technique by a great percentage of
the labour force. This rationalization of technique is not
new to individuals familar with the Taylorization of American
industry. In fact, Stalin himself, clearly suggested that the
Soviet work force should emulate American efficiency

(Stalin, 1965:20), while Lenin had a longstanding interest in
the system (Ulam, 1967:482). However, unlike Taylorism which
was a management-imposed system, there is a good deal of
evidence to suggest that the Soviet movement rose primarily
from the workers themselves and was termed the Stakhanovite
movement after the Donetz coalminer Alexi Stakhanov.

I do not wish to focus directly on the ramifications
Stakhanovism had for sport since I have argued this point
elsewhere[26]. However, it should be noted that the efficiency
of the Stakhanovites in industry did not appear to go unnoticed
by those individuals in the sports apparatus who were also
interested in developing highly efficient athletes. Moreover,
I do not believe it is fortuitous that the incentive program
among sportsmen paralleled that of Stakhanovites in industry.

Soviet Marxism is committed to the principle of total
employment. As such, it has virtually removed the uncertainty
of employment common to the capitalist state which relies on
a "reserve army of the unemployed" to compete for jobs with
those already working. Weber envisaged that this would occur
in a planned economy which would alter the compulsion for
productivity which characterized the market economy. In the
market economy, the legal contract was all that bound the
employer/employee together. The worker sold his labour power
for a specified wage and agreed to produce at a certain rate.
If he did not reach the agreed-upon production rate he was
replaced. These circumstances were considerably altered in
the planned economy which led Weber to suggest that if
efficiency was to be progressive in the planned economy something comparable to the market economy's quest for profit, or
the satisfaction of meeting effective demands must be
incorporated. This he believed could be filled in two ways:
by special material rewards; by perpetuating certain ideals

motives which can be used to stimulate a level of achievement in economic production (Weber, 1947:214).

In industry generally, increased material rewards could be accrued from the piece-work wage system. But given equal importance was the necessity of workers to emulate the rational efficiency of the Stakhanovites. Stakhanovites were individuals "who had completely mastered the technique of their trade, were able to make the most efficient use of their tools and equipment, work rationally and without waste and regularly exceeded the prescribed standards of output (Marcuse, 1936:11). The Stakhanovite characteristics became the ideal for which all workers were to strive.

Sport, like industry, was to be administered in a most efficient bureaucratic manner, with members of the sports bureaucracy expected to fulfill the plans like any other worker.

In 1929, the CPSU (b) reintroduced the state-controlled Ministry of Sport, citing lack of coordination within the physical culture movement as a major factor in this decision. The first F.Y.P. had served as a basis for future rationally-based industry and a similar consequence was evident in the sports administration. Intensification of state leadership in sport was imposed and the Ministry was organized on a hierarchal basis. Competition was to be organized under strict scientific controls and was to be an important instrument in attracting the masses to physical culture (Ivonin, 1972:20). But competitive sport was only one aspect of the physical culture movement. Another was the use of physical culture to create a disciplined labour force fit for work in the intensive drive towards rapid industrialization. In short, the Stalinist bureaucracy created the necessary

246

technical conditions for developing highly efficient worker/
athletes and athlete/workers.

For the worker, the Ready for Labour and Defence System
(Gotov trudu i oborone G.T.O.) was established in 1931. The
program was to develop "all-round ability in a number of
sports and knowledge of the rudiments of hygiene, first-aid
and civil defence" (Riordan, 1977:129).

The Uniform Rankings System was implemented in 1935 to
discover those with talent, "To categorize them according to
their level of ability in a particular sport and to give them
the incentive and amenities to realize their potential"
(Riordan, 1977:129). The talent discovery system coincided
with the rise of the 1935 Stakhanovite movement in industry.
Whereas the Stakhanovite was to inspire and encourage other
workers to adopt more scientific and rational techniques in
the industrial sphere, the athlete was to inspire the general
physical culturalists to continue their participation on a
regular basis, as well as to attract non-participants to the
movement. The institution of physical culture and sport[27]
was to develop the personal health and hygiene of workers,
and to prepare them for labour and defence of the country.
More importantly, the institution was reproducing the new
authority relationship patterns in which the rational rules
and norms developed by the Party were legitimated. This had
profound ramifications for both sport and labour.

Sport, like state industry, was administered in a most
efficient bureaucratic manner with athletes expected to fulfill
plans like any other worker. The 1937 Labour norms which
established Stakhanovite "records" in industry paralleled
those in sports but with one major difference. The Stakhanovite
records were peculiar to the U.S.S.R. since other industrial
states simply did not have worker/athletes with records for

labour output. The norms of the Uniform Rankings System were an entirely different matter. The sports record defined (and continues to do so) the "universal language of sport" (Gruneau in Ball and Loy, 1975:136). The universal sports records which objectively categorized "sports stardom" were sought after, not only by Soviet athletes, but athletes in every major industrial state.[28] The Soviet classificatory criteria was consequently established in accordance with records of Olympic and world competition. But unlike the ideational value system of Victorian Britain which greatly influenced amateur athletes in western states, the Soviet ethos defined excellence from a materialist perspective. Sport was contoured by the economic mode of production and in a planned socialist economy, assaults on the record were also planned in a scientific mater-of-fact way. Like the Stakhanovite in industry, the athlete was given time and expertise to train in the quest for the record; and again like the Stakhanovites, athletes were rewarded for meeting or surpassing the norms. But it is important to recall the 1925 basis upon which competition was institutionalized in the Soviet state. Competition was to aid in individual skill development but more importantly, was to attract the masses towards physical culture. The athletic elite were not nurtured for their own self glory but the betterment of Soviet physical culture generally. - - "Exposure to competition can improve individual performances but more importantly, the whole collective". (Ivonin, 1972:20 The athlete was pampered but only in so far as he was seen to be contributing to the overall improvement of the physical culture movement. In this regard, Baykov's comments concerning the Stakhanovite's obligation to the work force are equally applicable to the high performance athlete. Both not only achieve superior results in their chosen fields, but in so doing, improved the work "in order that others may profit by it, in order to stimulate others to work better and generally to raise labour productivity in a certain field" (Baykov, 1946: 359, emphasis added). The individual worker or athlete bent on self-aggrandizement and improving his lot at the expense of the collective was dealt with quickly and severely.

> Purely selfish motives were branded as
> grasping and self seeking, and if unmasked,
> closed any further possibilities of
> obtaining material advantage (Baykov, 1946:259).

The Uniform Ranking System allowed those with ability to achieve mobility within the sports hierarchy, to be rewarded accordingly but they were also expected to train efficiently and scientifically and to use their superior knowledge and training to improve the regimes of others in the physical culture movement. For this, the athletes were awarded with prestigious social incentives, such as the Order of Lenin, (recipients of which there were 50 athletes and sport workers in 1937) (Riordan, 1977:128). In addition, they were rewarded materially as were their Stakhanovite worker counterparts, and the norms clearly stated the amounts to be paid for surpassing the "record".

Olympic Involvement: How successful this athlete/worker program might have become both in surpassing world records and encouraging regular participation in physical culture, will never be known as the experiment was interrupted by the Second World War. The heroics of the Soviet people convinced the leadership that their mass fitness programs were worthwhile endeavours and should be continued.[29] As for the high performance program, there was one major change. Prior to the war, the Soviet authorities were highly critical of the Olympic movement, while following the war, the leadership

made overtures to join the I.O.C. The western nations were
anxious to return to a state of peace-time normalcy after the
war and sports competitions were seen as one way of achieving
this. At the same time, the massive American-USSR propaganda
campaigns that characterized the Cold War period of the 1950's
were beginning to be felt. For their part, the U.S.S.R.
pronouncements, both internally to Soviet citizens and
externally to non-aligned or developing nations, praised the
superiority of the socialist path. In part, these assertions
declared that as a result of the scientific rationality of
socialism, workers were more productive. There was one
fundamental weakness in such declarations - there was no way
of knowing if workers were more productive under the socialist
system. With no universal records of individual labour
productivity, it was impossible to discern if a Stakhanovite
worker surpassed his Taylorized opposite. As Mandell puts it:

> The Soviets learned ... that socialists citizens
> cannot cheer industrial Stakhanovites in stadiums
> and that there are no international festivals for
> steel workers. (Mandell, 1976:262).

The same was true of Soviet athletic activity. By not being
part of the international sports organization, records of
Soviet athletes were unrecognized. Not only were they
unrecognized, but they were often belittled as attempts to
suggest athletic supremacy where none existed. (Consider,
for example, the comments and attitudes that many Canadians
held prior to the 1972 hockey series between the NHL and
Soviety hockey teams). By joining the International Olympic
movement, the Soviet leaders had a reputable platform from
which to dramatize the superiority of the socialist path.
Soviet record-setting in ratified competition had to be
accepted and the Soviet authorities could lay claim to the

250

opportunity that socialism provided athletes to develop.
Further, the expected Soviet superiority could be won in the
relatively "safe" environment of the international sports
arena rather than in military conflict. What is also important
to the Soviet state internally, is that international athletic
superiority further legitimates the authority of the Party to
continue the legal/rational bureaucratization of greater
aspects of Soviet life. If mastery of technique, efficiency,
rational training and performance, and the willingness and
ability to continue the quest for the record produces
superiority in international sports competition, then the same
rationalized behaviour is appropriate in other aspects of life.

Ramifications for Sport: There are important ramifications
for sport generally which are a direct result of the
rationality and logic of Soviet sport. It is apt to recall
Herbert Marcuse's statement:

> The basic form of societal reproduction,
> once institutionalized, determines the
> direction of development, not only within
> the respective society, but also beyond it.
> (Marcuse, 1958:4).

The creation of a goal-directed state apparatus in which
action is increasingly governed by the dictates of scientific
rationality and efficiency, has indeed determined the direction
of Soviet physical culture. The apparatus is capable of
organizing the activity of specialists and athletes in such a
way that in a relatively short time, highly proficient
international performers are developed. The sport of ice
hockey is probably the best example of this. First introduced
in the 1930's and not seriously organized until 1946, the
Soviet Union is now the undisputed leader in the sport. However, this success does not stop with ice hockey but crosses
the entire Olympic and international sports spectrum,[30] and

251

this success has altered the ethos with which all athletes enter Olympic competition. The ethos, which now surrounds international competition, is one which has been implied in Soviet sport since 1917, but which was most clearly stated in the 1948 Party Directive concerning the development of international athletes. Progress in international sports is measured in strict linear terms. The Soviet athlete is nurtured in a situation whereby the preoccupation is with mastery of technique, efficiency, rational training and performance, and the willingness and ability to continue the quest for the record. This ethos has required other states to adopt similar regimes, some enthusiastically, others reluctantly. The end result is the same. Training regimes of international athletes, selected at younger and younger ages, have reached excessive levels; the elite amateur/ gentleman code of ethics of de Coubertin's Olympics has been replaced by the efficiency of rational Olympic work.

At the same time, the international athlete is seen to represent a particular political philosophy, as a mechanism of reproduction for particular authority relationships. In the case of the Soviet state, international victories not only have a political resonance at home and abroad, they also serve to legitimate authority relationships committed to greater rationality in all aspects of life.

The emphasis upon the high performance program, especially since the U.S.S.R. joined the I.O.C. in 1951, has, however, introduced a new pattern of ascription, namely, ability. The quest for the "record" requires increased funding for research, coaching, facilities, etc., while improvement becomes progressively harder to attain. Consequently, there is a growing separation between participants and potential champions in terms of the activities

in which they engage, their exposure to coaching, and the
opportunity for participation. To participate means engaging
in a few mass sports, tourism, but most commonly the G.T.O.
program.[31] To engage in sports implies working through the
sport classification system, striving for ever-improving
performances which will ultimately result in an international
Master of Sport ranking. Social and material incentives
accrue as long as there is continued success, either as an
athlete or a coach; success which is measured in linear terms:
greater productivity, intensity and rationalization of athletic
labour. In this regard, those with ability must receive
preferential treatment and it might be added, reproduce and
legitimate an authority relationship which allows a political
elite to exert their authority as the "Vanguard of the
Proletariat".

Throughout this paper, I have built my argument on the
thesis of Max Weber which suggest that a legal/rational
bureaucracy is virtually indispensable for the creation of
modern industrial capitalism and that even in a socialist state
with its planned economy, there is not only a need but an
increased growth of this rationalized apparatus. This is a
fact of the Soviet Union which cannot be denied but how it is
interpreted is of paramount importance. One can adopt a
pessimistic stance and suggest that the growth of impersonal
domination is inevitable under socialism, truly a "new iron
cage of serfdom", in which sport becomes a reproductive agent
for reinforcing this impersonal domination; or one can broach
the subject along the lines of Anthony Giddens in which
rationalization "in the sense of the rational transmutation
of the modern cultural ethos, provides men with the understanding necessary to control 'rationalization' in the sense of the
dominance of technical rationality in social life".
(Giddens, 1973:277, Emphasis added). Sport then could become

an instrument of transformative importance in allowing man
to realize his true potential. Surely the latter must be the
stance to adopt.

NOTES

1.	Since entering Olympic competition in 1952 at the
	Helsinki Games, the U.S.S.R. has been declared the
	unofficial Olympic "points champion" in all but the
	1968 Summer and Winter Games. The popular sports
	periodical Sport v SSSR (No. 9, 1977:22-23) implies
	that this is a result of the large massovost' program
	in the Union Republics. Of the 15 Republics Estonia has
	the greatest participation rate at 23.5 percent while
	Turkmenia is lowest at 16.5 percent. At the same time,
	the former has 101 international master of sport
	athletes while the latter has ten.

2.	For a discussion of the state of Russian industrialization
	in 1917, c.f. Dobb, 1948; Lyashchenko, 1949; McKay, 1970;
	Trotsky, 1971. A well-written popular account of the
	Russian people can be found in Miller, 1973, while Weber,
	1968, specifically deals with the tsarist patrimonial
	apparatus in his theoretical discussions of bureaucracy.

3.	c.f. Weber, 1968:953.

4.	Weber's concept of rationalization is most clearly
	articulated in his essay, "Science as a Vocation",
	Weber, 1948.

5.	For a more complete discussion of the types of authority
	and the basis of legitimacy, c.f. Weber, 1947.

6.	For Weber's particular use of the ideal-type concept for
	research in sociology, c.f. Weber, 1949.

7.	c.f. Weber's essay "Socialism" in Weber, 1970.

8.	For example, Weber's most specific article, "Socialism",
	was delivered in the form of a speech to the Austrian
	Officiers in Vienna, in 1918. c.f. Weber, 1970

9. The most comprehensive account of the Bolshevik Revolution is Carr, 1950 (published im three volumes). Reed, 1919 provides a fascinating account of the first days of Bolshevik rule.

10. c.f. Trotsky, 1971 and McKay, 1970.

11. c.f. Dobb, 1948:94.

12. Lenin reorganized the two institutions in the spring of 1918.

13. Ulam, 1965:438 states that "The fact that so many professional officers of the Tsar were ultimately enlisted in the Red Army cannot be ascribed solely to compulsion or the need for employment and livelihood. There was also the attraction for the military mind of Trotsky's "New Model": an army where professional competence and discipline were to be the ruling considerations." This attraction may also account for the enthusiasm with which NCO's agreed to act as Instructors in the Vsevobuch

14. The following Soviet texts: Stolbov, 1977; Samoukov et al, 1967; Stolbov and Chudinov, 1970; Moskalev and Spasskii, 1967; and the three volumes Entsiklopedicheskii Slovar' po fizicheskoi kul'ture i sport, 1963: edited by G.I. Kukushkin. These have been supplemented by Riordan, 1977, the most comprehensive English language work dealing with sport in the U.S.S.R. as well as the dated (although useful) Morton, 1963, text.

15. For a concise description of the historical development of the British code, c.f. McIntosh, 1968.

16. For Lenin's account of the survival of the tsarist state

bureaucracy, c.f. his recommendation to the Twelfth Party
Congress, "How We Should Reorganize the Workers and
Peasants Inspection" in Lenin and Trotsky, 1975. His
reference to the inability to control the car is found in
the same source in his "Political Report to the Eleventh
Party Congress."

17. This basis for recruitment has now been institutionalized
into the nomenklatura system. For a discussion of the
nomenklatura and its implementation in the physical
culture apparatus c.f. Cantelon, 1972.

18. The All-Union Sports Society Dinamo was established in
1923. This organization, along with the Central Red Army
Sports Club (TsSKA) develops the majority of competitors
who represent the U.S.S.R. in international and Olympic
competition.

19. A Russian anagram for Proletarian Cultural and Educational
Organizations.

20. c.f. Riordan, 1977, for a detailed account of one of the
Socialist workers' game: "Indians, British and Reds."

21. Lenin had pointed out to the Proletkul'tists that "What
is important is not the invention of a new proletarian
culture but the development of the best forms, traditions
and results of existing culture from the viewpoint of
Marxist philosophy." Cited in Riordan, 1977:103.
Emphasis in the original. The movement was abolished and
most of its leaders purged by 1932.

22. This paper is most valuable in that it cites Russian
sources that are not readily available to authors outside
the Soviet Union.

23. It is not being argued that administrative terror is a
    current vehicle to insure efficiency is the norm in the
    state apparatus. However, it cannot be denied that it
    was widely used during the 1930's in order to more
    rapidly transform the orientation of the labour force
    into goal directed activity. Once such an orientation
    was dominant in the work force, it gradually became
    institutionalized as the standard to be met. Contemporary
    members of the labour force consequently strive for
    efficiency not out of terrorist coercion but because
    efficiency is the legitimated norm.

24. The Red Sport International had been organized on June
    22, 1921, in Moscow "to unite all worker and peasant
    gymnastic and sport organizations." It was to be "a
    worthy standard of the proletarian class struggle,
    educating and physically strengthening the working
    masses of the city and countryside." This physical
    development was to be implemented so that the proletarian
    class struggle would include "those who are gifted in
    resistance, physical dexterity, alertness and full of
    determined struggle." (Kukushkin, 1963:42, Vol. II).

25. During the 1930's, this was not the prevalent Party
    attitude towards the Olympic movement. It was condemned
    as a "bourgois" institution and valiant attempts were made
    to attract the international worker movement to the Red
    Sport International. It attracted members of the Canadian
    Worker's Sports Union and the American Workers' Sports
    Union to international events such as the 1931 Berlin
    Spartakiad and the 1937 Antwerp Workers' Olympiad.
    c. f., Kukushkin. Vol. II, 1963 :43.

26. "Stakhanovism and its influence on the Development of Soviet International Sport." Proceedings of the Fourth' Canadian Symposium on the History of Sport and Physical Education, June 25, 1979.

27. Physical culture is described by contemporary Soviet authorities as "a system of physical education (<u>vospitaniya</u>) with special scientific knowledge, the development of sport and levels of sporting achievement; it includes social and personal hygiene, the correct regime of labour and health, utilizing the natural strength of nature - sun, water and air - in the matters of hygiene and the tempering of the organism. In the first days of the existence of the Soviet State, the Communist Party and Soviet leadership attached paramount state significance to the development of physical culture in developing personal health of workers, preparation towards socialist labour and the defence of the Mother-land." (Kukushkin, Vol. III, 1963:226-227).

28. Richard Mandell, 1976, provides an excellent socio-historical discussion of the invention of the sports record.

29. James Riordan, who is the foremost western authority on physical culture in the Soviet Union, has a concise account of the thinking of the Party and State authorities concerning the benefits of the mass fitness program during the Second World War. (c.f. Riordan, 1977:153-160).

30. Since 1952, Soviet Athletes have dominated both the Summer and Winter Olympics. Using the "unofficial" point total, the U.S.S.R. has finished first in every Olympics with the exception of the 1968 Summer and Winter Games.

31. This was first initiated by the <u>Komsomol</u> in 1931. It has undergone a good deal of revision but primarily consists of a number of skills for overall physical development.

REFERENCES

Aron, Raymond, <u>Main Currents in Sociological Thought</u>, in two
    volumes translated by Richard Howard and Helen Weaver.
    Middlesex, England: Penguin Books, 1965.

Baykov, Alexander. <u>The Development of the Soviet Economic</u>
    <u>System: An Essay on the Experience of Planning in the</u>
    <u>U.S.S.R.</u> Cambridge: The University Press, 1946.

Bendix, Reinhard. <u>Max Weber:</u> An Intellectual Portrait.
    London: Methuen and Co., Ltd., 1959.

Bunchuck, M.F. <u>Organizatsiya fizicheskoi kul'turi</u>.
    Moscow: Fizkul'tura i sport, 1972.

Cantelon, Hart. The Political Involvement in Sport in the
    Soviet Union Unpublished M.A. Thesis, University of
    Alberta, Spring, 1972.

Cantelon, Hart. "Stakhonovism and Its Influence on the
    Development of Soviet International Sport." Proceedings
    of the Fourth Canadian Symposium on the History of Sport
    and Physical Education, June 25, 1979.

Dobb, Maurice. <u>Soviet Economic Development Since 1917</u>.
    London: Routledge & Kegan Paul Ltd., 1948.

Dobb, Maurice. <u>Soviet Planning and Labor in Peace and War</u>.
    New York: International Publishers, 1943.

Fisher, Jr. Ralph Talcott. <u>Pattern for Soviet Youth: A</u>
    <u>Study of the Congresses of the Komsomol, 1918-1954</u>
    New York: Columbia University Press, 1959.

Giddens, Anthony. <u>Capitalism and Modern Social Theory: An</u>
    <u>Analysis of the Writings of Max. Durkheim and Max Weber</u>.
    Cambridge: Cambridge University Press, 1971.

Giddens, Anthony. <u>The Class Structure of the Advanced Societies</u>.
    London: Hutchinson University Library, 1973.

Gruneau, Richard S. "Sport, Social Differentiation and Social
    Inequality". in Donald W. Ball and John W. Loy, <u>Sport</u>
    <u>and the Social Order: Contributions to the Sociology</u>
    <u>of Sport</u>. Massachesetts: Addison-Wesley Publishing
    Co., 1975.

Ivonin, V.A. (ed) Sputnik: Fizkul'turnovo Rabotnika
    Moskva: Fizkul'tura i sport, 1972 Excerpts: pp.19-21.
    1. Resolution of the C.C. (R.C.P. b) 13 July, 1925
    2. Resolution of the C.C. (A.U.C.P. b) 23.09.1929
       "About the P.C. Movement"
    3. Resolution: C.C. (A.U.C.P. b) 27-2. 1948
       "Concerning the motion and directive instructions
       of the Party and Gobernment to the Physical
       Culture and Sport Committee Concerning the
       Development of mass physical culture in the rural
       areas and the increased mastery of Soviet
       sportsmen." (EXCERPTS)

Kukushkin, G.I. Entsiklopedicheskii Slovar' pro fizicheskoi
    Kul'ture i Sportu, in three volumes.
    Moscow: Fizkul'tura i sport, 1962

Lenin, V.I. & Trotsky, Leon. Lenin's Fight Against Stalinism
    New York: Pathfinder Press, 1975. Edited with an
    introduction by Russel Bloch

Lyashchenko, Peter I. History of the National Economy of
    Russia to the 1917 Revolution. translated by L.M. Herman.
    New York: The MacMillan Co., 1949.

McIntosh, P.C., Dixon, J.G., Munrow, A.D. and Willetts, A.F.
    Landmarks in the History of Physical Education.
    London: Routledge and Kegan Paul, 1957.

McIntosh, P.C. Sport in Society
    London: C.A. Watts & Co., Ltd., 1968.

McKay, John Pioneers for Profit: Foreign Entrepreneurship
    and Russian Industrialization 1885-1913.
    Chicago: University of Chicago Press, 1970.

Mandell, Richard. "The Invention of the Sports Record."
    Stadion Vol II (No. 2) 1976. pp.250-264.

Marcuse, Herbert. Soviet Marxism: A Critical Analysis.
    London: Routledge & Kegan Paul, 1958.

Markus, B.L. "The Stakhanov Movement and the Increased
    Productivity of Labour in the U.S.S.R." International
    Labour Review Vol XXXIV (July-Dec., 1936) pp. 5-33.

Miller, Wright. Who are the Russians?: A History of the
    Russian People.
    London: Faber and Faber, 1973.

Mommsen, Wolfgang J. The Age of Bureaucracy: Perspectives
    on the Political Sociology of Max Weber.
    Oxford: Basil Blackwell, 1974.

Morton, Henry W. Soviet Sport: Mirror of Soviet Society.
    London: Collier Books, 1963.

Moskalev, V.M. and Spasskii, O.D. Sport i Vek Moscow:
    Fizkul'tura i Sport, 1967.

Reed, John. Ten Days that Shook the World.
    New Hork: International Publishers, 1919.

Riordan, James. "Political Functions of Soviet Sport: With
    Reference to Ritual and Ceremony." Stadion, Vol. III
    (No. 1), 1977, pp. 148-172.

Riordan, James. Sport in Soviet Society: Development of
    Sport and Physical Education in Russia and the USSR.
    Cambridge: Cambridge University Press, 1977.

Riordan, James. Why Sport Under Communism?: The 'Physical
    Culture vs Sport' Debate After the Russian Revolution.
    Unpublished paper, n.d.

Samoukov, F.I., Stolbov, V.V. and Toropov, N.I.
    Fizicheskaya Kul'tura i sport v SSSR.
    Moscow: Fizkul'tura i sport, 1967.

Stalin, J.V. The Foundations of Leninism: Lectures
    Delivered at the Sverdlov University.
    Peking: Foreign Languages Press, 1965.

Stolbov, V.V. Istoriya Fizicheskoi Kul'turi i Sport.
    Moscow: Fizkul'tura i sport, 1977.

Stolbov, V.V. and Chudinov, I.G. Istoriya Fizicheskoi
    Kul'turi Moscow: Fizkul'tura i sport, 1970.

Trotsky, Leon. 1905. Hamondsworth England: Penguin Books,
    1971.

Ulam, Adam B. The Bolsheviks New York, Collier Books, 1965.

Weber, Max. Economy & Society: An Outline of Interpretive
    Sociology. 3 Vol. Edited by Guenther Roth and Claus
    Wittich. New York: Bedminste Press, 1968.

Weber, Max. <u>From Max Weber: Essays in Sociology</u>. translated, Edited and with an introduction by H.H. Gerth and C. Wright Mills.
London: Routledge & Leyon Paul Ltd., 1948.

Weber, Max. <u>On Law in Economy and Society</u>. Edited and annotated by Max Rheinstein. Translated by Edward Shils and Max Rheinstein.
New York: Simon and Schuster, 1954.

Weber, Max. <u>The Methodology of the Social Sciences</u>. Translated and Edited by Edward A. Shils and Henry A. Finch.
New York: The Free Press, 1949.

Weber, Max. <u>The Protestant Ethic and the Spirit of Capitalism</u>: The Relationships Between Religion and the Economic and Social Life in Modern Culture. Translated by Talcott Parsons.
New York: Charles Scribner's Sons, 1958.

Weber, Max. <u>The Theory of Social and Economic Organization</u>. Translated by A.M. Henderson and Talcott Parsons. Edited with an introduction by Talcott Parsons.
New York: The Free Press, 1947.

Weber, Max. <u>The Interpretation of Social Reality</u>. Edited and with an introductory essay by J.E.T. Eldridge.
London: Michael Joseph, 1970.

9

Sport and the Soviet State

Response to Morton and Cantelon

James Riordan

I think it deserves to be said that Henry Morton is a pioneer in Soviet sport for English speaking audiences and, indeed, he has helped to smooth the way for Hart and myself and other people who have come later.[1] In this sense he very much deserves the respect and gratitude of all of us for what he has done. I think also that a pioneer has serious responsibilities and obligations in creating as clear and true a picture as possible and it is here that I part company with Henry for I feel he has created a whole set of myths about Soviet sport that may well be comforting to many westerners, but in fact may actually have retarded our understanding of the role and place of sport in Soviet society.

It reinforces our prejudices to form a picture of Soviet society, for example, by reading Solzhenitsyn and by not reading even one non-dissident Soviet writer. Indeed, if you ask most people present, or if you ask your students what Soviet writers they have actually read who have written since 1917, you know the answer you are likely to get. The kinds of myths that Henry has presented enable us to discourage any of our students of physical education or sociology from actually learning Russian to see what the Russians themselves are actually writing about in the field of sport. And, it is all very nice and cosy. If things are just as bad or, indeed, even worse in the Soviet Union we don't have to question western institutions or values or we don't have to fight for change.

Well, I think that the main thrust of Henry's argument is that Soviet leaders have built up a red sport machine to win success and prestige at home and abroad and I certainly agree that this is an important factor. It is clear that the pattern of foreign sports competition involving the USSR has closely followed the course of Soviet foreign policy. With the control of the sports system, the Soviet leadership has been able to mobilize resources to achieve maximum efficiency in its sports challenge, hence to perform what it believes to be paramount political functions. While sport in the west is by no means free of politics or foreign policy aims, in a planned society like that of the USSR, sport clearly occupies a focal position and its functions and inter-relationships with a political system are more manifest than in western societies.

I would argue that the Soviet Union has demonstrated that the highest realization of human potential can be most effectively achieved through the planned application of a society's resources. It has attained this goal in sport and in many other fields of human endeavour, for example, in musicianship, and its achievements have been motivated by the deliberate and quite plausable intention of demonstrating the superiority of its system. In general, in the western world the whipping up of popular fervor in sport has, by accident or by design, often resulted in the sacrifice of the sporting and the Olympic ideal on the altar of national or ethnic chauvinism. In the USSR, thanks partly to the multi-national population that both Henry and Hart mentioned, this has been largely avoided; it is not some innate ethnic or national superiority that has been seen to triumph, but a political system. So the Soviet leaders, I agree, see sport as important in terms of prestige and moral leadership.

Yet, I personally don't see this as necessarily sinister or, indeed, as greatly different from the aims of the sport of western states. But, in any case, it is just one factor in Soviet sports policy and its relationship to the state. As Henry has said, and Hart said afterwards, Soviet domination began in 1952. The USSR joined the International Olympic

Committee in 1951. So I have to ask what the motivating
factor was in the thirty five years prior to 1952. It may
be flattering to some Americans that the whole period from
1917 was devoted to building up Soviet sports eventually to
defeat the USA, but I think this is too facile. Such a
view avoids any real examination of the role of sport in the
USSR and how it differs from western sports developments.
Soviet sport would seem important, I think, for a number of
very important reasons that apply to virtually all developing
societies; for health, for hygiene, for defence, for
patriotism, for integration, for productivity, for international recognition, even for nation building. And, this
experience of sports development, by the way, may have more
relevance to cultural revolutions in the emergent nations of
Asia, Africa and Latin America than does our own. In societies
of scarcity and societies striving to build a new life from
illiterate and impoverished peasant populations, western
commercialized sports on the one hand, and the gentlemanly
sport for sports sake on the other, may be looked on as
entirely unsuitable even immoral. Sport, or physical culture
as it's known in the USSR, may indeed be used as a means of
social change, not simply a weapon with which to defeat one's
ideological opponent.

The second point that I would like to make concerns the
speculation on the decline in Soviet sport fortunes. I rather
put this in the same category as the western press's
obsession with the impending death of Mr. Brezhnev. It could
be indeed that sport in the Soviet Union may spread its
international success and move into rugby and baseball and
American football and field hockey and motor racing and golf.
If the Japanese can do so, I don't see why the USSR can't.
But let's concentrate on what we know and not use speculation
as a substitute for serious study.

People in the West have a penchant for speculating about the Soviet Union and this penchant seems reflected in the number of unsubstantiated remarks I have heard here regarding Soviet sports. I think it is comforting also to equate the negative features of western sport with Soviet sport and there is no doubt that Soviet sport has its share of problems. But the comparison is very misleading. It avoids the fundamental differences that exist in Soviet sport and western sport; in Soviet sports development and western sports development. Can we really compare the commercialization of some western sports with a system that has no basis for exploitation based on private profit; or can we compare the star obsession of the western mass media with the Soviet press, TV and radio which are generally free of this obsession; or the treatment of women; or the high priced private clubs and even expensive public sports centres, with the free trade union sports societies of the Soviet Union; or the actual or simulated violence of some western sports; or the often evasive money stakes for top athletes in the West? Two weeks before I came here by the way, there was a world golf match championship at Wentworth and the winner took home 73,000 Pounds. That is not bad money for just a week's work. Now, this doesn't exist in the USSR and never has been. These and other fundamental differences are obfuscated in the comparison which has been made.

I would like to make two more related points. One example of what I have just mentioned is Henry Morton's treatment of "elitism" which he claims is the primary characteristic of Soviet sport and which works against the equality of sport experiences for the masses. The fact is that he offers no evidence whatsoever for this bold statement. I think it is important here to distinguish between elitism and excellence. Although some Soviet sportsmen enjoy a lifestyle beyond the reach of the common man, nonetheless, there exists a number of strong official and social sanctions (for instance, within the press and trade unions and youth organizations and the sports clubs) that militate against the cult of sport stars and the development of elitism in Soviet sport. On the other hand excellence is unquestionably accepted and given every possible encouragement in all areas of human endeavour. The Soviet Union tends to regard talent in sport like talent in music, or art, or mathematics, or ballet, as meriting special attention from an early age. Talent is nurtured within the state system not in private clubs. It is, therefore, free and open to all. The official view in the USSR is that sporting excellence should be complimentary, even secondary, to sport for all. Indeed there are serious reasons that I have mentioned already why it is considered important to involve citizens of all ages in regular and active physical recreation.

On the whole, people at least in the towns, can and do pursue the sport of their choice using facilities free of charge. To sporting leaders the word "star" is deliberately avoided and athletes are constantly urged to be models of good conduct since their main task is said to be to attract more people into sport. So although it would be naive to assume that all citizens of communist countries are sporting enthusiasts,it's likely the communist athletes do well in world sports, not because they themselves are a privileged elite, but because the society they live in makes the widest possible provision for general participation in sport and the development of sporting skills.

Now to the last point I wanted to make about Henry's paper. Henry argues that Soviet athletes lack the freedom "to see what the markets will pay for their services abroad and are greatly underpaid by western standards". He cites

Ilie Nastase as an example of the freedom that Soviet
athletes lack. I think this point, and the underlying
attitude of it to sport in the Soviet Union, is symptomatic
of our radical differences. There is a certain school of
thought that suggests it is quite right for the richest
countries in the world to buy up world talent and import
it for the delectation of its already pampered consumers.
This indeed is done in America and in Britain and in
Canada and in France; in ice hockey, in soccer and cricket
and in athletics often attracting talent from the economically
depressed nations of Africa, Asia and Latin America. It is
also done, incidentally, in terms of doctors and engineers.

Now, it's undeniably appealing to some individuals to
escape poverty, to escape various restrictions including
political restrictions and the lower standard of living at
home, and make a 'fast buck' in an advanced industrial
western state. I think it is important to recognize,
however, that the once almighty dollar or pound cannot buy
everything it wants, that some governments refuse to permit
this brain drain except to help those countries poorer than
themselves, even that to some athletes, human dignity and
patriotism are more important than selling themselves to
the highest bidder. When Henry says Soviet athletes are
greatly underpaid by western standards, I wonder what
standards he is referring to. Probably those that make the
top western professionals in golf, tennis, baseball and ice
hockey near millionaires while the vast majority of the
competitors get nothing at all - standards that encourage
the type of moral outlook and behaviour precisely associated
with a person like Ilie Nastase who surely will be remembered,
if at all, more for his gross lack of sportsmanship than for
his skills. Well those western standards are not the

standards of everyone in the west and they are not mine.
In fact, I personally would say, "good for the USSR", that
it gets its priorities right in rewarding its sportsmen.
I am not saying that the top Soviet athletes don't get
'perks' as Henry has rightly said. They do receive cash,
though by no means the sort of earnings of western athletes;
they receive a town apartment, high prestige, travel at
home and abroad, but it would be a mistake to ignore
another set of considerations; the motivation that produces
a mixture of self discipline, patience, dedication,
patriotism, a genuine desire to do well for the good of
one's team, one's people, and one's country. Many westerners
conditioned to seeing money values as the stimulus to
sacrifice find this aspect of an athletes' motivation hard
to understand, but in a country where a sportsman owes his
allegiance to the community rather than to a private club
or institution, and where a successful athlete is rewarded
and respected by the country he represents, patriotism can
indeed be a strong motivating force. So I suggest that we
try not to look at the USSR through 'red white and blue'
eyes, not to impose the worst values of western sport upon
the Soviet Union, but rather to study Soviet sport with an
open mind; to try to understand it as an agent of social
change in a developing society which is fundamentally
different, despite certain superficial similarities, from
western societies and their development.

Now, as far as Hart is concerned, he differs both
from Henry and myself in being a physical educationist who
has come to Russian studies.[2] As we know, it is very
difficult to understand the sport of the country if one
doesn't understand the soul of that nation, the history,
the social background. He has learned Russian and been to
the USSR several times and turned himself into a student of

Soviet society. I think his paper personally is a serious
comparative study of Soviet sport; an attempt to set it in
a sociological framework. It is to my mind an interesting
and perceptive study. But I have a dilemma and I better
state my dilemma and my bias right away. I, as other
people have said in the other direction, am not a Weberian
and I find it hard to take issue with a set of ideas whose
very premises I reject.

It is a brave thing to apply Weber to a society whose
ideology is at least instantiably based on Marxism. What
I think is unfortunate is that Weber is used generally to
disprove Marx without quoting Marx and using Weber's and
others' interpretations of Marxism to demonstrate its
limitations. Marx and Marxists never have claimed that
socialism in its early stages means the end of bureaucracy
or even the beginning of complete freedom. Only in the
future when certain prerequisites have been satisfied and
complete communism has been achieved will the realm of
freedom be reached and the withering away of the state
bureaucracy begin. No communist leaders in the world today
will claim that they have got any where near that ideal
society. What I'm saying really to Hart is that I think
that the legal-rational bureaucracy in the Soviet Union may
be a different quality that the legal-rational bureaucracy
in western society.

I'd like to take issue with Hart, and Weber too, that
the actions of the Soviet leaders have been altogether
motivated by rationality. Indeed much of Stalinism was
entirely irrational. It is the over-riding theme of Hart's
paper that the Soviet regime is committed to greater
rationality in all aspects of life, including sports, and
here I think it is important to distinguish between the

273

actions of the Soviet government and the actions of the communist party. One is concerned with executing policies and running the country efficiently, the other is, if you like, an ideological conscience or ideological watchdog concerned also with the long term goal of building a communist society. So the party is constrained by moral judgements.

In sport, I think, a rational decision has obviously been taken or was taken after the last war to demonstrate the superiority of the Soviet version of communism through sports victories over the west, particularly over the leading western states. The sports committee has the task of carrying this policy out in the most rational way possible, but the party often intervenes in a way that cuts across the rational execution of this policy. I think it has done so, for example, in or over the apartheid situation. The Soviet Union has withdrawn and indeed often has not taken part in competitions where it could have demonstrated its superiority because of its abhorence of apartheid. I think it has also done so in the case of professional boxing and wrestling which it has never (for certain ideological reasons) gone into, or at least stopped as soon as the revolution occurred. I think the non-rational character of Soviet sport can also be seen in the late development of sports boarding schools. One sees how they developed in the German Democratic Republic in 1949, the very year of the foundation of that state. In the USSR it wasn't until the early fifties that they began, haltingly, to develop in the USSR, partly because of the ideological dilemma that the party was in about their development. I think the non-rational side of Soviet sport is also evident in the emphasis on mass sport. I think it is evident in the cooperation with (and the aid to) other socialist countries

274

and developing societies in Africa, Asia and Latin America. At the same time I see much that is irrational in capitalism such as unemployment and inflation, the investment by big business in South Africa rather than at home, the pouring of billions of dollars or pounds into the bottomless pit of the armaments industry.

The last point I want to make is that in looking for sport success in terms of an efficient bureaucracy one tends to obscure the fundamental differences between Soviet and western sports systems. One also diverts attention from other important considerations that I mentioned in discussing Henry Morton's paper. I would certainly agree with Hart that the dominant pattern of organized sport in any society tends to dramatize the major values and requirements of that society and constitutes part of a sometimes highly elaborate apparatus for its legitimation. Indeed, I would maintain that the dominant pattern of sport in western societies is very much a microcosm of western society. Sport is a source of profit, something to package up and sell, a medium for football pools in Britain and betting shops, cigarette advertising and the booming sportswear and equipment industry as well as being a distraction for the populace, a new opiate of the people; a piece of the Hollywood dream factory; pop music and the sex scandal; the sport tittle tattle of much of the mass media promoting a vicarious and largely fantastical experience. I agree with Hart about all of this . Hart didn't exactly say this but I agree with him anyway. Its always a good ploy of mine to agree with people when you're actually putting your own views forward and imposing them on them. But he did say, and I agree with him, that sport helps to insure conformity with the consensual status quo. However, it is essential to distinguish between this and the development of sports in Soviet state socialist society.

I think the Soviet leaders have consistently affirmed
their allegiance to Marxism and Leninism in general. They
adhere to a number of Marxist goals in respect to recreation
in particular, emphasizing the provision of recreation for
all in the need for the new Soviet person, the builder of
communism, to have every opportunity for harmoniously
combining spiritual wealth, moral purity and perfect physique,
a healthy mind and a healthy body for everyone. But party
affirmation not withstanding, actual practices often diverge
substantially from official theory in the USSR, and the
forms of recreation which have developed in the Soviet
society have not coincided with the prediction of Marxist
writers about playful activities in the society of the
future. As far as recreation is concerned the reasons for
the divergence between ideals and practice may be assumed
to parallel those in other areas of life. In the early
post-revolutionary period, as Hart referred to, genuine
efforts were made by certain future-oriented groups to move
in the direction foretold by Marx. But, as Hart was saying,
Civil War and national poverty made them impossible to bring
to fruition and from the late 1920's command over the
repressive state apparatus, disposal of material resources
and sources of information were in no real sense under
popular control. Rather, they were in the hands of members
of the leading group, in the ruling party which, in the
absence of help from the revolution in the industrial west,
was pursuing a policy of building a strong nation state
using these instruments of power.

Now some Marxists might argue that the fetishization
of recreation in the form of competitive sport, which indeed
offers vast opportunities for the manipulation of peoples,

is one of a number of defects of a society in transition to communism, still stamped with the birthmarks of the old society from whose womb it emerges, as Marx put it. Such defects might be regarded as inevitable as long as the individual still remains subordinate to the division of labour; as long as an antipathy exists between mental and manual labour; as long as labour is primarily a means of livelihood; as long as the forces of production are at too low a level to permit the all round development of the individual; that is, as long as the USSR remains at the first stage of communist society. We might speculate further on whether, given Russia's overall backwardness in 1917, any road to socialism other than a state which pro-longed bureaucratically-enforced development would be possible. We might also speculate whether Russian society is even yet ripe for genuinely socialist or communist human relations, including those of free recreation, and whether, the original social goals can have remained uncontaminated in the minds of any leaders given the class or the elite differentiation actually involved in the process of bureau-cratic state socialist construction.

It is here, perhaps, that we should seek the key to an understanding of the fetishism of sport developed in the USSR as I think Hart has done this. In western society the fetishism of sport was a consequence of market factors, offering the possibilities of profit making and turning out, characteristically, without any conscious purpose of intent, to be a highly appropriate means of distracting the masses from class conscious politicization. In Soviet society it characteristically resulted from centralized planning and administration designed to subordinate areas of social life, such as sport, to the political and economic tasks of building a strong state.

I think this distinction is very important in terms
of the potential dynamics of the two systems. It is certainly
true that the actions of the Communist Party leadership
often appear contradictory. On the one hand their policies
reinforce the fetishism of sport by an increasing stress on
international success and on the training of even faster,
stronger and more skillful professional sportsmen in an ever
growing range of highly organized institutionalized sports.
At the same time, the false consciousness of the mass of
people is reinforced through a cultivated obsession with mass
produced media-oriented spectator sports. On the other hand
the Party leadership is increasing the amount of free time
available to people, providing an ever wider range of
amenities and equipment for citizens to pursue recreational
activities of their choice. It is encouraging people to be
active participants rather than passive spectators and is
increasing opportunities for individuals to enjoy recreational
activities in a non-institutional setting: fishing, hiking,
rock climbing, boating, pot holing, water skiing, horse-
back riding and skin diving. They even tell me that golf
and certainly squash are now being developed in the USSR.

It is too early to prophecy which trend will prevail.
There has been no obvious sign in the field of recreation of
a movement towards transparent demystified social relationships. At the same time no fundamental obstacles such as
excessive commercialism exist to prevent recreational
activities from being liberated from fetishism and
manipulation so that they will become freely chosen and
pursued for their inherent pleasure rather than for the
utilitarian ends that Hart was talking about quite rightly.
As some Marxists would argue, the profound cultural
revolutionary changes of this sort could be brought about

in Soviet conditions by comparatively minor political
changes. New men at the top; (I have to use the word men
because there aren't any women at the top of the Party in
the Soviet Union.) Others would incline to a view that
the present course is more systemic, all possible candidates
for the leadership having common class or quasi-class
relations to the means of production different from the masses
and so resulting in vested interests in the status quo.
Whatever the interpretation of the present and perspectives
for the future, we should make fundamental distinctions
between the pattern, the purpose and the place of sport in
socialist and capitalist societies.

NOTES AND REFERENCES

1. See Morton, Henry W., _Soviet Sport: Mirror of Soviet Society_, New York: Collier Books, 1963.

2. See Cantelon, Hart, _The Social Reproduction of Sport: A Weberian Analysis of the Rational Development of Ice Hockey Under Scientific Socialism in the Soviet Union._ Ph.d. dissertation, University of Birmingham, 1981.

10
Sport, Dependency and the Canadian State

Bruce Kidd

"To achieve higher levels of participation and fitness, and excellence in sport, will be of great value both for the image we have of ourselves and for our national spirit".

-- Iona Campagnolo, _Green Paper on Sport_, Oct. 1977.

"Once again, Americans have taught us what it means to be a Canadian".

-- Fred Mooney, _The Toronto Clarion_, Oct. 3, 1979.
apropos of the excitement generated by the
Montreal Expos' drive to the pennant.

Despite the idealist's hope (and many participant's perception) that forms of sport are separate, and represent a "respite" from everyday reality, each of these cultural forms carries within it the typing or "genetic stamp" of the mode of production and particularly the social relations of the society or societies in which it is created and played. Whatever the extent to which forms of sport become reified and take on a semi-autonomous existence, we must never forget that they were created, and then elaborated, redesigned and streamlined by groups of humans in specific human societies: these innovators and players -- the George Beers, Bobby Orrs, and Al Eaglesons -- could not dream up or improvise their contests, rules, norms, favourite "plays" and associated mythologies on any other basis than from their own experience. Thus, we can see in the amateur code, which continues to have force even today in sports like track and field, the vestiges of an attempt a century ago by the largely aristocratic and bourgeois ruling groups in sport to limit working class participation, an attempt which both reinforced and drew inspiration from similar confrontations in virtually every sphere of economic, political and cultural life. We can see in the nineteenth-century prohibitions against Indian athletes in Canada, in part, a specific statement of the widespread belief that the native peoples were innately different from "civilized" whites and therefore had to be banished to reservations in marginal areas.[1] It is for this reason that forms of sport can play such a significantly ideological role: despite their seeming innocence -- they invariably contain within them statements about social relations, which in turn serve to reinforce or, as the case may be, contest the dominant social relations or arrangements of power. These statements tend to encourage some kinds of behaviour and discourage others. Thus the amateur code, with its eloquent affirmation of participation for participation's sake, has not only served to exclude many talented working class athletes, but also to discourage its many adherents from questioning the ethical basis of wage labour under capitalism and from even demanding full remuneration from the sports entrepreneurs or governments for whom they toil.[2] To the extent that beliefs acquired and elaborated through sport are transferred by participants to their other activities, the entire inter-connected system of social relations, including under capitalism, wage labour, political beliefs, and even the teaching of the social sciences in universities, is reinforced, further developed, or contested.

Previous papers in this volume, have discussed the inter-relationships between sport, the state, class and the logic of production in advanced state monopoly capitalism. In this paper, I would like to explore the ideological role of sport, as it is affected by the state, in connection with the question of nationalism or independence. Specifically, I will consider the role that forms of sport have played in the disintegration of English-speaking Canada as a distinct national community. Although "nation" can never be separated from "class", it will be instructive to study sport as ideology from this perspective.

Let us briefly consider the interrelationships between forms of sport and national communities. By "nation", I mean an ethnic community with certain specific characteristics: a common language, territory and economic life, a common culture and sense of identity. It is not necessarily synonymous with a nation-state.[3] Those of you familiar with Canadian history and political affairs will readily recognize this terminology. Both Quebec and the Dene are "nations", although neither have formed their own nation-states. English-speaking Canada is also a "nation" in this sense, although it's becoming more difficult to define its unique characteristics. Perhaps this distinction is clearest in the present referendum debate in Quebec -- both René Lévesque and Claude Ryan are in agreement that Quebec is a "nation"; they differ on what is its best relationship to the present Canadian state.

In the capitalist era, forms of sport have often strengthened or accelerated the development of national communities, especially those which become nation-states. This is a well-argued thesis. Roland Barthes, to take one example, contends in his National Film Board essay, Of Sport and Men, that many games not only express national characteristics, but do so in a way that enables people to discover and articulate these characteristics for themselves. Hockey captures both the passion, and the struggle of life in the Canadian winter; La Tour de France is a catechism of the geographical and cultural majesty of France.[4] Although many of these sports are now played -- and refashioned -- by other national communities, distinctive styles are still very much in evidence, as Soviet Hockey, Brazilian samba soccer, and West Indian cricket dramatically attest. In

some cases, forms of sport served to express and solidify
the idea of a national community well before it enjoyed
common political boundaries. The Turner movement which
grew out of the gymnastics curriculum of Friedrich Ludwig
Jahn after the Prussian defeat by Napoleon in 1799,
consciously articulated the aspirations of pan-German
unity, even during 23 years of state prohibition. Although
this movement would later be appropriated by both the left
and the right -- the workers' sports movement and the Nazis
-- in many of the feudal German principalities in the nineteenth century, it was simultaneously an expression of the
liberal bourgeoisie. In 1848, when the Prussian Emperor
invaded Hesse to put down the provisional government
declared by the Frankfurt Assembly, it was the Turners who
first sprang -- unsuccessfully, it turned out -- to the
defense of the fledgling republic.

Forms of sport have contributed to the development of
national culture in at least one other significant way:
by providing a format -- international competition -- in
which the national community can be symbolically represented.
Pierre de Coubertin was right: the prospect of national
victories in sport has proven to be a powerful stimulus,
to which the survival of the modern Olympics, despite many
problems, is striking testimony. To the extent that these
performances developed and reinforced beliefs in the national
community, they served to strengthen and buttress a whole
range of economic and social policies and behaviours, from
protective tariffs, selective purchasing and hiring to the
explicit concern with autonomy. In Canada, long before its
respective national communities could win complete autonomy
in political affairs, the English-speaking community, and
particularly the professional classes of Montreal and the

manufacturing centres in southern Ontario, avidly sought to articulate a national interest in the growing accomplishments of Canadian athletes. In the 1880s, Ned Hanlan won a string of sculling races that, in the approving words of the Toronto Globe, "carried the name of Canada around the world". Hanlan was better known than Prime Minister Macdonald and his victories were widely perceived to be an example of the growing strength of the young Dominion.[5] The career of Tom Longboat, the Onondaga marathoner who was the most famous athlete in the land in the decade prior to World War I, is also instructive. Throughout his life, Longboat would be smeared by the charge that he never trained, that he exhibited -- in the words of the Globe -- "all the way- wardness and lack of responsibility of his race."[6] But when he won against runners from other countries, he would be toasted as an example of Canadian courage and determination. "This man Longboat has done more to help the Commissioner of Industries than any other Canadian," a Toronto City Controller told the press the day after Longboat's victory in the 1907 Boston marathon.[7] Increasingly, the state has been active in fostering sport as a symbol of the national community. The first such attempts came during WWI when the army staged a number of exhibitions and competitions in an effort to stimulate recruiting and arouse the patriotism of Canadian soldiers.[8] In recent years, the most prevalent form of state intervention has been direct and indirect subsidization of national teams.[9]

Many people today, on both the left and the right, regard nationalism as a restrictively conservative, if not a reactionary force,[10] and to the extent to which the slow-to-change forms of sport reinforce it, particularly in cases of hegemonic national communities, they regard

sport as inherently reactionary as well.[11] But we should
not conclude that forms of sport are necessarily conservative,
that they can never serve as an outlet or part crucible for
progressive ideas, or what Rick Gruneau calls the "transformative power of play". According to C.L.R. James'
account of cricket in the West Indies, Beyond a Boundary,
the black players' struggle for full recognition on
representative teams selected and dominated by white colonial
administrators ebbed and flowed in counterpoint harmony with
the larger struggle for independence until in Trinidad it
finally broke out in riot in early 1960 and gave the
independence movement the final push to remove all remaining
forms of colonial rule.[12] Forms of sport are much less
suited to the expression of conflict, as John Hargreaves and
Rob Beamish have argued, but they have and can express
progressive ideas as well as conservative ones.

Like other ideological forms, forms of sport not only
reinforce certain categories in the mode of production, but
also challenge or question them. In each of the examples
already cited, the ideas about national community spread
through sport gradually supplanted ideas that reinforced
kinship, feudal and regional practices and institutions.
What can be described in approving terms as articulation,
development and reinforcement can simultaneously be described
as denial, under-development, and subversion. Although the
native peoples of Canada once enjoyed a wide variety of
highly developed games, they gradually altered -- and in
many cases, eventually abandoned -- these games and the
beliefs which accompanied them in the face of the pressure
and encouragement to do so from the more numerous and
economically advanced white invaders. At the international
level, the two faces of this single process are imperialism

and disintegration.[13]

Few generations in English-speaking Canadian history
have not puzzled over the distinct nature of their national
identity: apart from our now challenged ability to subjugate
Quebec, what is it that we share that defines us as a nation?
Whatever the disagreement about the national characteristics,
there is now little debate that many common economic patterns,
political institutions, and cultural forms are rapidly
disintegrating with the advance of American and other forms
of state monopoly capital, with the result that in each of
these spheres, groups of Canadians are losing control over
the forces shaping their lives. The examples are well known.
What's so terrifying is that the details indicate further
deterioration every day. The economy has never emerged from
its reliance upon staple exports as the leading sector,
leaving it vulnerable not only to the boom and bust cycles
necessitated by the size of investment in staple extraction,
but the fluctuating prices characteristic of international
commodity markets. Foreign control of the strategic, non-
renewable oil and gas resource, and the political influence
associated with that control, has exacerbated inter-regional
tensions and has militated against a two-tier price system
for Canadian products that could stimulate Canadian
manufacturing. (U.S. producers and consumers get Canadian
oil from $6.00 to $9.00 per barrel below the world price.)
On the eve of this conference, the Governor of the Bank of
Canada told a House of Commons committee he had no choice
but to raise interest rates -- now a record 14 per cent --
in step with an earlier increase by U.S. banks. Culturally,
U.S. books, periodicals, films, television sit-coms and
musical entertainers so dominate Canadian stores, libraries,
radio and television stations, and theatres that many

Canadians recognize U.S. authors and entertainers more readily than our own. At last year's hearings on the renewal of the CBC's radio and television license, a commissioner of the CRTC, the national regulating agency, asked CBC President Al Johnson: "Do you really believe, Mr. Johnson, that the average citizen in this country really wants to be a Canadian?" Johnson, to his credit, answered in the affirmative,[14] but the question illustrates the extent to which "English-Canadian" has become a minority culture. Politically, the federal Liberals were long able to govern Canada by adroitly mediating between popular and nationally articulated needs and aspirations and American state monopoly capital,[15] but as that task has become increasingly difficult, if not impossible, they were defeated in May. The new government threatens to dismantle even more of the institutions which Canadians have tried to manage for their benefit as a national community.

In sport, the styles of play, norms of behaviour and team loyalties which once combined to enunciate a national sense of identity have now become co-opted by the very forces that seek to undermine it. Consider the case of hockey, the game Al Purdy once called "the Canadian specific", Ralph Allen, "the national religion". In 1926, Conn Smythe purchased the Toronto St. Pats from a syndicate of mining entrepreneurs headed by J.P. Bickell. Smythe had heard that Bickell's group was planning to sell the team to a partnership in Philadelphia for $200,000. He raised $160,000 and approached Bickell. "How can you, a group of loyal Canadians, sell the team to the United States?" he is alleged to have told Bickell. Smythe got the team for $160,000. Renamed the Toronto Maple Leafs, the team quickly became a highly visible symbol for English-speaking Canada. During the 1930s, its

games -- against Quebec's national team, Les Canadiens, and
representative teams from several U.S. cities -- were broadcast live on the growing national radio network, and as a
result of this, shrewd public relations, and the ruthless
buying and selling of players, the Leafs gradually replaced
prominent local and regional teams in the loyalties of
English-speaking Canadians. During one playoff game against
Detroit, Hockey Night in Canada is said to have drawn more
than six million listeners, almost three quarters of the
entire English-speaking population. But the Leafs not only
created new national loyalties, particularly in the estranged
prairie provinces, the team also encouraged beliefs which
would ultimately undo the sense of national identity it had
created. The commodity market in players, which it visibly
engaged in and celebrated during the radio intermissions on
the Hot Stove Lounge, seriously qualified the community
loyalty that could be developed by representative teams.
Athletes and spectators were still expected to go all out
for "their" team, but if its composition could be arbitrarily
changed and local players replaced by players from another
region -- or today, from another continent -- it suggested
that the community didn't really have much to boast or care
about. If the majority of players could only find playing
jobs across the border, to the extent that local fans
transferred their loyalties to New York, Chicago, Detroit
and Boston, the national symbolism expressed by hockey was
further divided. Lead operations undercut the sense of
national community in further ways. Its hockey broadcasts
were sponsored by Imperial Oil -- one of the most successful
early attempts to give imperialism a Canadian face -- and
the mass audiences they created provided markets for a string
of American radio shows, from the racist Amos and Andy to

the progressive Mercury Theatre of Orson Welles. The state
played a not unimportant role in this process -- the creation
of the CBC and the abdication of editorial control of Hockey
Night in Canada to McLaren's Advertising gave the national
radio network to commercial hockey in the 1930s. During
WW2, the exemptions it provided individual hockey players
and teams travelling across the border kept the NHL in
operation while its competitors in the Canadian Amateur
Hockey Association were forced to fold. By the war's end,
with its influence and economic power, the NHL was able to'
reduce the CAHA to what Gordon Juckes called the "Gold Coast
slave farm of hockey", with the control of rules, revenues,
style of play, player development, and even the national
team entered in international tournaments firmly in its
hands.[16]

Two aspects of this process warrant emphasis. In his
ideological history of advertising in the 1920s, Captains of
Consciousness, Stuart Ewan shows how young people were
systematically singled out as advertising targets in the
attempt to transform them into models -- teachers -- for
the new patterns of consumption. For those who believe the
ruling class doesn't have an explicit strategy for social
control, the book provides powerful evidence to the contrary.[17]
The extent to which the NHL had a consciously ideological
marketing strategy still must be determined, but the
player cards, team sweaters, special bank accounts and other
widely advertised souvenirs all contributed to the weakening
of a national sense in hockey-playing youth. Long before
multi-national brand logos became a popular decoration on
clothes -- another indication of the extent to which western
peoples have internalized their role as commodities --
generations of Canadian boys grew up wearing (and never
taking off) sweaters celebrating the cities of another country,

while living in ignorance of their own. Secondly, while these processes were shaped in step with similar changes -- the continuing penetration of U.S. capital, and the concomitant shift in exports from east-west to north-south -- they did not simply mirror or reflect these other changes, they interacted with them with a force of their own. They reinforced each other, together accelerating the disintegration of the beliefs and practices which had once supported and nurtured autonomous Canadian institutions.

Of course, explanation lies neither in U.S. expansion nor national betrayal, but in the dynamics of capital. Once sport became a sphere of commodity production, a process supported from the very beginning by the state, then it was almost inevitable that the best Canadian hockey would be controlled by the richest and most powerful aggregates of capital and sold in the richer and more populous markets of the U.S. The disappearance of community control over Canadian hockey strengthened a much larger process -- the centralization of all popular forms of culture.

The case of Canadian football is distinctly different, but the ultimate impact very similar. Its early development -- the articulation and continuous amendment of rules, the design and redesign of strategies and plays, equipment -- was largely in the hands of the southern Ontario and English-speaking Montreal professional classes, centered around the universities and private clubs. But when its adherents tried to transform it into a national game with uniform rules from coast to coast, it became the object of long and bitter intersectional disputes, in the course of which the western representatives, always aided by one or two eastern mavericks, were successful in streamlining the rules in ways which encouraged teams to bring in Americans

who had played under similar rules.[18] The first athletic
director of the School of Physical and Health Education at
my own university, for example, came to Toronto after one
such rule change permitted the forward pass. In the warm-
up of his first home game, Stevens threw the first forward
pass ever seen in Toronto. The crowd gave him a standing
ovation and when he retired his fame was such he was
immediately hired by the university. When post-war incomes
permitted the full professionalization of the game and
rational-instrumental norms replaced community ties, the
Americanization became explicit: seasoned U.S. pros, whose
only advantage over their Canadian counterparts was that
they had previously played on a full-time basis, were hired
in increasing numbers. When team management became almost
universally American a decade later, the belief developed
and spread that Canadians were naturally inferior. When
Russ Jackson retired, the Roughriders announced they would
have to look for a replacement in the States, despite the
fact that Jackson played his college football at one of the
weakest teams in Canada. The CFL now has a rule -- now
challenged in the recent Jamie Bone appeal before the Ontario
Human Rights Commission -- which penalizes a team with a
Canadian quarterback. The so-called national championship
Grey Cup is proudly proclaimed by its sponsors as a vehicle
for Canadian unity, but the claim is vitiated by the lowly
status of Canadian players,[19] and its dependence upon and
subordination to U.S. commercial football.[20] There has never
been a truly national English-Canadian game of football,
played on the same basis from coast to coast, directed and
controlled by Canadians.[21] Although the Canadian Amateur
Football Association has begun to fight for greater autonomy --
it no longer uses the CFL rulebook, for instance --

financially, and ideologically, the commercial league effectively controls the game. In every way, it undermines the belief in Canadian independence.

During the last decade, U.S. dominated commercial sport has expanded further into Canada, assisted increasingly by the state. Liquor interests in Montreal and Toronto have brought U.S. baseball franchises to their respective cities, greatly encouraged by federal tax laws, heavily subsidized municipal stadia, and CBC broadcasts. The entrepreneurs enjoy the free advertising from the spillover of the U.S. media, and they also benefit from the development of another symbol for their beverages which can circumvent provincial restrictions on alcohol advertising. In 1974, the federal government did step in to stop the expansion of the now defunct World Football League in Toronto -- "We know what 'world' means," Toronto Alderman Karl Jaffary said at the time -- but the bill in question (which died after second reading when the election was called) neither changed the structure of the CFL, despite the promise to lower entry requirements for teams in other Canadian cities, nor prevented dumping of NFL telecasts by the CBC.[22]

But while the Canadian state has unwittingly assisted the process of cultural disintegration in those sports which have been heavily commercialized, it has attempted to foster the Olympic sports as a symbol for national unity, defined by and equated to the pan-Canadian state. Although the federal government began making financial contributions to national teams in 1920, Mackenzie King told the House of Commons in 1936 that Canadian athletic teams should not be considered as representative of government.[23] This was during the all-too-brief period when Canadian political institutions were not subordinate in any significant way to

those of the United Kingdom or the U.S. At the same time,
Canadians dominated international hockey with ridiculous
ease, enjoying what seemed almost to be an advantage of
natural selection (in the same way the Finns dominated
distance running and javelin throwing during this period,
the English, soccer). But Canadian international hockey
supremacy came to an end in 1954, the result of Soviet
sport science and the depletions of senior hockey by the
war and the NHL. In sports like track and field and
swimming, where Canadians had competed successfully in the
interwar years, they were now falling further and further
behind. The war and its sovereignty-ending defense production
agreement with the U.S., the spread of American television
and the invasion of a new wave of U.S. branch plants all
contributed to another crisis of Canadian identity. In sport,
the Diefenbaker Government's Fitness and Amateur Sport Act
was in part a response.

But the Conservatives' FAS Directorate not only provided
a new source of funds for the national teams fielded by the
volunteer amateur sports governing bodies, it also attempted
to stimulate local sport participation and non-competitive
fitness and recreation, through a program of shared-cost
provincial grants. It continued to leave the responsibility
for the success of national teams in the hands of the sports
governing bodies. It was only with the return of the Liberals
and the ascension of Pierre Trudeau in 1968 that international
success in sport -- as an explicit means of strengthening
national unity -- became stated state policy. With John
Munro at the helm, provincial programs were terminated, non-
competitive programs sharply curtailed, and the level of
spending for what came to be known as "elite" sport
dramatically increased. Although Ottawa did not intend

that Montreal should stage the Olympic Games, after the
award was announced it made a significant contribution to
both operating and construction costs and stepped up its
assistance to national teams. The sports governing bodies
were nominally still in charge, but Sport Canada increasingly
assumed direction and control, to the point that on the eve
of the 1978 Commonwealth Games, the responsible minister, Iona
Campagnolo, announced detailed medal quotas for Canadian
athletes.[24] Few steps were omitted that would enhance
performance, or the desired image of national success. Last
year, Sport Canada subsidized the salaries of at least two
journalists to file regular reports to the Canadian media on
Canadian performances abroad.[25] The latest scheme, an
official told a Toronto conference last spring, is to sub-
sidize the efforts of the national associations in those
sports where success depends upon subjective judging to
pack technical committees and lobby for favourable judges.[26]
The success of these measures was demonstrated by Canadian
successes at the Edmonton Games, several of which were
accompanied by ardent flagwaving and nationalist cheering of
a type never seen before among members of a Canadian team.

It is my contention that the state's assumption of the
direction of these national teams can best be explained in
relation to the crisis of legitimacy which has faced it, the
federal Liberal party and the loose alliance of ind genous
and multi-national capital which supported it, since the
mid-1960s. The Quiet Revolution in Quebec has unleashed a
nationalist sentiment so powerful that a political party
would subsequently be formed, committed -- not to a restructuring of the pan-Canadian state along the lines of
deux nations -- but to a distinct Quebec state. In English-
speaking Canada, the expansion of American imperialism into

even more areas of human existence, the simultaneous erosion
of Canadian autonomy, the stimulus of Quebec nationalism and
the youth radicalization of the 1960s all gave impetus to a
new surge of English-speaking Canadian nationalism. This
movement was divided in several key ways, but it served to
pressure the federal state in both economic and cultural
policy areas. Finally, the growing industrialization,
unemployment, and regional disparity of the 1970s, all in
large part the result of the vulnerability of the Canadian
economy to the multi-nationals, aggravated class tensions.
In this situation, the Liberals adopted as one solution a
long-standing proposal by many in the sports community:
greater state assistance for national teams. Other factors
contributed, to be sure. The support of national teams was
also linked to the staging of international games -- the Pan
Ams in Winnipeg in 1967, the Olympics in 1976, the Commonwealth Games in 1978 -- facility construction for which
provided an important means of capital accumulation for the
construction industry, some short-term employment for
construction workers. In fact, the prospects for capital
accumulation and corporate legitimacy were so great at the
Olympic Games that major multi-nations like GM and Esso, as
well as the large Canadian-controlled companies, "contributed"
in one way or the other to the Games. When a group of
Canadian athletes threatened to boycott the Games if their
demands for increased living allowances were not met, the
Canadian Olympic Association paid the requested grants, not,
in the opinion of the program administrator, because national
pride was at stake, but because the adverse publicity was
hurting Olympic-related sales.[27] In 1978, the COA, now
financed by a trust representing both foreign and domestic
capital -- proposed that donations to national teams be

given tax exemptions at a rate of 125 per cent.[28]

But the success of the Liberals' attempt to solve national, economic, political and cultural discontents by accentuating the role of sport as a symbol of "One Canada" was compromised by the same forces that led it to do so in the first place. The success at events like the Edmonton Games was more than matched by their repeated failure, in the face of continuous NHL opposition, to develop an adequate national hockey team. In the 1960s, the CAHA had tried to develop such a team, but after mixed results, Fitness and Amateur Sport joined with the NHL to kill it. Future national teams became the property of the state-NHL partnership, Hockey Canada. It was only Paul Henderson's last-minute goal which saved Pierre Trudeau from the ignominy of the "goat's" role in the first Canada-Soviet series. Trudeau had been powerless to stop the NHL from banning four WHA players, including Bob Hull, from Team Canada. The effort to make sport a symbol of national vitality has also been compromised by the use of publicly funded Games facilities for U.S. - dominated commercial sport (and not local athletes), its increasing reliance upon multi-national sponsors like Imperial Oil, its inability to fund fully those athletes who are now competing at the inter-national level (so that the Edmonton successes will not be repeated in Moscow), and its outright refusal to redress any of the great inequalities of income and opportunity that divide the Canadian sport "community". With the election of a new government, the future of Sport Canada is up in the air. If further cutbacks are imposed, perhaps in the name of reducing elitism, even this short-lived attempt to provide a focal point for Canadian identity will disappear.

There is much to add to what I have sketched in here. The mechanisms of cultural disintegration in sport must be studied in greater detail. Take the U.S. athletic scholarship. Why do some athletes head south unquestioningly, while others pay their way to study in Canada? What backgrounds do they come from? What considerations are foremost in their minds? What is the result of this experience on their subsequent behaviour? If they return to Canada, do they lobby for similar opportunities in Canada, or do they become part of the conduit for Canadian athletes to U.S. colleges? Answers to these and similar questions would enrich our understanding of the process.

It would also be useful to consider the interactions between forms of sport and other categories at key moments in Canadian history. Rick Salutin, in his award-winning play Les Canadiens, has suggested that the hockey team sustained the hopes and combativeness of Quebec nationalism during many long and hopeless periods, only to evaporate as cultural symbol the night le Parti québécois won the election. Nick auf der Maur has often said that the Québécois press coverage of the Canada-Soviet hockey series differs markedly from that published in the English-language press. These suggestions merit more careful study and similar questions should be investigated for English-speaking Canada. What role have forms of sport played in strengthening English-Canadian hegemony over Quebec?

The programatic response is difficult. In the first place, nationalism can be a reactionary force, even in a dependent country, if, as in the Liberals' version, it encourages the continued denial of the rights of self-determination to subordinate national minorities, and masks the systematic underdevelopment of local sports organizations. There is "no way" a team of foreign players like the Expos can represent a sports community like that in Montreal, especially when the public funds poured into the stadium in which they play could have been used much more effectively by local athletes. Secondly, although nationalists of all stripes have looked to the Canadian state for assistance -- and with some success, I might add -- that path is fraught with booby traps. As a life-long lobbyist for increased state funds for sport, I am embarrassed to see the extent to which Canadian teams have been manipulated to carry the message of "One-Canada", and to which athletes, now underpaid state workers, are less and less the subjects of their own activity, but increasingly the raw material for a vast scientific cadre of coaches, doctors, psychologists and bureaucrats.

The problem is that strategies for the democratic control of Canadian sport cannot be posed solely in terms of nationalism, for classes as well as peoples are oppressed, and increasingly the state plays an active role in the process. Strategies for change must therefore address all of these contradictions, not just one of them. It means that the struggle for the Canadianization of the NHL must be linked with the struggle for social ownership of the game and a measure of player control. Struggles in sport must be linked to other struggles in the community (as several athletes in the pre-Olympic period linked their demands for improved opportunities to specific struggles in the city of Montreal) and a more generalized campaign for better public fitness and recreation programs everywhere.[29] The task of defining a strategy of this complexity is difficult, but not impossible. All of these concerns are linked by a common desire for individual and collective autonomy or self-control.

NOTES AND REFERENCES

1. In the years immediately following Confederation, when
    the idea of the Indian as 'noble savage' still held
    many adherents, the native athlete faced two contra-
    dictory forms of racism: either he was oonsidered a
    'natural' and therefore provided unfair competition
    or he was 'inferior' and not worthy to play with
    whites. Both ideas led to his exclusion. Bruce Kidd,
    Tom Longboat (Toronto: Fitzhenry and Whiteside, 1980).

2. "I know it's crazy, but I felt guilty during the five
    weeks of intensive training I took, even though it
    helped me immensely," national discus champion Carol
    Martin told this writer a year before the 1976 Olympics.
    "Amateurism Dies Hard", Weekend, July 19, 1975.

3. Stanley B. Ryerson, Unequal Union (New York:
    International Publishers, 1968), p.23.

4. This brilliant film is no longer in distribution, but
    a copy of Barthes' commentary, dated September 8, 1961,
    is available from the NFB.

5. Frank Cosentino, "Ned Hanlan -- A Case Study in 19th
    Century Professionalism: Canadian Journal of History
    of Sport and Physical Education, V (2), 1974.

6. The Globe, Jan. 22, 1909.

7. Toronto Daily Star, April 20, 1907. Prior to the 1908
    Olympics, the secretary of the Amateur Athletic
    Federation of Canada, one of two rival sports
    federations, travelled to London to support the
    American AAU's charge that Longboat was a professional
    and therefore ineligible to compete. This "treasonous"
    action angered so many of its own supporters that it
    soon was forced to disband, leaving the Amateur Athletic
    Union of Canada as the sole multi-sport governing body.

8. Kevin Jones, "The Effects of the First World War on
    Canadian Sport", Proceedings of the Second World
    Symposium on the History of Sport and Physical Education,
    Banff, May 31 - June 3, 1971.

9. For the best summary of state assistance to sport, see
    Eric Broom and Richard Baka, Canadian Governments and
    Sport (Calgary: CAHPER, 1979).

301

10. E.G. Harry G. Johnson, The Canadian Quandry (Toronto: McClelland and Stewart, 1977); Eric Hobsbawm, "On 'The Break-up of Britain'", New Left Review, 105, 1977.

11. E.G. Alex Natan, "Politics and Sport" in Natan (ed.), Sport and Society (London: Bowes and Bowes, 1958). Jean-Marie Brohm, Sport. A Prison of Measured Time (London: Ink Links, 1978).

12. C.L.R. James, Beyond a Boundary (Kingston, Jamaica: Hutchinson, 1963).

13. In Canada, the process has variously been described as "continentalization", "colonization", Americanization" and "disintegration". Although each of these terms contains a measure of accuracy, I much prefer the latter. "Continentalization" obscures the unequal power relations that have developed, while "colonization" seems to ignore the fact that the Canadian state retains at least the form of independent political institutions. "Americanization" obscures the essential role that capital has played in the process.

14. Joyce Nelson, "The Global Pillage", This Magazine 13 (2), 1979, p.32.

15. James Laxer and Robert Laxer, The Liberal Idea of Canada (Toronto: Lorimer, 1977).

16. Bruce Kidd and John Macfarlane, The Death of Hockey (Toronto: New Press, 1972).

17. Stuart Ewen, Captains of Consciousness (New York: McGraw-Hill, 1976).

18. Frank Cosentino, Canadian Football (Toronto: Musson, 1969).

19. Donald W. Ball, "Ascription and Position: A comparison of 'Stacking' in Professional Football", in Gruneau and Albinson, Canadian Sport: Sociological Perspectives (Don Mills: Addison Wesley, 1976).

20. Bruce Kidd, "The Continentalization of Canadian Sport: football", Canadian Dimension 6 (2), 1969.

21. Even in the host city, significant class differences
     in "Grey Cup behaviour" have been observed. See Alan
     Lystiak, "'Legitimate Deviance' and Social Class: Bar
     Behaviour During Grey Cup Week", in Gruneau and
     Albinson, op. cit.

22. Both public and private media have played a key role
     in educating Canadians about the relative importance of
     U.S. sport and the insignificance of Canadian sport,
     as a glance at any newspaper or sports telecast will
     show. The prevalence of this kind of coverage is best
     explained by the active ideological and financial
     partnership between the media and commercial sport.
     See Bruce Kidd, The Political Economy of Sport
     (Calgary: CAPHER, 1979), pp.32 and 40-49.

23. Canada, House of Commons Debates, Feb. 13, 1936.

24. The Globe and Mail, Aug. 5, 1978.

25. Personal communication from Abby Hoffman.

26. Marion Lay, "The Role of Sport in International
     Relations", presentation to the International Studies
     Association, Toronto, March 21, 1979.

27. Personal communication from Abby Hoffman.

28. Canadian Olympic Association, Toward a national policy
     on amateur sport (Montreal: COA, 1978).

29. Bruce Kidd, "Canadian athletes should support the
     Olympic Games and help defeat Jean Drapeau", Canadian
     Dimension 9 (4), 1973 and "Olympics '76", Canadian
     Dimension, 11 (5), 1976.

11
Sport, the State and Dependency Theory

Response to Kidd

Colin Leys

Bruce Kidd's paper is a fluent and fascinating account of the way in which the major professional spectator sports have been implicated in the subordination of Canadian society to American economic, cultural and political domination, and of the contradictory role of the Canadian state in this process.

In response to the force of Bruce's characterization of this process, I will simply say that it illuminates many aspects of the third world experience of imperialism for me. The planned transfer of tastes from metropole to periphery includes the transfer of sports, and notably of sport as a field for capital accumulation in the shape of professional teams, which both reinforce and accentuate the division of countries into rival and even hostile regions - for instance tribal football teams, sponsored by foreign-owned companies, in Africa; multinational corporation finance to prime the pump for state spending on Olympic entries; the commodification of sport in general, as part of the capitalist (subordinate or under-) development of the periphery, including the implication of the periphery economies in the world division of labour in the sports goods industries; and not least, sport as the medium of a profound cultural imperialism of the kind Bruce Kidd describes.

There is also an important difference. The role of the state in third world countries has to be bigger in this respect, as in others. In spite of what has been said already about the role of the state in Canadian sport, I think that non-state apparatuses of hegemony are more important here than in the third world. In most third world

countries most of the population is still caught up in
pre-capitalist production relations, not fully proletarian-
ized or urbanized, relating more directly with other (small
commodity) producers, related more directly to nature, and
living a correspondingly different symbolic life.
Consequently sports imperialism of the kind we have been
discussing operates on a narrower front (mainly in the
cities and towns), meets more cultural resistance, under-
goes more complex cultural modificafions. In Canada, as Leo
Panitch has argued,[1] the fundamental form of U.S. hegemony
tends to be the assimilation of the Canadian classes to the
U.S. classes (the bourgeoisie through the corporations,
the workers through the international unions, and everyone
through commercial television, to put it with gross over-
simplification); but in Africa especially, but also in many
other parts of the third world, the state must be the chief
instrument of the introduction and reproduction of sports,
as of other modes of capitalist life.

Having indicated some of the ways in which Bruce Kidd's
paper seems to me stimulating in relation to other settings,
as well as making important points about Canada, I would
nonetheless like to enter some reservations about his
analysis.

The most general form of this criticism is that the
analysis is cast predominantly within the problematic of
'dependency'. There are indications of the presence of a
different problematic as well, and there is a tension or
contradiction between the two, but the clearly predominant
one is that of dependency. That is, the problem is presented
as one of subordination of <u>Canadian</u> society, economy,
culture and state policy to <u>American</u> control - with a
consequent concern with the possible destruction of the

possibility of forming a Canadian _nation_, and the possibility
of a break-up of the Canadian _state_.

While these preoccupations refer to real phenomena I
think this way of looking at the matter suffers from problems
common to all dependency theory:[2]

a) the implied aim and solution is non-dependency -
i.e. 'autonomy'. But autonomy of what, to do what? By
implication, autonomy of the _Canadian_ economy, society,
state, etc.; i.e. the capitalist character of the society,
economy etc. is either ignored or taken to be of secondary
interest. Non-dependency implies, in fact, autonomous,
home-controlled capitalism. But would all the problems
Bruce Kidd has identified in sport - would any of them -
be soluble under 'national capitalism'?

b) Because 'dependency' theory doesn't reject the central
categories of bourgeois thought, it tends not to see
capitalism as essentially _contradictory_. Hence the process
of dependency seems to unfold in an ineluctable sequence.
It flows, as Bruce says, from 'the dynamics of capital'.
But these dynamics appear here only as an inexorable
process of accumulation, not a contradictory one, and so
the focus is only on its victories, not on the struggles
it constantly generates and not on the possibility of
defeating it. (We might label this tendency 'mechanism'.)

c) This links to the distinctly 'residual' role played in
the analysis by social classes. This flows naturally from
making the 'nation' and 'state' the main focus. Classes
appear only as the source of particular forms of cultural
hegemony in sport - the amateur code, and so on. The
struggles of the working class, in particular, don't figure
in the account. As an example of the consequences of this

307

within the paper, Bruce cites Salutin's observation that the national project previously symbolized by the Montreal Canadiens was abruptly transferred to the PQ but he doesn't comment on what this meant for the prospect of solving the problems of sport in Quebec; yet it seems clear that this poses the problem of the 'class character' of the PQ and its specific political project.

d)   Less necessarily (i.e. logically), but nonetheless contingently connected with the dependency approach, the paper tends to see the problems of sport as a sphere susceptible to analysis, and by implication, to resolution, at least to some extent 'autonomously'. Whereas it seems to me that it can only be understood, and its problems prospectively resolved, in the context of a very broadly conceived social analysis and practical struggle.

It is only fair to add that Bruce also uses the term 'imperialism', and so far from being insensitive to some of the elements to which the concept of imperialism directs attention, he describes some of these very clearly. But the concept of imperialism is not really 'active' in his paper, and the point is that all-important practical-political consequences flow from the conceptualizations we use. The concept of imperialism does focus on the contradictions of monopoly capitalism, the forms of class struggle it entails, and the perspective of social revolution. Whereas the concept of dependency directs our attention to the mere assymetry of power between two regions, economies and states, without a clear standpoint on the necessity and prospects for reform or revolution.

Towards the end of Bruce's paper some of the ambiguities of the dependency perspective come home to roost

in the shape of a radical pessimism. This is not to say
that a revolutionary perspective based on an analysis in
terms of imperialism would result in optimism. But it does,
I think, focus attention firmly on the long-run necessity
of overthrowing bourgeois production relations, and on the
shorter-run contradictions in which the opportunities for
struggle are most favourable (see below). I suppose this
is what Gramsci meant by 'pessimism of the intelligence,
optimism of the will'.

As a possible example of the sort of shift which such
a change in analysis might produce, I would refer to the
fact that in Bruce's paper, the possible break-up of the
Canadian state through Quebec independentism features as a
purely negative consequence of dependency. But it is clear
that U.S. capital and the American state are hostile to the
break-up of the Canadian state. Apart from strategic and
international considerations, they recognize that more or
less any form taken by the independence movement jeopardises
the unity of the Canadian market and the stability of the
bourgeois state in Canada. So Quebec independentism is a
contradictory consequence of imperialism, threatening not
only a significant loss of a field of accumulation for U.S.
capital, at a time when this is least affordable, but more
seriously, a unique loss of stability and a breach of
ideological hegemony. This does not make the prospect of
independence for Quebec unambiguously positive, but it
reminds us that it is not necessarily negative for the
prospects of a socialist transformation in North America,
or, therefore, for the prospects of self-activity in play
and recreation with which the last part of Bruce's paper is
concerned.

If 'dependency' is an ideological concept, i.e. a concept
which represents real phenomena but in a way which conceals
their essential nature, their real determination, it seems
to be probable that 'sport' is too. Bruce Kidd remarks
that forms of sport have the dominant social relations of
specific historical social formations stamped on them; but
should we not go further and see the concept of 'sport'
itself, which was developed early in the sixteenth century,
as precisely the concept of a pastime subjected to and
expressive of bourgeois production relations? No doubt this
is a familiar thought for specialists in sport studies
(cf. J.M. Brohm)[3]; but it raises the question of how much of
what we now mean by 'sport' would be compatible with a
society freed from class oppression, where spectacle as the
opium of the people was at a discount, where individualism
and competition were subordinated to cooperation, and so on.
How much of 'a magnificent spectacle like hockey' referred
to by Bruce presupposes a class-divided, alienated
society, in which the commodification of play and its
subjection to the principle of systematic elitism has become
internalized as entirely 'natural'? Probably it has been
done, but it would seem valuable to study the historical
development of a fairly recent play activity (e.g. swimming?),
not technologically dependent on industrialism, from pastime
to sport, from play to measured achievement, from the sphere
of self-activity to increasing subordination to bourgeois
rationality and organization; with a view to exposing the
full ideological significance of the concept of 'sport'
itself. Perhaps not the liberation of sport, but the de-
sportification of play, would be a slogan consistent with
such a perspective.

One of Bruce Kidd's assumptions is that sport is
important in the imperialist domination of Canada because of
the importance of sport in the exercise of ideological hegemony
over the working class. The idea is that cognitions of the
dominant social reality achieved through sport, or at least
'naturalized' through their reflection in sport, are
transferred in a reinforced form to other spheres of life
(work, consumption, etc). This formulation probably needs
qualification in various ways but in general it seems
correct and important. But it raises the question of what
it is about sport that makes it so important to the workers:
why do they read the sports pages first, why are team loyalties
so central in peoples' consciousness, why should sports be
an important arena or focus for the violence through which
the frustrations of working class life are partly expressed,
etc.? Perhaps the answers are obvious. I see at least four
main reasons:

a)   In an advanced capitalist society organized sport is
a form of expression of some basic aspects of human nature -
elements of our biological make-up which are transhistorical,
present, however mediated, in all historical social formations
which, in bourgeois society, are denied expression in work,
and to a large extent in alienated work's obverse, 'leisure'.
John Hargreaves referred to this and perhaps most sport
sociologists take it for granted.

b)   The possibilities for the real subsumption of labour to
capital are limited precisely by the fact that spectator
sport must express these qualities. Hence it retains a
strong element of individual, human input which is and
appears real. (The appearance of being subject to a truly
random distribution of chance, of 'luck' which John Hargreaves

referred to as an important element in the ideological significance of sport, seems in large part due to this).

c) Because of this the mental component in sports labour, while very important, can't be fully academicized. Hence it remains accessible to workers - in fact in some spectator sports a 'middle class' education and socialization may to some extent disqualify people for success.

d) The character of sport as drama or theatre.

Supposing these reasons are accepted (the list is not meant to be in any sense exhaustive), we might try to bring together this line of analysis with the earlier discussion of contradiction: i.e. to look at each of these dimensions in terms of its characteristic contradictions.

a) When a sport becomes most fully subjected to capitalist relations of production, as for instance with football, the pressure of competition can easily push the capitalists - the team owners and their executives, the managers, coaches, etc. - into competitive innovations which begin to undermine the expressive function on which sport as spectacle depends (Bruce Kidd's well-taken remarks about hockey and football mercenaries are a case in point and it is a fair bet that a contradictory development is occurring with the increasing acquisition of foreign players in European soccer).

b) Dependence on the talent and temperament of the individual players provides opportunities for organization of players as sports labourers, the effective formulation of progressive demands and for raising both player and supporter consciousness. For various reasons, largely connected with the team character of sport, players have not produced many parallels with Jane Fonda, Vanessa Redgrave or Tom Jones (Rock Against Racism), but this is not the decisive aspect;

312

the question is what efforts have been or might be made to generate an appropriate form of player consciousness and player organization capable of using the powers placed in player hands by the nature of sports production.

c)   The critical importance of the working class as the prime consumers of sports spectacle implies the potential power of working class demands within sport - for accommodation at games, for access for policing methods, etc. - for raising consciousness of the ideological nature and social character of sport.

d)   Sport's character as drama is in principle subversible. Spectators are part of the drama, of course (chorus), The Loneliness of the Long-Distance Runner [4] is admittedly only a parable, pointed in its non-replicability in any literal sense, of the subversive possibilities of sports as drama. Black athletes showing the clenched fist at Olympic medal ceremonies are hardly a portent; but on the other hand the virtual monopoly of both the production and the criticism (TV and press) of sports drama by bourgeois ideologies does not seem so entirely inescapable as it is sometimes presented as being.   Both players and spectators - and only an organized few of either - have great possibilities for determining otherwise.

It seems to me that all these contradictory dimensions of sport lend themselves to effective forms of struggle, provided that, as with other fields of struggle, they are coordinated with parallel efforts in other fields of the class struggle.   In speaking of this 'coordination' I have in mind more than just organizational coherence, or something of that sort.   I am thinking more of the problem of linking the struggle of the working class for socialism, with the struggles of other non-class elements against bureaucratism, discrimination and other manifestations of the hierarchical and oppressive structures of state power, the so-called 'popular democratic' struggles recently emphasized by Ernesto Laclau.[5] An example of such links would be the success of the older elements of the Canadian bourgeoisie in linking the development of sport to their class ideology through the amateur code, as described by Bruce Kidd. A counter example might be the linking of the women's struggle with the workers' struggle by taking up the progressive implications of both for the question of women's participation in sport, e.g. in minor hockey. This is not, perhaps, an immediately persuasive example. It seems important to consider why this may be so, and the scope that exists for developing more.

NOTES AND REFERENCES

1. See Leo Panitch, "The Role and Nature of the Canadian State". In The Canadian State: Political Economy and Political Power, Toronto: University of Toronto Press, 1977.

2. For a broader critique of dependency models in Canadian political economy see Leo Panitch, "Dependency and Class in Canadian Political Economy", Studies in Political Economy: A Socialist Review, 6, Autumn, 1981.

3. Jean Marie Brohm, Sport: A Prison of Measured Time. London: Ink Links, 1978.

4. See A. Sillitoe, The Loneliness of the Long Distance Runner. London, 1959.

5. Ernesto Laclau, Politics and Ideology in Marxist Theory. London: New Left Books, Verso editions, 1977.

LIST OF CONTRIBUTORS

Rob Beamish   School of Physical and Health Education,
                     University of Toronto

Hart Cantelon   School of Physical and Health Education,
                     Queen's University

Wallace Clement   Department of Sociology, Carleton University

Rick Gruneau   Department of Sociology, Queen's University

John Hargreaves   Department of Sociology, Goldsmith's
                     College, University of London

Alan Ingham   Department of Kinesiology,
                     University of Washington

Bruce Kidd   School of Physical and Health Education,
                     University of Toronto

Colin Leys   Department of Political Studies,
                     Queen's University

Henry Morton   Department of Political Studies,
                     Queens College, New York

James Riordan   Modern Languages Institute, University of
                     Bradford

Ian Taylor   Department of Sociology, Carleton University